D0119944

La Nouvelle Agence
7, rue Corneille - 75006 PARIS
Tél. 01 43 25 85 60
Fax 01 43 25 47 98
RCS 308 256 015 00014

The Odd Man Karakozov

THE ODD MAN KARAKOZOV

*Imperial Russia, Modernity,
and the Birth of Terrorism*

CLAUDIA VERHOEVEN

Cornell University Press
Ithaca and London

First published 2009 by Cornell University Press

Printed in the United States of America

Library of Congress Cataloging-in-Publication Data

Verhoeven, Claudia, 1972–
  The odd man Karakozov : Imperial Russia, modernity, and the birth of terrorism / Claudia Verhoeven.
      p. cm.
  Includes bibliographical references and index.
  ISBN 978-0-8014-4652-8 (cloth : alk. paper)
  1. Karakozov, Dmitrii Vladimirovich, 1840–1866.   2. Alexander II, Emperor of Russia, 1818–1881—Assassination attempt, 1866. 3. Terrorism—Russia—History—19th century.   4. Political violence—Russia—History—19th century.   5. Russia—History —Alexander II, 1855–1881.   I. Title.
  DK219.6.K28V47 2009
  947.08′1092—dc22

                                        2008038072

Cornell University Press strives to use environmentally responsible suppliers and materials to the fullest extent possible in the publishing of its books. Such materials include vegetable-based, low-VOC inks and acid-free papers that are recycled, totally chlorine-free, or partly composed of nonwood fibers. For further information, visit our website at www.cornellpress.cornell.edu.

Cloth printing   10 9 8 7 6 5 4 3 2 1

For Paul, Martine, Heleen, and Stas

For not only is an odd man "not always" a particular and isolated case, but, on the contrary, it sometimes happens that it is precisely he, perhaps, who bears within himself the heart of the whole, while the other people of his epoch have all for some reason been torn away from it for a time by some kind of flooding wind.

FYODOR DOSTOEVSKY, *The Brothers Karamazov*

CONTENTS

Appendixes

ACKNOWLEDGMENTS

Of all those who supported me in the writing of this book, I would like first of all to thank three of my teachers. Irina Paperno inspired my pursuit of nineteenth-century Russian history, David Sabean taught me how to become a historian, and Stephen P. Frank was a great and generous advisor.

For their thoughtful comments on this work, I am very thankful to Peter Baldwin, Victoria Frede, J. Arch Getty, Marcy Norton, Teo Ruiz, and especially Carlo Ginzburg. Additionally, two anonymous readers read an earlier version of this book for the press, and I thank them for their shrewd suggestions.

At UCLA, of my graduate cohort, I would like to acknowledge Andrea Mansker, Kelly Maynard, Britta McEwen, Peter Park, Jared Poley, Courtenay Raia, Patricia Tilburg, Gabriel Wolfenstein, and Amy Woodson-Boulton. For their insight and interest, my thanks also to the participants of the European History Colloquium and to the members of David Sabean's seminars and reading groups, particularly Sung Choi, Sean Guillory, Ben Marschke, Dan Ryan, Tami Sarfatti, Daniela Saxer, Simon Teuscher, and Tamara Zwick. Hopefully David Sabean knows that when he opened his house for group dinners and discussion in the spring of 2003, he saved this work.

In Russia, I thank for their magnanimous, patient assistance the staffs of the State Archive of the Russian Federation, the Russian State Historical Archive, the State Historical Library, the Russian National Library, and the Russian State Library, and particularly Viktoria Zakirova, Irina

Zasipkina, and Elena Cherkova; for the kindness and expertise with which they facilitated my stay in Moscow, Elena Drozdova, Leonid Veintraub, and Galina Kuznetsova; for archival camaraderie, Miriam Dobson and Kathleen Addison; and for their friendship, Kiril Asse and Liuba Chumak Harris.

In the Washington, D.C. area, I would like to thank my new colleagues at George Mason University and the staff of the European Reading Room at the Library of Congress.

At Cornell University Press, I thank Karen Laun and Gavin Lewis for editing the manuscript, Carolyn Sherayko for creating the index, and John Ackerman for supporting this book from the start.

For financial assistance of this project, I am grateful to the UCLA Center for European and Eurasian Studies, the Center for German and European Studies at UC Berkeley, the International Studies Overseas Program, the UCLA Department of History, the Fulbright-Hays Doctoral Fellowship program, and the Graduate Division at UCLA. I would also like to thank the Robert Schuman Centre for Advanced Studies at the European University Institute, where during my year as a Jean Monnet fellow I was able to complete the final revisions for this book.

I have no idea how to adequately thank my family—Paul, Martine, and Heleen Verhoeven—and Stas Shuripa, but to them, I dedicate this book.

Note on Transliteration, Translation, Dates, and Dramatis Personae

I have used the Library of Congress system of transliteration, but adopted the traditional −*sky* and −*y* for well-known personal names. All translations are mine unless otherwise noted. Dates in this book refer to the Julian or Old Style calendar, which, during the nineteenth century, was twelve days behind the Gregorian or New Style calendar.

Because of the large number of individuals featured in this text, a list of dramatis personae will be found in Appendix A at the end of the book. In the text, the first appearance of an individual listed in the appendix is marked with an asterisk.

THE ODD MAN KARAKOZOV

INTRODUCTION

The epigraph to this book comes from the preface to *The Brothers Kara-mazov* (1880). It is Dostoevsky's preemptive strike against readers who will say that the book's hero, Alyosha Karamazov, is not much of a hero at all: "What has he really done? To whom is he known, and for what? Why should I, the reader, spend my time studying the facts of his life?"[1] Dostoevsky concedes the critique and admits that Alyosha is "a strange man, even an odd man," but then he turns around and comes back with the argument that in fact the odd man "bears within himself the heart of the whole."[2] It is exactly an argument, this Parthian shot, and not just a conviction. The Russian for "odd man" is *chudak*, a term that is etymologically related to the word for miracle, *chudo*, and this linguistic link grounds Dostoevsky's logic: the odd man in history, one may say, is homologous to the miracle in theology. Just as the miracle betokens a world beyond this one that is more real, so the odd man signifies something beyond consensus that is more true. The odd man is thus not only the exception that proves the rule (because being odd, he implies the even), but also, as the structural similarity with the miracle brings out, the example that enables the rule to exist in the first place. The odd man is heroic, in sum, since he holds in his heart the secret of history's sense.

And so it is for the hero of this book, the unlikely Dmitry Karakozov*: this is why it is possible to claim that we need precisely him, and no one else, to write a history that is more true than the history that we have (see figure 1). He is known to but a few, and even then fundamentally for his failure: on April 4, 1866, Karakozov shot at Tsar Alexander II,* but missed

Fig. 1. Dmitry Vladimirovich Karakozov. GARF, f. 1742, op. 1, d. 14778, l. 1. With permission from GARF.

Fig. 2. April 4, 1866. M. A. Antonovich, *Shestidesiatye gody.* Moscow: Akademia, 1933.

(see figure 2). This made him the first revolutionary to try to assassinate the tsar, but it hardly made him the last, and in the history of the revolutionary movement, the last mattered most: fifteen years later, with their spectacular and systematic "emperor hunt," the revolutionary organization *Narodnaia Volia* (People's Will) claimed the honor of having invented for the world a new political phenomenon: terrorism. A reasonable reader interested in the origins of terrorism might thus conclude that he need not spend his time studying the facts of Karakozov's life. But he would be wrong, because it is the odd man Karakozov who "bears within himself the heart of the whole."

As for the book's title: it would, perhaps, have been too bold to use "odd man" for Karakozov and thus to suggest, in some sense, a link between the terrorist and the miracle, except that when Dostoevsky created his odd man, Alyosha Karamazov, he had in mind this very link. "My pure Alyosha," Dostoevsky told his editor about the planned second volume of *The Brothers Karamazov,* "will kill the tsar."[3] Had he lived to write that volume, what Karamazov and Karakozov hold in common would not have seemed so coincidental at all—and then this book, perhaps, would have been written long ago.

Paradigm

There exists no general (historical) theory of terrorism: there is no comprehensive explanation or set of principles accounting for the origin, development, and—possibly—end of this political phenomenon. Another way of formulating the problem is simply to say that historians have no paradigm for terrorism the way they do for the civilizing process (Elias), or the public sphere (Habermas), or disciplinary society (Foucault). There is no norm to work with or against, for which to gather evidence, and with which to experiment. And so the question—given at least a century and a half of political violence that has been grouped under the term "terrorism"—is, why?

According to the mainstream of experts, *the* issue obstructing the path toward a general theory of terrorism is the notorious lack of agreement as to what terrorism is. Already long ago, scholars had concluded that there were so many definitions that we should do away with the notion of "terrorism per se" and speak rather of "terrorisms."[4] Nowadays, almost everyone has come to recognize the trouble with the term, as suggested by the renewed popularity of the phrase, "One man's terrorist is another's freedom fighter." Ultimately, it seems, what is shown by the multiple, divergent definitions of terrorism on the one hand and the refusal to define it on the other is this: whatever paradigm we are working with to determine political legitimacy is no longer being sustained by the reality of the world and its recent history. In other words, the exceptions have grown so numerous that we must begin looking for a new rule, one that will be able to explain why and how terrorism is part and parcel of the repertoire of modern political action.

This book, which is not a work of political theory, cannot contain that new rule, but it does offer a contribution, however modest, toward the writing of a novel history of terrorism. Such a history, it suggests, should start from the affirmation that terrorism—at least in its classical, revolutionary incarnation—is not simply a strategy, not a means towards this or that particular political end, but rather a paradigmatic way of becoming a modern political subject, and that its genesis can be understood only when analyzed in the material contexts of modernity.

Argument

The standard story about terrorism—and experts agree on this—is that it was invented in imperial Russia when, in the late 1870s, members of the revolutionary party *Zemlia i Volia* (Land and Freedom) had a falling out over the use and abuse of political violence. They organized a summit, had a debate, took a vote, and agreed to disagree: one faction persisted with peaceful propaganda; the other, *Narodnaia Volia,* wrote up a political program that explicitly embraced "terrorist activities," and then put this program into practice.[5] Thus was born terrorism: rationally, democratically, and systematically. My argument is that things were both more complicated and more interesting than that, for the simple reason that the birth of the new is never that simple.

The following, for example, has always seemed strange: *Narodnaia Volia*'s terrorism shocked everyone, of course, but it surprised no one. Bizarre, to say the least, that a radically new political phenomenon can come into being, yet immediately seem not only intelligible, but even self-evident. So self-evident, in fact, that within a year, Dostoevsky could suggest to his editor, apropos of what he had in store for his pure Alyosha Karamazov, that for anyone seeking the truth in modern Russia, the path from religion to revolutionary terrorism was natural.[6] In short, contemporaries—*Narodovoltsy* themselves included—reacted to the emergence of terrorism as if the idea of terrorism had already been there. And this is precisely the point: the idea *had* already been there—ever since 1866, when Karakozov first shot at the tsar.

Chronology binds the historian, so April 4, 1866, has in literature on the revolutionary movement always maintained an unofficial status as the "prologue" to terrorism. But because Karakozov was strange, sick, and suicidal, because he failed, and because his timing was off—according to the traditional historiography, the first modern tsaricide was fifteen years "too early" to be a "real" terrorist—he has largely been considered the odd man out of the revolutionary movement. "Miserable," "emotionally unstable," "insane," "not entirely responsible," and "far from healthy"— these are just some of the epithets Karakozov elicited with his awkward shortcut to terrorism.[7] April 4, 1866, correspondingly, is often dismissed as an antichronism, thought to reveal little about its time, and less about terrorism, other than that it foreshadowed what followed. The opposite is true though. And since scholarship has parenthesized April 4, 1866, as an untimely failure, this exceptional event not only casts an unfamiliar, yet unusually crisp light on a historiography that has grown rather torpid from repetition, but also discloses the hidden history of terrorism, starting with the story of its beginnings.

April 4, 1866, was unthinkable. No one expected it, and no one understood it. Karakozov's shot, as a matter of fact, was an event so unprecedented that it was long simply known as "April 4," and that day, to wit, news of the shooting so stunned Dostoevsky that he nearly collapsed into a hysterical fit, possibly followed by an epileptic fit.[8] Karakozov's violence— *exemplary* political action for which he coined the neologism *factual propaganda* (*fakticheskaia propaganda*)—was thus illegible. However: having caused a real rupture in understanding, Karakozov and his "unheard-of" act became the subject of a cacophonous onslaught of commentary. Law, literature, media, medicine, fashion, fine arts, and religion—none was left unaffected, all sought to make sense of what seemed a senseless story, and, in so doing, each contributed to the construction of what would eventually come to be known as terrorism. The most determinant ideas about this new form of political violence, indeed, were forged from the reception of April 4, so that it may fairly be said that in all but name, terrorism was born of 1866.

But—and this is the crux of the matter—this is also to say that terrorism as it is generally understood misses something of the essence of this political phenomenon. What grounds our understanding of terrorism is a reception of what was at that time something unthinkable—a reception, moreover, that was overdetermined by the devastating political reaction that April 4 unleashed. Our reading of terrorism, in other words, is rooted in what were often enough misinterpretations and sometimes deliberate distortions of Karakozov's factual propaganda. One of the tasks of this book, therefore, will be to interpret this idea of Karakozov's; for only if factual propaganda is understood will it be evident what was really at stake in this new form of political violence.

This was, as stated above, the emergence of a new, modern political subject. True, this is a subject that seeks, via violence, to generate fear and advance change. What matters more, though, and what matters especially in terms of modernity, is that by doing so, this subject desires to act in a historically meaningful manner, and does this without delay and without mediation. Ultimately, Karakozov's factual propaganda suggests a model of political action based on a subject that directly experiences and seeks to intervene in the historical process. That is, it suggests a reading of terrorism that roots this violence in the very rhythms and routines of life in the modern era.

The intimate bond between terrorism and modernity should become visible as soon as it is shown that April 4, 1866, exists entirely in relation to historical novelties. Karakozov himself, first of all, appeared only because he embodied the new: he enjoyed a "nihilist" education, had a revolutionary attitude towards religion, suffered a series of cityesque diseases, was treated according to the latest medical methods, and so on. Whatever is known of his appearance, moreover, is known only because his image was caught in the reflection of the modern: photography and fashion, social realist art and literature, news that was telegraphed or otherwise transported by train, reformed courts, and rewritten laws. Without all these things, there is no April 4, 1866. Only the modern makes terrorism both possible and intelligible: it is terrorism's precondition.

Modernity does not cause terrorism, clearly, but it does create the conditions for the coming of a historically conscious and politically sovereign subject, and when this subject's desire to act in accordance with its nature is blocked, terrorism can emerge. This is so for, principally, two reasons. First, modernity means the increasingly instantaneous experience of belonging to a community whose members are in synchronism with each other irrespective of the physical spaces that separate them. Technology and telecommunications connect what has happened, is happening, and will happen everywhere: doing so, they produce history, and position people in relation to this history. Thus, one can feel oneself to exist either in or outside of the historical process, and for moderns, who measure the value of their lives historically, the difference matters. Second, modernity implies action that—like goods and information—freely traverses spatio-temporal terrains, and constantly contributes to the renewal of the world. Therefore, in sum, the potential for universal redemption and autonomy is immanent to the materials of the modern, and modern subjects come to know this on a very elemental, everyday level—essentially, it is a knowledge that is inscribed on their bodies, simply because of their being in the modern world. When the tension between this knowledge of the coming community and the prohibition to participate in its construction becomes unbearable, the body may break out of its bind through action known as terrorism. Its form is determined by what modern subjects experience on any average day, namely that violence is promptly communicated to everyone everywhere, and that this message guarantees meaning: the act will have happened, and the world will not be the same. Violent to the extent it cannot be legitimate, terrorism is politics in becoming.

Plot

As for the facts of the case, they are these. At a quarter to four on April 4, 1866, just as Alexander II stepped out of Saint Petersburg's Summer Garden and onto the boulevard, a camouflaged Karakozov pulled out a double-barreled flintlock pistol and shot at the tsar. He missed, and was caught. Based on clues pulled out of the pockets of his peasant disguise, investigators concluded that there had been a conspiracy whose nets were so extensive as to have sprawled across the entirety of the Russian empire and the European continent. Karakozov was said to have been a member of a Muscovite socialist student group, "The Organization," at the center of which there sat a secret cell of suicide-assassins: "Hell." "Hell," in turn, had ties with extreme "nihilists" in Petersburg, exiled politicals in Siberia, and—most sinister of all—the European Revolutionary Committee, which had its base in Geneva, the age's haven for radicals. Ultimately, of thirty-six defendants, all but a few were convicted on counts of conspiracy, and Karakozov was publicly hanged on September 3, 1866.

Any additional information readers might need to understand April 4, 1866—including what was what and who was who in Russia at this time—will be covered in the chapters of this book. The following, though, they should know up front: the Karakozov case has not, ever, been definitively solved. Consider the contradictory interpretations that were advanced, then and since:

1. Karakozov was a member of "Hell," which sat at the center of "The Organization," which was connected with a revolutionary group in Petersburg, which was connected with (i) exiled politicals in Siberia and (ii) the European Revolutionary Committee in Geneva, which was either Karl Marx's First International or, more likely, Mikhail Bakunin's* *Alliance Internationale,* that is, "Hell" was one of the European Revolutionary Committee's terrorist cells.

2. Karakozov was a member of "Hell," which sat at the center of "The Organization," which was connected with a revolutionary group in Petersburg, but the groups parted ways precisely on the matter of violence: the Petersburgers were constitutionalists and/or gradualists, the Muscovites were socialists, radicals, and/or terrorists.

3. Karakozov was a member of "Hell," which sat at the center of "The Organization," but the decision to assassinate Alexander II was his alone, born of impatience, illness, and/or insanity.

4. "Hell" did not exist, though "The Organization" did, and Karakozov—because he was impatient, ill, and/or insane—took his friends' jokes about "hell" too seriously.

5. Neither "Hell" nor "The Organization" existed, and Karakozov—because he was impatient, ill, and/or insane—took his friends' jokes about "hell" and "organization" too seriously.

6. Some combination of the above—plus: Karakozov, via his doctor, had been brought into contact with an aristocratic-constitutionalist party in Petersburg that was plotting a coup and was headed by Alexander II's very own brother, Grand Duke Konstantin Nikolaevich.*

In short, since it has never been determined whether Karakozov acted alone or was part of a conspiracy, the Karakozov case contains a mystery at its core. This mystery is one of the principal reasons for the precarious status of April 4 in the history of terrorism, but it is also what makes the case so interesting: its natural plot an unsolved detective story, the history of April 4, 1866, is not really a textbook case of anything—except perhaps the conditions of contemporary historical research.

Plan

The plan of the book may be schematized as two sets of concentric circles linked by a line in the middle. The first set holds three chapters that analyze the reception of April 4 by—from the center to the periphery—the state (*gosudarstvo*, officialdom, the administration, plus the newly independent judiciary), society (*obshchestvo*,* the educated public), and the people (*narod*). The second set, likewise containing three chapters, treats —from the periphery to the center—the appearance, body, and psyche of the tsaricide. Between the sets sits a chapter that, via a reading of Dostoevsky's *Crime and Punishment* (1866), conceptually engages the novelty, or, to borrow Dostoevsky's famous phrase, "new word" that is Karakozov. The book ends with an epilogue on the political vision contained in April 4, 1866.

It should be said, though, that while there is this logic to the order of the book, the chapters need not necessarily be read in order. Chapter 1, for example, covers the basics in a more or less chronological fashion, but it is not required reading for what follows. Likewise, though the book's main methodological issues are worked out through the uncanny coincidence of Karakozov and Raskolnikov in the chapter on *Crime and Punishment,* one need not know this fourth chapter in order to understand the others. Each chapter narrates the case from its own angle, was written in such a way as to be largely autonomous, and can be read quite independently of the others.

CHAPTER 1

FROM THE FILES OF THE KARAKOZOV CASE

The Virtual Birth of Terrorism

> What chaos! A death, an execution, an absolute sovereign reigning
> over nothing absolutely, an immense lie about a conspiracy that's
> popped like a soap bubble . . . and then the mixed sounds of *Yankee
> Doodle* and *The Kamarinsky Peasant* . . . It's some sort of absurd, dis-
> mal assemblage, torn from Michelangelo's *Last Judgment* or stepping
> out of a *Non-Divine Comedy.* Where can we find a combination of
> Tacitus and Dante [to capture the history of the Karakozov case]?
>
> ALEXANDER HERZEN,* "The Gallows and Murav'ev," *Kolokol* (*The
> Bell*), 1 October 1866

Terrorism virtually emerged from the Russian autocracy's mishandling
of April 4, 1866. It was the government's slanted analysis of twenty-five-
year-old Dmitry Vladimirovich Karakozov's attempt on Alexander II that
brought into being this new political specter. This is true even though the
Karakozov case was tried before the empire's newly reformed and highly
respected justice system, and most people thought the Supreme Criminal
Court had checked and balanced the autocracy's reactionary reading of
the case. No doubt, had the case been tried before the notoriously corrupt old courts, many more of Karakozov's alleged co-conspirators would
have been sent to the gallows. But that is not the point. The point is that
however just the new court might have been, the government intervened
in the judicial process at precisely those junctures where, by law, the court
should have interacted openly with the public. Thereby, the government
set very specific limits on public knowledge of the case, and it was these
limits that eventually produced and publicized the specter of terrorism.
When over the course of the next decade this specter began to haunt,
first, the Russian empire, and, thereafter, the rest of the world, the form

in which it did so was directly determined by the government's earliest representation of Karakozov's unprecedented political challenge.

The Appearance of Difference

On August 31, 1866, the Supreme Criminal Court sentenced Karakozov to death, acquitted a young man alleged to have been one of his principal co-conspirators, and then announced that it would defer judging the remaining thirty-four defendants until the end of a second trial, which was scheduled to start in mid September.

After many months of anxious waiting for the conclusion of the case, some were doubtlessly disappointed by this delay, but overwhelmingly the court's pronouncements inspired confidence among the Russian public that justice would ultimately be served. "The acquittal of Mr. Kobylin* in spite of what had been printed about him," the liberal newspaper *Golos* (*The Voice*) declared, "represents a great, definitive guarantee for society that the Supreme Criminal Court will disclose the truth of each individual case—even if the investigation should have overlooked something or other."[1] And this was no pseudo-enthusiasm. It was a genuine response to the appearance of a highly charged and historically unheard-of divergence: for the first time ever, the judiciary seemed to have successfully separated itself from the state—and in the midst of a devastating political reaction no less.

The historic divergence was clearly manifested in the documentary record. On the one hand, there was the August 31 verdict pronounced by the Supreme Criminal Court. On the other, there was "what had been printed about him," which had appeared some three weeks earlier in a no less authoritative source: the official findings of the Investigative Commission, published on August 3 in the Ministry of Interior's *Severnaia Pochta* (the *Northern Post*). A crucial blueprint for future understandings of terrorism, the *Severnaia Pochta* article had been written by the head of the Investigative Commission, Count Mikhail Nikolaevich Murav'ev*—a tsar appointee also known as "the hangman" who sat at the epicenter of the post–April 4 reaction—and it had left little doubt that everyone involved in Karakozov's crime would be convicted on counts of conspiracy.

The liberal press had no trouble interpreting this split and choosing sides. If it was impossible to line up the truth of the court with that of the commission, this obviously proved the court's proper spirit of independence. The fact of the difference, that is, proved the truth of the court and thus, by extension, the lie of the commission: Kobylin's acquittal suggested that there had been no conspiracy at all, that this fable had been but a figment of Murav'ev's reactionary imagination, and that Karakozov had acted alone. And so, while awaiting the outcome of the second trial, society could rest assured: the guilty—if even any there were—would be punished, but the innocent would go free.

In a strange, poetic twist of fate, moreover, Murav'ev died quite suddenly of natural causes and was buried on September 2, only one day before Karakozov was publicly executed on Saint Petersburg's Smolensk Square. Did not this double death symbolically seal the end of the reaction? Perhaps even mark the demise of the old, autocratic world? With Murav'ev expired, Karakozov hanged, and Kobylin free, *Golos* proclaimed the beginning of a new reign of justice. And with a call for public vigilance to safeguard against "a repeat of the terrible event of April 4," the paper gladly signed off on the official sentence and liberally stamped it with society's approval.[2]

But all this optimism was rather misplaced: the Karakozov case—was April 4 the act of a lone assassin or a conspiracy?—was actually never conclusively solved, and the justice of the court's verdict remains dubious. Doubtlessly it is this irreducible unknown at the core of the case that is to blame for the precarious status of April 4, 1866, in the history of terrorism—although given that Karakozov was Russia's first modern tsaricide, it is nevertheless remarkable that his attempt has been so neglected by scholars interested in the development of terrorism. In a broader historical sense, the oversight is no less remarkable, given that it might legitimately be argued that along with the Karakozov case, the law itself had gone to trial.

If the outcome of this trial could—at least for some contemporaries—mark the beginning of a new reign of justice, this was because Karakozov's was the first major political case tried before Russia's newly reformed legal system. Ratified as early as November 1864, the judicial reforms were only inaugurated on April 17, 1866. No sooner had the ink dried on the new judicial statutes, that is, than the political violence of the Karakozov case challenged their efficacy and applicability. And as it happened, the law was not up to the challenge of this exceptional case.

Of course, to quote Porfiry Petrovich, the investigator in Fyodor Dostoevsky's *Crime and Punishment*—which was being serialized at this very time in *Russkii Vestnik* (the *Russian Messenger*)—"the average case, the case for which all the legal forms and rules are devised, which they are calculated to deal with, when they are written down in the textbooks, does not exist at all."[3] The Karakozov case, nevertheless, challenged the norm in more than the usual sense, bearing witness to legality in the making in a most exemplary fashion. Because it was partly handled in accordance with the new statutes, partly in accordance with the old, and sometimes even in accordance with none at all, the Karakozov case concurrently reveals the execution, violation, and creation of law: it is the exception that proves both more and less than one rule at once.

The purpose of this chapter is therefore threefold: it tells the history of the events surrounding April 4; it reconstructs the making of the case, and in particular of the idea of the conspiracy; and this provides the opportunity to evaluate the new judicial order and the relevance of the case for the history of terrorism.

Criminal Justice and the Paperwork Problematic

Despite repeated attempts since the early eighteenth century, the overhaul of the universally maligned Russian legal system proved impossible for more than 150 years. Peter the Great convened three commissions in the early 1700s; Catherine the Great penned her famous Montesquieu and Beccaria–inspired *Nakaz* (*Instruction*) in 1766; but only Mikhail Speransky, under Alexander I and Nicholas I, achieved a codification of Russian law so comprehensive that, in 1835, it could finally supersede the 1649 *Ulozhenie* (legal code). Real reforms, however, were not achieved until Alexander II ratified the *Sudebnye ustavy* (Judicial Statutes) in 1864.

Damning assessments of the old, inquisitorial judicial system litter the literature, but Herzen's famous quip is representative enough: "A common man who is brought to trial fears not the punishment, but the trial. He looks forward to being sent to Siberia."[4] Sundry were the reasons for this—corrupt officials, illiterate judges, and labyrinthine courts—but the most important one for our purposes was the old system's production of very peculiar paperwork: it was always chaotic, and more often than not, a charade. Because confession had a legal status as a prima facie guarantor of guilty verdicts, investigators and clerks regularly resorted to suggestive questioning, sometimes to (illegal) torture, and what they ultimately created was a written record one scholar characterized as "an unassailable screen between the accused and his judges [that] predetermined his fate."[5] Investigations culminated when the secretary of the court culled the record for enough essential facts to write an abstract that included counts of indictment and whatever evidence was necessary to ensure conviction. This abstract was then dispatched to courts whose task consisted not so much in trying or judging the case as in substantiating the police-recommended indictment: the separation between the executive and the judiciary was slight at best. Because of its formalism and essential immunity to external scrutiny, pre-reform criminal procedure existed virtually as a permanent occasion for the abuse of justice, and was widely perceived as such.

Deemed the most far-reaching and successful of all the Great Reforms enacted during the reign of Alexander II, the 1864 Judicial Statutes redressed many of the abuses of the old criminal justice system. They created a bar and introduced all the elements of adversarial justice: independent courts; counsel; oral proceedings; opposing presentations by counsel; publicity; trial by jury; and irremovable judges. Other than consolidating the office of the "judicial investigator," it should be noted, the Statutes did not alter the first stage of criminal cases: investigations continued to be run by the government, and the defense continued to be excluded from participation in the preliminary procedures. Finally, and significantly, the reforms both exposed the law to public scrutiny and began the public's legal education: newspapers like *Glasnyi Sud* (*Open Court*) and *Sudebnyi Vestnik* (the *Judicial Herald*) fostered legal consciousness, columnists jostled the court of public opinion, and the people—as jury or audience—began to serve as arbiter of worldly justice.

The history of the revolutionary movement shows, however, the extent to which the new legal system was still subject to arbitrary administrative abuse and autocratic intervention. Especially as the movement began to pick up speed, it became less and less unusual to escort revolutionaries directly toward closed-door military tribunals, deny them the amenities of the new justice, and execute them out of public sight. Even in the best-conducted of such cases, newspaper glosses provided the public with as dim a legal visibility and as superficial a juridical efficacy as had been given to judges by the pre-reform case abstracts.

In the Karakozov case, things were no different. Not only was the preliminary investigation essentially conducted under the old rules, but the law immediately suspended itself and withdrew behind closed doors: everything, trial included, took place in camera. There being no transparency whatsoever, external scrutiny was impossible. On the whole, the public was presented with, first, the commission's official findings and, second, the court's verdicts—and nothing else. These two documents provided the sum total of information on the basis of which the public could form an understanding of the Karakozov case. This is to say that public perception was based on about 1 percent of the actually existing documentation, and it need hardly be underlined that this was not just any 1 percent.

So that we may properly estimate the restraints set on the representation and reception of April 4, it is essential to revisit the written record of the Karakozov case. Following the paper trail, we can see that the case, though lauded as proof of a new type of justice, suffered much of the abuses of the old legal system—and that this had a definitive influence on the public image of the revolutionary actor, the revolutionary movement, and revolutionary violence.

The Karakozov dossiers in fact offer a unique occasion to view the layering of filters that goes into the formation of what ultimately comes to look like a case's calm, settled surface. Unlike later inquiries into revolutionary groups like *Narodnaia Rasprava* (People's Vengeance) or *Narodnaia Volia,* this thoroughly documented investigation was reasonably restricted both temporally and in scope. Over the course of five months, the official investigation produced approximately six thousand files directly relevant to thirty-six defendants, whose trials produced an additional pile of about one thousand folios, including some six hundred pages of stenographed court transcripts. The files include, but are not limited to, official memoranda; reports transcribed from oral interrogations; depositions written out by suspects themselves; investigative abstracts; indictments; trial testimonies; prosecution and defense speeches; verdicts; and eyewitness reports.

Through all of these run tensions and inconsistencies, some of which are related to the logic with which the materials were produced, some to deliberate distortion, yet others to political agendas, and so on.

Take the process of interrogation. Following the spoken interviews (the content of which has obviously been lost for the historical record), interrogations were conducted in writing: questions were neatly posed on the page's left side, and answers either transcribed by clerks or scribbled by suspects on the right (except in the case of "ochnaia stavka" or "confrontation," when two suspects accused and contradicted each other across a single page). Depositions given in a suspect's own hand partially addressed pre-reform problems such as that a transcription of oral testimony could often fairly be termed "distortion" or at best "translation," but of course the very format of these questionnaires and the formulation of the questions still imposed distinct narratives on defense testimony.

Beyond these bureaucratic restraints, this type of paperwork invariably reflected the unannounced socio-cultural filters of all parties involved and, finally, the planned and/or panicked deceptions typical of any criminal investigation. The anti-Catholic Polonophobe Murav'ev, for one, obsessively projected a Polish conspiracy onto the case. The testimonies of Ivan Khudiakov,* meanwhile, offer a clear example of lying: telling the history of his acquaintance with Karakozov, whom he knew well enough, Khudiakov, in the course of a single paragraph, calls him "Kozyrev or Korozov, Korazov . . . Kozyrev or Karozov . . . some sick guy. That Korozy or Kozyrev (or Kozyrev, ~~Koryzov~~, ~~Kozarev~~, *******, Korozovy)."[6] But hardly anyone else protests that much; most lies are much harder to ferret out, now no less—if not more—than then.

As for behind-the-scenes political intrigue, Secretary of the Supreme Criminal Court Iakov G. Esipovich* retrospectively reported that Chairman of the Court Prince Pavel Pavlovich Gagarin* was entirely suspicious of Murav'ev, and expressly requested of Esipovich that he not only sift through and summarize all materials produced by the investigation, but also take time to scrutinize the Count's conclusions: "[It] is imperative to verify whether this so-called organization of Murav'ev's really did put together an actual conspiracy."[7] Given that in 150 years no historian has been able to conclusively establish whether there really was a conspiracy and that Esipovich had a mere month for this task, Gagarin's request was all but impossible to fulfill. In a sense, nevertheless, this chapter mimics Esipovich's attempt to carry out Gagarin's request—albeit not "to verify whether this so-called organization of Murav'ev's really did put together an actual conspiracy," but rather to analyze how the idea of this conspiracy was put together and presented to the Russian public.

The White Terror

April 4 brought to a grinding halt whatever progressive tendencies still lingered during the later era of Great Reforms. Alternatively known as "the sixties," the era is conventionally dated from 1855 to 1866, that is, from the death of Nicholas I to Karakozov's attempt on the life of Alexander II. To be exact, "the sixties" were buried five weeks after the failed attempt, on May 13, when the tsar signed into law his "commitment to the protection of the Russian people from false and harmful doctrines that, lest their promulgation be halted, might in time shake the foundations of society."[8] Published by *Severnaia Pochta* the next day, the tsar's *profession de foi* urged the preservation of a firm moral order via proper upbringing; conservative, indeed religiously inspired education; loyalty to the government; respect for private property; and unity among social estates.[9] In other words, ideologically, it stood in diametrical opposition to the decade's undeniably progressive zeitgeist. To carry its spirit into action, Alexander II ordered the formation of a Special Council and charged it with the task of implementing administrative measures to curb the growth of harmful elements and halt the influence of "evil" on the young generation.[10]

A virtual who's who of reactionaries, the Special Council swooped down on the avant-garde of progressive journalism, forever closing down the progressive Petersburg publications *Sovremennik* (*Contemporary*) and *Russkoe Slovo* (*Russian Word*). It then tightened surveillance of the book market, determined to revisit the recently promulgated press laws, outlawed whatever student gathering the government deemed a threat to public safety or morality, and even prohibited public display of nihilist fashion.[11] By midsummer, the government's about-face had effectively increased the power of governors in the provinces, and in the capitals a broad reorganization of the police force was under way that included the formation of a special task force to protect the tsar's person.[12]

What April 4 inaugurated, in fact, was a period of such severe political reaction that it went down in history as the "White Terror" (*belyi terror*), a name taken from an article penned by N. A. Vorms and anonymously published in Herzen's *Kolokol* in early 1867. So many arrests had taken place in the aftermath of April 4, wrote Vorms, that "except for members of [Murav'ev's Investigative] Commission and affiliates of [Mikhail Nikiforovich Katkov's* conservative paper] *Moskovskie Vedomosti* [*Moscow News*]," no one felt safe.[13] Grigory Eliseev,* a regular contributor to *Sovremennik* and post–April 4 arrestee, noted that the whole world of journalism to the left of Katkov was subjected to searches and censorship. "Every day," he wrote, "news arrived that this or that literary man had been taken during the night."[14] "The censorship is so severe," read a letter from Kiev that was intercepted by the secret police, "that the only thing left to write are fairy tales, to print—ABCs, calendars, and handwriting samples."[15] In "Karakozov, tsar, and the public" (written by a certain "W" and also published in *Kolokol*), Russia was depicted as being in a near state of siege: "no one is certain that he will not fall into the hands of Murav'ev's horrible court for something said years ago . . ."[16] Between April and September 1866, indeed, Murav'ev's "horrible court," i.e. the Investigative Commission, censored, searched, questioned, arrested, and harassed thousands in the empire's major cities and provinces. In this atmosphere, not meeting the least bit of resistance, the commission made the case.

The Investigative Commission

The Third Section of His Imperial Majesty's Own Chancellery, or the tsarist security police, was created by Nicholas I in the wake of the 1825 Decembrist* uprising. Then in 1862, his reign increasingly challenged by political opposition, Alexander II ordered the formation of a special Investigative Commission in conjunction with the Third Section. Its task would be "to take the harshest and most decisive measures to avert and frustrate the harmful and dangerous intentions and actions of [political] criminals."[17] To this administrative body, at that time headed by General Lanskoi*, the tsar assigned the task of investigating the first, failed attempt on his own life. (A full list of the individuals involved in the investigation and subsequent trials can be found in Appendix B at the end of the book.)

Slow to produce results, however, the commission was reshuffled as early as April 7 and its leadership reassigned to Murav'ev, a lifelong reactionary at that time still (in)famous for his bloody suppression of the 1863 Polish separatist rebellions. His cruelty dreaded, Murav'ev reportedly said of himself that he was "not one of those Murav'evs who were hanged, but one of those who do the hanging"—whence also his sobriquet among radicals.[18] His appointment, reported a secret agent, caused "all nihilists and radicals to quiet down and sink in spirit," while "conservatives, to the contrary, livened up with hope."[19]

Until a few Guards officers were added to the case in late April to speed up the investigation, the commission's members labored tirelessly round the clock: "The number of arrests increased daily," wrote Murav'ev's protégé, Lieutenant Colonel Cherevin, "and it was physically impossible to successfully continue the questioning—even though we were at the Third Section without pause from 10 A.M. to 3 or 4 A.M."[20] During the day, members worked in teams of two or three to record testimonies; at night, in the presence of Murav'ev, the testimonies were read, compared, and gathered into a comprehensive whole that served as the basis for drawing up lists of new questions, suspects to be summoned, and the names of all those to be arrested between the early morning hours of 4 and 7 A.M. Cherevin noted that this procedure was "not entirely legal" since the law required the entire commission to be present during interrogations, "but this method enabled the quicker questioning of the mass of accused, which in three weeks had reached one hundred individuals."[21]

As was both widely suspected and in fact true, the commission applied other "not entirely legal" methods, as well. One log entry written by its original chairman, Lanskoi, noted on April 5 that the as yet unidentified criminal's "obvious lies and refusal to confess force the commission to the most active and energetic means."[22] Cherevin's notes both substantiate public rumors of torture and at least partly clarify the meaning of "the most active and energetic means": deprived of food, drink, and sleep, Karakozov was for days kept standing up straight (away from all walls against which he might have leaned and rested) and questioned incessantly.[23] What was done to Karakozov once Murav'ev was in charge was not recorded in the log, but "the hangman's" entry into the case is clearly manifested in its paperwork: suddenly Karakozov's handwriting becomes nearly indecipherable.[24] During the trial, finally, a number of defendants spoke of unspecified sufferings endured at the hands of the commission (as a result of which, some claimed, they had made false confessions, on which more below), and afterward Khudiakov, in his autobiography, claimed to have been severely beaten.[25] Therefore, notwithstanding what he called the "constant obstinacy" of those under the commission's scrutiny and no doubt thanks to "most active and energetic" methods, on June 9, 1866, Murav'ev was able to provide the tsar with a detailed report.[26]

Formally, Murav'ev's report to Alexander II was not the equivalent of the investigation abstracts regularly rubberstamped by the pre-reform judiciary. Containing neither criminal counts nor a catalogued presentation of evidence, this was not a legal indictment. Nevertheless, this document must properly be considered the crucial blueprint for perceptions of the Karakozov case. Not only did it enjoy imperial endorsement (Alexander II ordered the Special Council charged with implementing the imperial decree of May 13 to give Murav'ev's report careful consideration), and thus shape knowledge of the case among the upper executive echelons. In addition, in accordance with Murav'ev's recommendation, on August 3, a condensed version of the report was published in *Severnaia Pochta* and then reprinted by all major newspapers.[27] In other words, this was the reading via which the Russian public first encountered the facts of the Karakozov case: a reactionary's synopsis of a highly complex and contradictory paper trail. And since the report had the dominant shaping power as far as the image of the case was concerned, it is also this document that has most forcefully informed and set the parameters for historians— sometimes without their being aware of it. For all these reasons, it is Murav'ev's report that will now introduce the story of the Karakozov case.

The Murav'ev Report

Murav'ev's narrative unfolds over some forty pages, their perusal facilitated by marginal headings: "About the Person of the Criminal Karakozov"; "Karakozov's Membership of a Socialist Society in Moscow"; "Purpose of the Society"; "Methods of the Society"; "The Secret Circle named 'Hell'"; "Idea of the Attempted Tsaricide"; "Purpose of Tsaricide"; "About Ishutin*"; "About Khudiakov"; etc. Tacked onto his presentation of the crime of April 4 is a lengthy conclusion in which Murav'ev tracks the historical development of politically dangerous tendencies. What follows below summarizes Murav'ev's presentation of the Karakozov case— whence first took flight the specter of terrorism.

After days of posing as the peasant Aleksei Petrov, the criminal finally revealed his true identity: Dmitry Vladimirovich Karakozov, twenty-four years old (*sic:* twenty-five), a landowner's son from Saratov province, graduate of Penzenskaia gymnasium, and ex-student of Kazan and Moscow universities' law faculties. In Moscow, Karakozov had belonged to a society that had been "formed in 1863," consisted mostly of students, and intended to spread socialism, overthrow the government, and wreck the foundations of religion and public morality.[28] The society was called "The Organization."

To explain how "The Organization" intended to achieve these objectives, Murav'ev listed its activities under the heading, "Methods of the Society":

    a. propaganda among the rural population . . . the land belongs to the people,
    b. provocation of the peasantry against landowners, nobility, and power in general,
    c. building of schools, cooperatives [etc.] to get closer to the people and inspire them with the malicious doctrine of extreme socialism,
    d. establishment in the provinces of libraries, bookstores, free schools, and various societies on the basis of extreme socialist and nihilist principles . . . to attract and prepare new members and at the same time stand in a relationship of dependence on the central society in Moscow and receive further direction from it,
    e. the spread of socialism among the people,
    f. propaganda up and down the Volga (via steamships).[29]

"The Organization," Murav'ev went on, was divided into departments with names like "Mutual Aid," "Translators," "Publishers," and "Private Labor Incentive," which would eventually be covered by an umbrella agency for which it was planned to secure legal permission.[30] Financial backing was provided either by members themselves or, if need be, by "robbery, murdering the rich, and postal raids."[31]

While all of what Murav'ev asserted were the society's 72 members supported its ultimate political goals, they had clashed on the matter of a revolutionary timetable. It had been those wishing to unleash a revolution "sooner," so said the count, who had come to advocate tsaricide.

Now one of the central problems for the official investigation had in fact been the conceptual origin of tsaricide. Murav'ev's report promoted the theory that tsaricide had been a European import: Nikolai Ishutin, Karakozov's cousin, had introduced the idea in early 1866 after Ivan Khudiakov, a recent returnee from Geneva, told him of the existence of a regicidal European Revolutionary Committee that was willing and able to supply nascent oppositional movements across the continent with weapons, "Orsini bombs," and fulminate of mercury.[32] And it had been this very Khudiakov, according to the count, who had insisted that a kindred committee be established in Moscow.

Thus was founded "a small circle under the secret name 'Hell'" (*kruzhok pod tainym naimenovaniem "ada"*).[33] All members of "Hell" took an oath to murder whomsoever crossed their path—not excluding those belonging to "The Organization," should they prove too obstinate to follow directives. Equally rigorous rules applied to "Hell's" designated tsaricide: this "villain" was obliged to sever all ties binding him to proper society and delve into an underworld of debauched vagabondage so as to distract attention from his political activities (going so far as to turn agent provocateur if need be); upon execution of his crime, the tsaricide was to poison himself, leaving behind only an explanatory proclamation.

The purpose of tsaricide, explained the count to its intended victim, consisted in provoking "general unrest, revolution in the government, the extermination of the nobility and landowners in general, and the formation of a new government on the basis of socialist principles."[34]

Of all those in the society to whom it had been suggested to form the secret circle "Hell"—Petr Ermolov,* Ishutin, Dmitry Iurasov,* Karakozov, Osip Motkov,* Nikolai Stranden,* and Maximilian Zagibalov*—some had thought it still "too early" for tsaricide. Karakozov, however—"being, according to the testimony of his friends, always taciturn, an intense hypochondriac, who wanted, in his sick state, to commit suicide"—did not share these sentiments.[35] During the first week of Lent (in early February), Karakozov traveled to Petersburg, contacted Khudiakov, and told him of his tsaricidal plan.

Once Murav'ev's narrative has landed Karakozov at Khudiakov's doorstep, the exploits of the future tsaricide are momentarily abandoned in favor of a closer look at a man the text identifies as a writer "well known for his malicious teachings."[36] The count's reenactment stages Khudiakov as a personified nodal point of revolutionary paths stretching from Western Europe to eastern Siberia: Khudiakov was the "main agent" in Petersburg for all Moscow circles; his Geneva contacts included Herzen; he personally knew Polish separatists exiled in the empire's coldest hinterlands; and at home in the capital he had ties with *Sovremennik, Russkoe Slovo,* and with the recently deceased scientist Nikolai Nozhin,* whom Murav'ev cast as the founder of a socialist circle in Petersburg and a man closely connected with agitators abroad.

Khudiakov had also hatched a plan to free Nikolai Gavrilovich Chernyshevsky,* the hallowed author of *What Is To Be Done?* (*Chto delat'?* 1863), who had been exiled to Siberia after an arrest on trumped-up charges a few years back. Courtesy of Khudiakov's underground connections (listed are Ishutin and friends; Eliseev; and a nobleman named Alexander Evropeus,* who—although Murav'ev's report only reveals this later—in turn had contact with Karakozov's doctor, Alexander A. Kobylin), Khudiakov had been able to locate a willing agent, Organization member Nikolai Stranden, and supplied him with a false passport, poison, and letters of introduction to various people in Western and Eastern Siberia. All of this evidence left no doubt that, at the time of his arrest, Stranden had been poised to embark on his mission to rescue Chernyshevsky. In the same way, using his "ally" Alexander Nikolsky* as a go-between, Khudiakov had charged the Moscow circle with rescuing Nikolai Serno-Solov'evich,* who had been arrested along with Chernyshevsky.

Having thus fettered Khudiakov with a chain of names most dreaded by the tsar, the report swings its focus back to the figure of the tsaricide. From here on, the narrative sees Karakozov furtive: *sans-papiers*, he is forced to live nomadically, landing first somewhere on Nevsky Prospect, then on one of the city's northern islands, then in the Hotel Znamen-skaia, and, finally, with his doctor, Kobylin.

When Karakozov, "in peasant clothing," showed up at the clinic where Kobylin worked, according to Murav'ev's narrative, the latter had denied him medical attention and yet—even though he was well aware of Kara-kozov's illegal status—not only sheltered him at his private home for several days, but even discussed socialist propaganda with him. Obviously, this cluster—an incognito, a doctor denying a patient medical treatment, sheltering an illegal stranger, and socialism—was meant to imply a conspiratorial tie between Kobylin and Karakozov. Karakozov had testified, the report continued, that Kobylin had told him that there existed in Petersburg, as Murav'ev put it, "various circles and a Konstantinian party"; mentioned the names of two literati, Evropeus and Alexander Putiata*; and supplied him with poison.[37] Kobylin's counterclaim that Karakozov had stolen the poison from him, Murav'ev prompted his imperial reader, "should not be considered probable": during Karakozov's last days in Petersburg, Kobylin had helped him financially and been concerned to find him living quarters.[38] Probably, the report implies, the doctor had willingly supplied the tsaricide with the pharmaceuticals necessary to kill himself after committing his crime.

When he did not place Karakozov alongside either Khudiakov or Kobylin, Murav'ev had him vagabonding his way through Petersburg, associating with unidentified Medical-Surgical Academy students and distributing his proclamation, "To My Worker Friends" (*Druz'iam rabochim*). As regards this proclamation, the count assured the tsar, besides one sent anonymously to Saint Petersburg's governor (Suvorov) "as far back as March" and another that was evidently tossed out by a factory worker, no copies had been found.[39] Vagabondage, poisons, a proclamation . . . : Karakozov, Murav'ev meant, had acted out "Hell's" program.

The Muscovite secret circle, so the report went, was aware of Karakozov's plans, but worried about his carelessness and his timing. During the fourth week of Lent (late March), therefore, Stranden and Ermolov were dispatched to Petersburg to fetch Karakozov. They found him, "near the Winter Palace, in peasant dress," a bit of information Murav'ev clearly inserted to show Karakozov lurking incognito near the tsar's home.[40] During their conversation, Karakozov told Stranden and Ermolov about his relations in Petersburg, "mainly with students from the Medical-Surgical Academy"; then they persuaded him to abandon his plan; and then Karakozov finally "gave his word" that he would return to Moscow.[41] Then

Stranden and Ermolov left, but Karakozov himself did not; he did not quit the capital until he was coaxed once again, this time by a letter from his cousin Ishutin. A few early Easter days were consequently spent in Moscow, but no later than the next Wednesday, March 29, Karakozov was back in the northern capital, reestablished contact with Khudiakov and Kobylin, and devoted the last weekend before April 4 to securing his weaponry.

In the remainder of the report, Murav'ev provided a few more biographical details on Ishutin, Ermolov, and lesser-known society members, but, having narrated the history of the crime, he principally turned to underline its immediate cause as the "moral depravity" wrought by the overexposure to socialist, nihilist, and democratic ideas through free media and popular education. Establishing a direct link between April 4 and the unchecked dispersal of "exile, Russian, and foreign books and the essays of Herzen and company," Murav'ev warned that, given the "present frame of mind" in the empire, the likes of Karakozov might be numerous.[42] In a move that still remains characteristic for approaches to the revolutionary movement, Murav'ev proclaimed a direct, one-to-one relation between the words (or theory) of radicals and the acts (or praxis) of revolutionaries.

The *Severnaia Pochta* Publication and the Official Response

A few points must be made about the extract that was drawn from Murav'ev's report and released by the Ministry of Justice's *Severnaia Pochta*. These concern the editorial process that took place between Murav'ev's June 9 recommendation that his report be submitted to *Severnaia Pochta* and the article's August 3 publication date.

The original document was, first of all, almost entirely shorn of names. Not only the proper names of suspects, but also, in the severely cropped section on Khudiakov, those of Herzen, Eliseev, Evropeus, Nikolsky, and even of *Sovremennik* and *Russkoe Slovo* were censored. Khudiakov's own presence was rendered ghostly: he haunts the text as a macabre "agent of the Moscow circles" and disseminator of corrupt popular literature.

Three names remained, however, and a string of others was added. The first of the three was Nozhin. Having recently died, he evidently no longer posed a threat; it was even safe to identify him as "an extreme nihilist . . . with contacts and in correspondence with foreign agitators." The two others were Chernyshevsky and Serno-Solovevich, the meaning whereof was apparently assumed stable enough to always and forever conjure up visions of otherwise unimaginable revolutionary horrors. Arguably, moreover, given that Chernyshevsky and Serno-Solovevich were both in Sibe-

rian exile, they were as harmless as the dead Nozhin. The additions were
of Polish origin and consisted of convicted politicals whose ties with the
Muscovites were said to have involved shady politico-financial dealings directed by a Moscow-based Polish committee, *Narodowa Opieka* (*The People's
Welfare*)—a small bit of information that went a long way in providing support for everybody's favorite theory that the conspiracy was Polish in origin (see Chapter 2).

The section on Dr. Kobylin was also sanitized. Most notably, Karakozov's testimony about having been told by Kobylin of "various circles
and a Konstantinian party" in Petersburg became a generalized reference
to "social circles with political goals." Understandably, the government
did not wish to give credence to any rumors of court intrigues involving,
of all people, the tsar's own brother, the constitutionally inclined Konstantin Nikolaevich Romanov. It is worth emphasizing that these editorial
changes did not diminish the report's originally strong suggestions of
Kobylin's guilt—hence the public shock when he was acquitted.

Details implying administrative negligence and ineptitude, of course,
were gone. Several pages detailing the Moscow society's semilegal grass-
roots practices went missing, as did mention of the "completely unre-
stricted distribution" of socialist, nihilist, and revolutionary ideas among
Russia's youth. And such, too, was the fate of a paragraph noting that "as
far back as March," a copy of Karakozov's proclamation had been sent to
Saint Petersburg's governor.

Lastly, someone rewrote tsaricide's political purpose, amputating most
of the specifics and leaving only "general unrest and revolution in government."[43] Thus having its real enemy and *raison d'être* subtracted, this
revolutionary violence is blind, unjustified, and anarchic.

Officialdom's response to the *Severnaia Pochta* publication was mixed.
No doubt the very fact that Murav'ev's article was published meant that
Alexander II endorsed its content, but it hardly met with approval from
the entire government. According to Esipovich, for example, the publication much grieved Prince Gagarin. It was entirely possible, Gagarin
supposed, that the court might see the case differently than had the commission, which would mean that the judicial verdict would not coincide
with what had appeared in print. Said Gagarin, "[Murav'ev's article] has
already condemned all of them to death. Of course, they are serious criminals: I told the emperor that for three of them, at least, his mercy is unattainable. . . . Well, it's clear that Karakozov, his cousin [Ishutin], and
[Khudiakov] must be executed, but the minister of justice [Zamiatnin,*
also the case's prosecutor], on the basis of Murav'ev's essay, suggests
executing eleven, eleven or ten, I can't remember . . ."[44] The reader will
recall that because he did not trust Murav'ev, Gagarin had expressly requested of Esipovich that he scrutinize the commission's conclusions.

Hence Gagarin's grief: before anything had been verified by the court, after months of absolute secrecy—and therefore guaranteed to make an impression—Murav'ev's version was being publicized by the official newspaper of the Ministry of Interior. The *Severnaia Pochta* publication, in other words, was a clear attempt by the executive to domineer, to impress its version of events onto public consciousness. And since this version was influencing the minister of justice to write up certain indictments, moreover, it obviously did not bode well for the separation of powers that the judicial reforms were supposed to have secured. Minister of Interior Petr Valuev* even noted in his diary—with disapproval, to his merit—that Chief of Police Feodor Feodorovich Trepov* was busy building eleven gallows as early as August 20, before the first trial had even been concluded.[45]

A further upset took place just a few days later, when *Moskovskie Vedomosti* carried Katkov's critical and, it should be added, partisan reading of the *Severnaia Pochta* article.[46] "Nowhere else in the world," an outraged Esipovich claimed to have told Gagarin, "would any journal or any newspaper dare pronounce in public its verdict on a case being considered by the court and known only through rumors and gossip."[47]

All this provides evidence of serious confusion, indeed strife, with respect to political sovereignty. Who decides life and death here? The official sovereign, Alexander II? Chairman of the Court Gagarin? Minister of Justice Zamiatnin? The judges? The head of the Investigative Commission Murav'ev? Perhaps even the journalist Katkov? And lest it be forgotten, all this confusion occurred in the aftermath of the fact that an ordinary man had taken it upon himself to decide that the time had come for the emperor to die and that, as Murav'ev had noted in his report to Alexander II, given the "present frame of mind" in the empire, the likes of this man might be numerous. The question of sovereignty, in other words, needed not only to be practically decided and structurally agreed upon, but also, for appearances' sake, publicly resolved.

The Supreme Criminal Court

What conceivably exacerbated the confusion over and contestation of sovereignty was that Russia did not have a permanent Supreme Criminal Court until the late 1880s. Before then, a court would be convened temporarily to try state criminals of the magnitude of Emelian Pugachev,* the Decembrists, the Petrashevtsy,* or indeed Karakozov and company, but then disbanded immediately afterward. On June 28, 1866, therefore, Alexander II decreed that a Supreme Criminal Court be formed for the specific purpose of examining and judging the findings of the Investigative Commission.[48] Fully formed, the court consisted of five judges; a prosecutor; counsel for the defense; three religious authorities (of Orthodox, Evangelical, and Catholic faith); a secretary plus assistants to keep minutes; and the first ever stenographer for a Russian trial. As mentioned, Secretary Esipovich later wrote up his recollections of the trial, as did Ishutin's defense lawyer, D. V. Stasov.*

"Oh, how regrettable!" Esipovich claims to have opined upon hearing that the trial would proceed behind closed doors.[49] At first, this regret seems to have been a matter of principle ("Oh, how illegal!" he might have claimed to have said); later, Esipovich became convinced that the accused were so vile and idiotic that they could only have provoked disgust or laughter among the public, even among possible sympathizers, and that the government had missed a very real opportunity to stamp out whatever had caused this crime by keeping the case under wraps.[50]

Because it so pleased him, however, Alexander II decided against an open court and, moreover, because his future daughter-in-law was due to arrive in Saint Petersburg for an early September wedding, insisted that the trial be brought to a close with the utmost expedition.[51]

Also telling of the tsar's thinking was his wish for the trial's setting, namely the grounds of the empire's most dreaded prison, the Peter-Paul Fortress, which was at that time stuffed to full capacity with the hundreds arrested in connection with April 4.[52] Asked about on-site accommodations for the court, the governor of the Peter-Paul Fortress, General Sorokin,* symbolically offered his private dwellings, the very premises where the Decembrists had been tried in 1826 and the Petrashevtsy in 1849.[53]

The First Trial (August 18–31, 1866)

The first trial was in session on August 18, 20, 22, 24, and 31 and involved, besides Karakozov, ten defendants, i.e. those "ten or eleven" whom Zamiatnin suggested executing, according to Gagarin, on the basis of Murav'ev's report. Their names were Petr Ermolov, Nikolai Ishutin, Dmitry Iurasov, Ivan Khudiakov, Alexander Kobylin, Osip Motkov, Petr Nikolaev,* Viacheslav Shaganov,* Nikolai Stranden, and Maximilian Zagibalov. At the end of the first trial, however, only Karakozov and Kobylin heard their verdicts; the other nine were judged a month later, along with the remaining twenty-five defendants.

On August 10, the court convened for a pre-trial "administrative session" in which indictments, witness lists, and a choice of counsel were distributed to defendants, and the court officially announced its decision to try the case behind closed doors. The next day, each of the defendants met for the first time with his lawyer. One week later, on August 18, the first trial began.

It has been noted in the scholarship that the Judicial Statutes continued to exclude defense from the preliminary investigation and pre-trial decisions, but in this case, the temporal constraints were particularly acute: counsel had exactly one week to get acquainted with the material and prepare a defense.[54] Khudiakov, in his autobiography, writes that he had occasion to meet his lawyer for the first time exactly three days before the trial and was told, "I don't know what I can do in light of these accusations . . . the case is enormous; I won't even succeed in reading part of it; there are so many testimonies, and they all contradict one another."[55] Moreover, although the accused were not necessarily defended badly, closing statements by the defense indicate that none of the lawyers was especially eager to defend his client, so widely feared and eagerly avoided was the case. Expressing the hope that "this cup pass from him" before he was charged with the duties of secretary of the court, Esipovich leaves little doubt that he originally saw the case as political suicide, and he quotes Gagarin as repeatedly expressing the dramatic conviction that he, Gagarin, and not the emperor, had been hit by Karakozov's bullet, and that this case would end up putting him in the grave.[56] And neither of these two, unlike counsel, was even charged with the task of defending the tsaricide and his alleged co-conspirators. "In my personal opinion," said Karakozov's lawyer, Aleksei P. Ostriakov,* "there can be no discussion whatsoever here about mitigating circumstances . . . ; nevertheless, if the law put me in this place to defend someone who stands accused . . ."[57]

Karakozov stood accused of attempted tsaricide, of course, but this was not the crux of the trial (he had been caught on the spot, after all, and so was obviously guilty). The crux of the trial, rather, was "Hell." In fact, excepting Kobylin, who was only charged with having known about Karakozov's tsaricidal plans, the most damning count against all of the principal defendants was having inspired, having founded, or having been a member of "a secret revolutionary society, "Hell," having tsaricide as its exclusive goal." And yet the court's verdict—released by the newspapers at the very hour Karakozov was being publicly hanged on September 3— avoided "Hell" altogether.

Barely two pages long, the verdict first lists the two counts of which Karakozov stood accused: attempted tsaricide and belonging to a secret revolutionary society. At the outset, it states that Karakozov had pled guilty to a crime he had acknowledged was "so great that not even the morbid, nervous condition he suffered at the time could justify it," and then adds that he had nevertheless, during the trial, sought recourse to a psychological defense.[58] The verdict then contests this defense both legally and empirically. As for belonging to an (unspecified) "secret revolutionary society," the verdict certainly implies Karakozov's guilt and explicitly states that his extremism had been a secret to none who knew him, but it also explains that Karakozov's unmitigated guilt of attempted tsaricide alone is enough to condemn him to death. Whether or not Karakozov was guilty on this second count had no bearing whatsoever on the degree of his punishment, and thus the court found the question to be irrelevant. Karakozov's "belonging to a secret revolutionary society, "Hell," having tsaricide as its exclusive goal," and by extension the very existence of this society, were therefore left undiscussed.

In sum, given that the only details from the crime's prehistory that peppered the Karakozov verdict were already known from the *Severnaia Pochta* article published a month earlier; and that the Kobylin not guilty verdict (also published September 3, 1866) mentioned nothing at all about any "secret revolutionary society" (since he had not been accused of having inspired, having founded, or having been a member of "Hell"); the public, at the time of Karakozov's execution, still did know whether that sinister circle of suicide assassins, "Hell," really existed or not. Which also explains why the court postponed handing down judgments for the remaining nine defendants until the end of the second trial: this bought the court extra time to decide the question of "Hell's" existence.

The Second Trial (September 7–12, 1866)

The second trial was in session on 7, 8, 10, and 12 September, and involved twenty-five more defendants. For the record, their names were Aleksei Bibikov, Feofan Borisov, Varlaam Cherkezov, Viktor Fedoseev, Alexander Ivanov, Dmitry Ivanov, Konstantin Kichin, Nikolai Kutyev, Adolf Langhaus, Fedor Lapkin, Pavel Maevsky, Alexander Malikov, Orest Malinin, Maximilian Marks, Fedor Nikiforov, Alexander Nikolsky*, Leonid Obolensky, Nikolai Peterson, Apollon Polumordvinov, Aleksei Sergievsky, Boleslav Shostakovich, Vasily Sobolev, Boleslav Trusov, Dmitry Voskresensky, and Alexander Voznesensky.

The verdicts on these twenty-five and on the nine whose cases had been heard during the first trial were all read on September 24. As the only documents to be released for public consumption, they were more carefully worded than anything else produced by the court. What follows below concentrates on those aspects of the verdict that are relevant to the subsequent discussion on the nature of conspiracy and secret societies.

The verdict opens with the crimes with which the accused had been charged:

> The charges against Khudiakov included (1) enabling Karakozov to commit his crime, (2) knowing Karakozov's intention, and (3) instigating Ishutin to establish a secret revolutionary society with tsaricide as its goal.

Ishutin was charged with (1) knowledge of Karakozov's tsaricidal intention and not reporting this information to the authorities, and (2) instigation of his friends to found a secret revolutionary society, "Hell," intended to create a revolution by means of tsaricide.

Ermolov, Stranden, and Iurasov stood accused of (1) knowing of Karakozov's intention, and (2) belonging to the secret society "Hell."

Zagibalov, Motkov, Shaganov, and Nikolaev also stood accused of belonging to the secret society "Hell."

The other defendants were charged with (1) belonging to a secret revolutionary society, "The Organization," whose goal was the overthrow of the government, and (2) knowledge of the existence of another secret revolutionary society, "Hell," and not reporting this information to the authorities.[59]

"As far back as 1863," the text states after listing the formal crimes and beginning to narrate their history, "a circle of young people infected with socialist ideas formed in Moscow."[60] Already, this circle of affected adolescents projects far less of a threat than would, for example, a simple sentence reading, "a society was founded." Next, the judges see this circle building "schools and various associations, a bookbinding institution, and a clothing company," and founding "societies of translators and of mutual aid," some of which were established without permits, and some of whose activities were outright criminal. The document lists no activities more specific than that the school's teachings were subversive of power, however, and tucked among bookbinders and dressmakers, the translators and mutually helpful people seem less threatening, too. "Some members of these societies," the text goes on to declare as if referring to a multiplicity, "wanted a more definitive base for action and started to gather at meetings to discuss various questions and proposals and to compose draft regulations."[61] Unannounced, formal membership of what was initially but a circle of young people has now crept into the text. The verdict goes on to state that while none of the drafts was officially adopted as their program, they included such criminal outrages as (1) unleashing not just an economic, but a veritable social revolution, (2) freeing Chernyshevsky so that he could lead the revolution, and (3) enshrining the credo that "the end justifies the means." In sum, this history implies that there existed an increasingly radical society whose members were in the midst of adopting a formal structure and whose intentions were revolutionary, criminal, and amoral. Finally,

in a small circle (*v nebol'shom kruzhke*) there were discussions about whether it would be worthwhile, following the example of the European Revolutionary Committee, to permit tsaricides and the extermination of governments in general as one of the means toward a general revolution. . . . Some rejected [tsaricide] outright, others postponed it for an indefinite time, except Karakozov . . . [62]

The secret revolutionary society of tsaricides from the start of the document has been reduced to discussions and arguments, albeit criminal in nature, within the confines of not just a circle (*krug*), nor even a diminutive *kruzhok,* but a "small *kruzhok.*" Moreover, within this tiny enclave of radicalism, besides the instigator Ishutin, no one unreservedly granted that violence be permitted. No one, that is, but the by now dead Karakozov and the non-Russian European Revolutionary Committee. The vision of "Hell" unleashed by the *Severnaia Pochta* article was thus partly demystified.

On the basis of both the preliminary investigation and the trial proceedings, as the text goes on to explain, the court had concluded that,

1. Ishutin, Ermolov, and Stranden were the main personages involved in the formation of circles with criminal goals,
2. Ishutin had first "stirred up discussions" about the *European Revolutionary Committee* and suggested that a similar society be founded in Moscow,
3. Ermolov, Stranden, Iurasov, Zagibalov, Shaganov, and Motkov had all participated in those discussions, although they all opposed the idea of tsaricide,
4. Ishutin, Ermolov, Stranden, and Iurasov had all known about Karakozov's intention,
5. Khudiakov neither had knowledge of Karakozov's intention, nor helped him carry it out, but he did first introduce the information about the *European Revolutionary Committee* and, although he had not instigated the founding of a similar society in Moscow, he did know that there existed in Moscow a revolutionary society whose goal was an upheaval in the government,
6. Malinin, Dmitry Ivanov, Lapkin, and Alexander Ivanov were all members of "The Organization" and were aware that its goals were illegal. All they knew about the formation of "Hell," however, they had heard from Motkov, and none of them had been certain whether it had really been suggested to found such a society,
7. Kichin, Sobolev, Sergievsky, Borisov, Voskresensky, Kutyev, Polumordivnov, and Prince Cherkezov were also members of "The Organization," but were rarely at meetings, had but a dim understanding of socialism, nihilism, and communism, and their motivation to join had essentially been poverty and the hope that their financial situations might improve.[63]

Thus, at this point in the reading of the verdicts, the court has officially reduced "Hell" not even to discursive existence, but an inconclusive philosophical exercise: some six or seven friends had debated whether it would or would not be beneficial to invent "Hell."

The existence of "The Organization," however, was affirmed: the court named it a secret, illegal, criminal, revolutionary society with actual members.

It is worth underlining this once more: the verdict affirms the existence of "The Organization," and nowhere states that "Hell" did not exist. Doubtlessly, this was because stating so would have meant dismissing the major count against the nine principal defendants: one cannot be found guilty of having inspired, having founded, or having been a member of "Hell" if "Hell" did not exist.

Normatively, however, the difference in status between the societies had little bearing on the fate of the accused. As the verdict notes, according to articles 241, 242, and 243 of the Criminal Code, *every* plot against the life of the emperor—*executed, attempted, prepared, planned, written, spoken, or however else*—was a state crime punishable by death, as was participation in any such plot or not reporting one's knowledge of any such plot to the authorities. Among the punishable acts via which one could proceed "to whatever preparation" (*k kakomu libo dlia prigotovleniiu*) for this first of six state crimes under Russian law, article 242 specifically listed establishing or joining a conspiracy or society.[64] The relevance of this clause, the verdict explained, was that article 318, which defined as a state crime membership of "secret societies of whatever denomination" (*tainye, pod kakim by to ni bylo naimenovaniem, obshchestva*) aiming to harm the peace and safety of the government or its lawfully decreed order, required sentencing in accordance with article 242.[65] Thus, members of "The Organization" (criminalized under article 318) who had—in the context of discussions about their revolutionary goals—spoken about the possible use of tsaricide (criminalized under article 241) or a secret society of tsaricides (article 242) were subject to the death penalty because the very initiation of such discussion could fall under the "whatever preparation" mentioned in article 242. The combination of articles 318, 241, and 242, therefore, allowed the court to circumvent having to decide the question of "Hell's" actual existence but nevertheless use its potential as an idea to ensure legitimate convictions and death sentences.

Based on this logic, on September 24 the Supreme Criminal Court meted out sentences to all but Malikov, Bibikov, Obolensky, Nikolsky, and Nikiforov, who were acquitted (but nonetheless placed under surveillance), and Voznesensky, whose name resembled someone else's and who had mistakenly been arrested, jailed, and tried. Sentences divided up as follows: one defendant was sentenced to death by hanging (Ishutin); seven defendants to hard labor (Iurasov and Stranden to life; Ermolov to twenty years; Zagibalov, Shaganov, and Nikolaev to twelve years; Motkov to eight years); nine to exile in Siberia (Khudiakov, Malinin, D. Ivanov, Lapkin, A. Ivanov, Fedoseev, Marks, Maevsky, Shostakovich); and eleven to prison terms of six to eight months (Langhaus, Kichin, Sobolev, Sergievsky, Borisov, Voskresensky, Kutyev, Polumordvinov, Trusov, Cherkezov, Peterson).[66]

According to Esipovich, Alexander II was displeased with the verdicts: they were too mild to leave comfortable room for his imperial right to show clemency.[67] Nonetheless, on October 2 he reduced some of the sentences. Stranden and Iurasov had their life sentences of hard labor reduced to twenty and ten years respectively; Ermolov, Zagibalov, Shaganov, and Motkov each had theirs reduced to ten, six, six, and four years; and Nikolaev's twelve-year sentence was cut by a third. The terms of settlement and exile for A. Ivanov, D. Ivanov, Shostakovich, and Lapkin were also altered; they either were exiled to places less dreary than Siberia, or tossed into military service.[68]

At 7 A.M. on October 4, 1866, exactly half a year after Karakozov's failed assassination, eleven black carts carrying eleven prisoners entered a crowded Smolensk Square for the execution of the Supreme Criminal Court's sentences: physical death for Ishutin, civil death for the ten others. As Ishutin already stood blindfolded and roped on the scaffold, Alexander II "suddenly" sent word that the condemned man's life would be spared. All eleven prisoners were then carted off to the Nikolaevskaia railroad line leading to Moscow and beyond, and rolled toward years of exile, hard labor, prison, and, in some cases, insanity and/or death.[69]

Sources

In this way, the materials of the Karakozov case were not exposed for public viewing, but rather filtered through official readings of a revolutionary conspiracy. But what happens when the case's unseen materials are brought out?

To repeat: no one, including historians, has ever conclusively demonstrated whether there did or did not exist a conspiracy to assassinate Alexander II in 1866. Even by combing through the thousands of pages of testimony that were written by the hundreds of people who were arrested in the tens of cities of the empire after April 4, and by making an encyclopedic reconstruction of their social networks, it is probably not possible to ever get a definitive answer to the question of "Hell's" existence. One particular aspect, though, should always be kept in mind, namely the nature of the sources of the information about "Hell," such as whether a particular source was an actual member, or a friend on the fringes of their "organization" who picked up a rumor. Which brings us to a figure heretofore unmentioned: the ex-student Ignaty Ignat'evich Korevo,* who knew Nikolaev, Ishutin, Stranden, and Shaganov, but was not centrally positioned in their social network.

On April 19, Korevo voluntarily turned himself in to the authorities in Moscow and requested that he be placed under arrest and deported to Saint Petersburg, where he wished to have a personal interview with Murav'ev.[70] Four days later, Murav'ev reported to Alexander II that Korevo had testified that there existed a secret society in Moscow whose members were called *mortusy* ("dead men"), whose goal was "tsaricide and the annihilation of authority with murder and poison," and which had ties to the Polish underground.[71]

Korevo's testimony was reprinted in the Soviet journal *Krasnyi Arkhiv* (*Red Archive*), along with a note by its editor, A. A. Shilov, stating that what had happened to him was unknown.[72] In all of the nine hundred–plus pages of trial records and documentary notes edited under the auspices of M. M. Klevensky and K. G. Kotel'nikov, there is not a single mention of Korevo: evidently, he was not involved in the trial. Finally, there is a note from June 16, 1866, written by Murav'ev and addressed to Alexander II, suggesting that Korevo be awarded one thousand silver rubles from the State Treasury.[73] Nothing else. Sometime between June 16 and late August, Korevo disappeared, and there is simply no information about the life of this figure other than what he told the Investigative Commission: that he was born into the nobility in 1841, orphaned after the death of his father in 1844 or 1845, and then, thanks to his talents, made his way to Moscow University.[74]

At any rate, it was Korevo, on April 22, 1866, who first made mention of "Hell" and its *mortusy*. After that, obviously in response to a question formulated on the basis of Korevo's testimony, Khudiakov told the commission on April 25 that "about '*mortusy*,' i.e. people obliged to sacrifice their lives, he [Ishutin] told me nothing."[75] Three days later, on April 28, Karakozov was asked for the first time about "a secret society calling itself "Hell" or *mortusy*.[76] By the time the indictments were written up, "Hell" had become a secret revolutionary society having tsaricide as its exclusive goal. Turning to the trial transcripts, that is, to all those pages not presented to the public, will clarify just how the notion of "Hell" crystallized—and bring out in starker relief the difficulty involved in determining, then as now, the (non)existence of a conspiracy.

Transcripts

A number of terms referring to student and/or revolutionary gatherings were used in nineteenth-century Russia, some of which were foreign borrowings: *skhodka* or *sobranie* (meeting), *kruzhok* (circle), *obshchestvo* (society), *agentura* (agency, intelligence), *assotsiatsiia* (association), *komitet* (committee), *organizatsiia* (organization), *partiia* (party), *klub* (club), *firma* (firm), and *artel'* (cooperative).

Several considerations need to be borne in mind concerning the usage of these terms. First, *obshchestvo* is indeed the term for *a* society or social circle, but also, much more broadly, for polite society or society in general. Second, the lack of articles in the Russian language can lead to a confusion whenever the word "organization" is used: read as if preceded by *an* or *any,* "organization" can substitute for any of the above-listed terms, but if the word is read as if *the* were implied, it comes to signify "The Organization," that is, a specific organization under this name. Indeed, and this is the third point, the referents of most of these terms are in fact very vague. *Skhodka,* for example, which originally was reserved for village meetings, derives from the verb *skhodit'sia,* to meet, converge, gather, come together, become friends, or agree. As in other languages, such terms do not exactly guard their meaning jealously, and precisely herein lies both their advantage and disadvantage.

Throughout the investigation and the trial, the efforts of the government and the court were directed toward making the diverse meanings of all these terms coincide, smoothing out discrepancies, and stuffing the remaining gaps with polemics. To understand how this process worked, it is necessary first of all to examine some of the discrepancies in meaning that became invisible once access to this data was officially barred.

1. "Hell" as Talk

a. ERMOLOV: When Ishutin went to Petersburg, he brought back news of the European Committee, and that started various sorts of talks and suggestions, which afterward were called "Hell." [The talks concerned] the extent to which tsaricide was useful and how to commit it.[77]

b. SHAGANOV: There were just talks (*tolki,* also "rumors"), and the society "Hell" was nothing organized.[78]

c. PRESIDENT GAGARIN TO STRANDEN: Can you say anything about "Hell," about the existence of the intention to carry out a tsaricide?
STRANDEN: We had some vague talks apropos of the European Committee, rumors of which were brought to us by Ishutin, who, in turn, had found out about its existence from Khudiakov. The goal of the European Committee, as Ishutin told it to us, was the extermination of monarchical families. After Ishutin told us, there were a few talks about the European Committee. Ermolov was there and he called the European Committee "*Hell.*"
PRESIDENT GAGARIN TO STRANDEN: What was the name of that circle formed from the society "The Organization" for the surveillance of the activities of members of the organization?

STRANDEN: We had no such circle; there were just some arguments about it among some people.[79]

d. ISHUTIN: "Hell" did not exist; it was no more, no less than some stupid speeches made under the influence of wine. . . . If I acknowledged ["Hell"], then only because they [members of the Investigative Commission] demanded that I do so, stressed that my friends had already admitted everything, and that if I said everything straight away I'd lighten my sufferings, role, and situation. I said that, really, "Hell" did not exist, but that talks about it only took place at the time of fun and games.

GAGARIN: This is not about games; this is about Karakozov appearing to everybody as a member of the circle "Hell."

ISHUTIN: He was not a member of the circle "Hell," since "Hell" itself did not exist, but he was there during our talks, though in his morbid condition he did not participate at all.[80]

2. Suggestive Questioning and the Co-Authorship of Conspiracy

a. GAGARIN TO MOTKOV: How can you say that you don't know the circle "Hell" when in your testimonies before the commission you acknowledged the existence of such a circle?

MOTKOV: In my testimonies I said that an idea about the necessity of the formation of a society "Hell" had been expressed, but that idea was not put into practice. I drew up a list of members of "Hell," but explained that it was a list of people who wanted to form the circle "Hell."

MINISTER OF JUSTICE: How could you make a list of a society you don't know?

MOTKOV: I heard from the commission that the society exists.[81]

b. ISHUTIN: They [the commission] said: Write about "Hell" and about "The Organization," and it will be just a formality, neither more nor less. . . . I wanted to say that "Hell" did not exist, but they told me, "you'll explain that in court."[82]

c. IURASOV: The heading ["Membership List of the Society 'Hell'"] about "Hell" was given to us directly by the commission. I signed my name under that heading, but when they told me afterward what meaning they ascribed to this list, I protested, saying that I did not understand "Hell" as a society, but had just put down names on that list of people knowing about the talks about "Hell."[83]

d. GAGARIN TO STRANDEN: Did you belong to the secret society "Hell"?

STRANDEN: No.

GAGARIN: It seems to me you acknowledged as much. You admitted that you belonged to the society "Hell," which had as its goal tsaricide, and put yourself on the list of members of "Hell."

STRANDEN: I'm saying that we rejected tsaricide, and those lists have no meaning because they were presented to us by the commission. . . . They told us that we were making a list to facilitate checking people at the commission. . . . I thought that I was drawing up a list of members of "The Organization" and the mutual aid society.[84]

    e. POLUMORDVINOV: At that time, when I came into contact with the cir-
cle, my understandings about "Hell" were not considerable and based
only on phrases; and if there formed some understanding about
"Hell," then only at the time of the interrogation.[85]

    f. DMITRY IVANOV: I was under the influence of a conversation with
Timashev, a member of the commission . . . under "Organization," all
we understood was associations, schools, and libraries; herein consists
our whole socialism, our whole revolution, our whole secret society.[86]

    g. NIKOLAEV: About the society "Hell" I only know what I found out from
the indictment.[87]

3. The Trouble with Terms

    a. Khudiakov, at his trial, denied relations with the European Revolu-
tionary Committee, knowledge of "The Organization," and ever having told Ishutin or anyone else that he belonged to a society of
revolutionaries in Petersburg.

GAGARIN: About which society did you tell Ishutin?

KHUDIAKOV: I didn't tell him about any society.

GAGARIN: Ishutin positively testified: "My connections with Khudiakov
were such as with someone from the Petersburg socialist party, etc."

KHUDIAKOV: Aside from telling him that I was acquainted with Nozhin, I said nothing about any party.

GAGARIN: Yes, now it's easy to point to Nozhin, now that he's dead.

KHUDIAKOV: Yes, he was my close friend, and I knew him well, but we
had no society of any sort.

GAGARIN: Here it talks of your belonging to a socialist party.

KHUDIAKOV: Yes, well, I did belong to a socialist party.

MEMBER OF THE COURT PINSKY: A socialist party constitutes a society.

KHUDIAKOV: Ah, no. There's a big difference. A meeting of people,
organized in a certain order, that's what constitutes a society. But a
party is just a meeting of people thinking along a certain line.

PINSKY: So finally a party is a meeting of people who meet to discuss
various questions, various measures.

KHUDIAKOV: Ah, no, if there will be meetings, it'll already be an organization. We had nothing of the sort.

MEMBER OF THE COURT OLDENBURGSKY: Who's "we"?

KHUDIAKOV: Nozhin, Nikolsky, and I.

PINSKY: Every party has a goal, without [a goal] it's not a party.

KHUDIAKOV: We did not have any sort of party; we were just people
who saw eye to eye.[88]

    b. MALININ: I didn't know what to call those meetings, whether to call
them a society and ascribe certain activities to it. . . . We, we members,
did not have a single goal, did not agree on any means, [and] were
not in any way committed either to each other or to the society.[89]

    c. MOTKOV: ["The Organization" did not exist.] That name was a syn-
onym for a society. We'd say: "so we're entering into an organization,
we're organizing."[90]

    d. SOBOLEV: I don't even know whether that society ["The Organization"] existed as a project or not. I only know that we met at meet-ings.[91]

Finally, Voskresensky, an entirely impoverished Petrovskaia Academy student, related that he learnt from Ishutin and his roommates about a society that could get him some tutoring jobs. Though information was sparse, he resolved to attend a meeting of what turned out to be a mutual aid society. Some meetings later, however, he still had no work, complained, and claimed to have been told:

> "You understand nothing; after all, we're just talking theoretically here, at this point our words cannot yet be put into practice." . . . Then they started calling it "organization" and began to discuss various goals, though each only his own, there were no common goals whatsoever. . . . Finally, I began to notice certain arguments of Ishutin's about the need to discuss associations. Maybe there's some point to associations, but the way they were talking, it positively went nowhere. . . . They said that if associations would be built, it would mean equality on earth. Why, I didn't understand too well. So in this way our whole time was spent discussing strictly theoretical questions.[92]

Given this chaos, it is little wonder that the court circumvented the question of "Hell's" ontologico-legal status—and that the Karakozov case ultimately forced the reformulation of law. In early 1867, along with articles 318–324 of the penal code, articles 166–169 of the fourteenth volume of the Code of Laws were revisited in order to eliminate the problem of societies so secret that they contemptuously denied their own existence or covered it with inconspicuous names.[93] Law No. 44402 reformulated article 318's "secret societies of whatever denomination" as "whatever unlawful societies" (*kakie by to ni bylo protivozakonnye soobshchestva*), and then redefined these in articles 166–169 as follows:

1. All secret societies (*tainye obshchestva*), with whatever aim they might be established;
2. All gatherings, meetings, groups, associations, circles, collectives, etc. (*sborishcha, sobraniia, skhodbishcha, tovarishchestva, kruzhki, arteli i proch.*)— under whatever name (*pod kakim by naimenovaniem*) they might be existing—pursuing a harmful goal and established or acting under an agreement among several persons;
3. All those societies that, after the appropriate permission for them has been issued, shift away from the goal for which they were established, or begin to cover up with seemingly appropriate actions a tendency that in whatever respect might be harmful to the well-being of the state or to public morals.[94]

Thus, in order to eliminate any future threat, whatever unprecedented forms of organized popular political life the Karakozov case presented for the legal system were unhesitatingly captured by the law. Henceforth, "whatever" concord among two or more individuals groups of people seen to be acting in "whatever" way against the state was a crime punishable by death; which is to say that, henceforth, potentially, all such concord was criminal, and all friends—enemies. The new norm thus constitutes the birth of optics that has the potential—literally and legally—of everywhere perceiving virtual exceptions to its own rule, and that, by populating the whole of the world with spectral enemies, creates the conditions of possibility for terrorism.

Whatever Logic

Porfiry Petrovich's paradoxical claim in *Crime and Punishment* that the only "average" component of criminal cases is exactly their equal claim to being exceptional signals the potential of each case to force a rewriting of the rules. All cases being singular, this implies, no case is ever truly captured by existing law. Lest each case receive its own amendment to the law, therefore, it can be only incompletely rendered intelligible, namely by reference to a forged average—a reductive procedure that covers up with the phantasm of precedence whatever breaks and discontinuities might exist. The Karakozov case exemplarily illustrates this reductionism through the court's creative use of "whatever" clauses (e.g. *kakie by to ni bylo, pod kakim by, k kakomu libo, ili inym obrazom*), which are generalities extracted from exceptions so gross that they could be not be subsumed under existing rules. The case illustrates, in other words, the logic of the rule in the face of the exception.

The epigraph to this chapter suggests that Herzen felt no less challenged than did the law in finding an approach to this unprecedented case, whose totality seemed to have outstripped all the usual narratives. Suturing with "whatever," however, would not suffice: until the various threads of its story would be disentangled and woven anew by what might have to be a whole new poetics, the clashing styles of the case's constituent parts would refuse to synthesize, and continue to show but "an absurd, dismal assemblage." As far as properly narrating the Karakozov case is concerned, perhaps it was in fact Herzen himself who came closest when he managed at least to identify its narrator as a strange hybrid form of Tacitus and Dante, writers respectively celebrated for their talent for distilling order from the chaos of the past and for creating a rational poetics from the circles of hell.

CHAPTER 2

THE REAL RAKHMETOV

The Image of the Revolutionary after Karakozov
(Being Also an Episode in the Reception History of
What Is to Be Done?)

"But you astonish me, Rakhmetov.
You're not at all what you seem to be."

VERA PAVLOVNA, *What Is to Be Done?*

Regarding the Archimedean point he made with his *Black Square* (1913), the artist Kasimir Malevich once noted, "Today it is God, tomorrow Nitrogen, the day after a new X, and all names and X-s will form the sum total of misunderstandings."[1] In the wake of Karakozov's attempt on Alexander II, one of the main "X-s" society mobilized to mend meaning and make sense of what had happened was "conspiracy." Around this notion public discourse fluttered feverishly, and when it finally settled, there appeared, following the form of a particular type of conspirator, a decisive image of the revolutionary.

Not that this image will surprise anyone. It shows a revolutionary whose amoral, all-or-nothing, end-justifying-means modus operandi can be recognized in later, better-known figures such as Sergei Nechaev,* Andrei Zheliabov,* and Lenin—those making up the violent "vanguard" or terrorist strand of the revolutionary tradition. What's more, scholars have long identified the source of this strand, and insisted that it predates Karakozov: it is Rakhmetov, the "extraordinary man" (*osobennyi chelovek*) of the 1863 novel universally known as the socialist gospel, Chernyshevsky's *What Is to Be Done?* Thus, some may say, rather than having first emerged from the Karakozov case, the revolutionary conspirator had long existed in the pages of a book whose status as a "catechism for the revolutionary" is beyond doubt.[2] If the image of the revolutionary after Karakozov resembled Rakhmetov, in other words, this must be because Karakozov had learned his catechism well.

In 1866, in fact, the authorities saw precisely this relationship between *What Is to Be Done?* and April 4. "The novel of that criminal," concluded the verdict of the Supreme Criminal Court, "had the most destructive influence on many of the defendants, inspired absurd antisocial ideas, and, finally, invited them to take as a maxim, *the end justifies the means.*"[3]

Since then, scholarship has confirmed that, like so many other young Russians at the time, Karakozov and his friends indeed imitated the novel, and specifically modeled themselves on the "rigorist," as Rakhmetov was dubbed for what the narrator calls his "special sin" (*osobennyi grekh*).[4] If Rakhmetov disciplined his body, denied himself love, restricted his diet to the food of the poor, read only "original" books, and slept on nails to prepare for the worst, then so (more or less) did they. "It was probably a lunatic," said one of their acquaintances about the April 4 assassin, "wanting to take up the role of Rakhmetov from the novel *What Is to Be Done?*"[5] In the beginning, therefore, were Chernyshevsky's words—and then came the act, and the act was a form of violence eventually known as terrorism.

All this being the case, why bother—as this chapter does—to analyze the reception of April 4 only to prove, once again, the existence of this well-known image? Because something is not quite right. Because strangely, of all the figures offered by the historiography, the sick and suicidal Karakozov probably *least* resembles the strong and spirited Rakhmetov, a character Chernyshevsky sketched as "an exemplar of a very rare breed."[6] Who could be farther removed from one another than the odd Karakozov and the extraordinary Rakhmetov? And yet one of the tsaricide's alleged co-conspirators, Petr Nikolaev, later wrote, "Karakozov was a lot like Nikitushka Lomov," using the more honorable of Rakhmetov's two aliases to describe the tsaricide.[7] Once upon a time, this means, Karakozov, like Rakhmetov, was unflinchingly likened to a legendary folk hero and soldier saint. Or was this comparison only possible *later*, when Nikolaev, then a veteran revolutionary, squinted backwards across decades of time, his view obscured by a discursive storm first unleashed on April 4?

What happened is this. Reactions to the attempt on the life of the tsar rearranged meaning in such a way that it became almost impossible to notice a very real and vital discrepancy between the original literary composition and its later social incarnations. It is not the case that the image of the revolutionary after April 4 resembled Rakhmetov because Karakozov incarnated him. Rather, it was the image that settled after April 4— an image that emerged from an overdetermined interpretation of Karakozov's peculiar reading of the professional revolutionary—that was mapped back onto the original. The Rakhmetov we know—the one the secondary literature generally characterizes as cold, cruel, and calculating; ascetic and austere; rational and regimented; utilitarian; and, finally, "Machiavellian"—this Rakhmetov only came into being after April 4. In short: what has always looked like the source for all of Russia's ruthless revolutionaries up to and including Lenin, Rakhmetov the "rigorist," only looks that way because he is seen through a filter based on the reactionary reception of Karakozov's political action. And so decisively did this image of the revolutionary settle after April 4, moreover, that it obscured something deeply essential that has been forever in plain sight, yet rarely seen, namely that Chernyshevsky's original figure was *funny*.[8]

What is funny about the revolutionary conspirator can only be brought to light, however, after scraping off the layers of dread, intimidation, and fear that accumulated on top of the original figure after Karakozov happened to Russia on April 4. The aim of this chapter is to excavate the original for its own sake—that is, because of what it reveals about the true source of the revolutionary movement, which is not malice, but mirth—and for the sake of the perspective it will offer from which to best appreciate the changes later made to its form.

Visions of Chernyshevsky's Vision

No sooner had the recently installed telegraphs brought the governor of Eastern Siberia news of April 4 than Chernyshevsky was locked up tighter in his cell; the government's suspicion that he may have been responsible for the day's attempt on the life of the tsar was instant.[9] "The revolutionary movement in ideology and politics was sometimes, in all earnestness, ascribed to Chernyshevsky's influence alone," writes Irina Paperno of the writer-critic's extraordinary political influence.[10] The fact of his arrest on charges of subversion in 1862 had not lessened this perception; for if anything, Chernyshevsky's martyrdom increased his prestige and powers: "After Chernyshevsky was sent into exile, every time the government uncovered either state crimes or harmful political circles," wrote Head of the Police Count Shuvalov* about the 1860s, "it was noticeable that their origins served [his cause]."[11] In revolutionary eyes, indeed, the author's absence was an interregnum, his return would mark the dawn of a new age, and his liberation, therefore, became a leitmotif of the underground.[12]

After several years of a stellar career as a radical critic and editor of the age's most influential journal, *Sovremennik*, Chernyshevsky wrote *What Is to Be Done?* in a few months while incarcerated in the Alekseevsky Ravelin of the Peter-Paul Fortress. The work was smuggled out and, through a legendary censorship slip-up, published in *Sovremennik* in the spring of 1863.

What Is to Be Done? which carries the subtitle *Tales from the Lives of the New People* (*Iz rasskazov o novykh liudiakh*), is a boulevard bildungsroman. It tells the story of Vera ("faith") Pavlovna (a patronymic referencing St. Paul) Rosalskaia, who escapes despotism and ignorance via a fictitious marriage to one of the "new people," Lopukhov; achieves independence and social equality for herself and her seamstress employees through a cooperative venture; finds love with her husband's best friend and fellow "new person," Kirsanov; dreams four prophetic dreams of a Red dawn; and along the way transforms into a new person herself. A second narrative strand tells the history, life, and disappearance of the "extraordinary" Rakhmetov, and projects his possible return as coinciding with the start of the revolution.

Unarguably, according to most, *What Is to Be Done?* is one of the worst pieces of literature ever written. Nevertheless, none other than Mikhail Bakhtin decided that the work invented polyphony; it brazenly experiments with mixing genres; and its temporal layering (dream sequences, rewinds, flash-forwards, etc.) achieves near-cinematic effects. Moreover, *What Is to Be Done?* is rationalist, feminist, materialist, socialist, and literary pedagogy (through its pages trots a canonical parade that includes the likes of Newton, Condorcet, Sand, Feuerbach, Dickens, and Gogol), a revolutionary manifesto, and a conspiratorial manual: from Rakhmetov readers learn how to become revolutionaries, and from the "new people," how to be free in a time of unfreedom.

Above all, though, *What Is to Be Done?* is an ethics. One of the most unflinching visions of the nineteenth century, Chernyshevsky's work exposes a world from which the old gods have been ejected, and although the possibility of transcendence is maintained, essentially it teaches readers how to live while waiting for the possible to become real. *What Is to Be Done?* preaches immanence, and it is a joyful book.

Conspiracy Theory, Secularization Theory

About two weeks after April 4, when the public had just found out the assassin's name, newspapers reported that, according to those who knew him, the twenty-five-year-old university drop-out and adherent of the most extreme variety of socialism had long suffered from melancholy and hypochondria, had had a stint in a clinic, "had already had enough of [Life], and hated people."[13] The testimonies Karakozov scribbled over the course of the investigation and gave at the trial are largely consistent with these assertions: he invariably underlined that he would not have committed his crime but for the terrible state he had been in "since the time of my grave nervous illness in the Moscow clinic," a time since when he had constantly been pursued by the thought of death.[14]

But April 4 had already produced too many rumors that its criminal had donned a disguise and given nothing but false testimony, that the crowd had been unusually dense near the gates of the Summer Garden that afternoon, that mysterious carriages had been present, and that a pale young man had been seen fleeing the scene of the crime ... [15] No one found the tsaricide quite believable in the role of a melancholic suicide.[16] Evidently, it was far more natural to suspect that Karakozov was part of a conspiracy.

Given that there had been tsars before who had become the victims of conspiratorial intrigue, this suspicion was not altogether strange. What was strange, however, was that this conspirator, unlike the traditional tsaricides, had attempted to assassinate the tsar in public. The major problematic introduced by this fact can be easily ascertained from what was at that time a standard rendition of the event:

> On April 4, 1866, around 4 o'clock in the afternoon, when the emperor, upon finishing his walk in the Summer Garden, exited onto the banks of the river Neva, an unknown man, standing in the crowd of people that had gathered by the gate, approached his carriage and shot at the holy person of His Imperial Majesty.[17]

What Karakozov did was to complicate the Russian experience of tsaricide by introducing new elements of danger: publicity, anonymity, and the crowd. And what April 4 revealed, therefore, was not only that public display would henceforth be dangerous to the sovereign, but also, and more importantly, the existence of a new, as yet undefined, irregular enemy.

The assassin's anonymity, which made it impossible to determine the nature of the crime, long severely strained public nerves. Reportedly, he had initially identified himself as the peasant Aleksei Petrov, but this was exposed as a lie no later than April 8: "Fine," *Moskovskie Vedomosti* cited the criminal's response, "then I'll call myself Petr Ivanov. It makes no difference to me."[18] By trumpeting a cacophony of utmost outrage across the pages of periodicals (*unprecedented, unheard-of, the most horrible, the worst ever, etc.*), society attempted to drown out its fears, but despite its show of all-Russian unity in the face of an unidentified enemy, public discourse was marked with a nervous flutter. "Serious meaning," one writer worried, could be attributed to what he called "most anxious and troubled rumors": the criminal had been writing his testimonies in a style that was not only grammatically correct, but even literary.[19] A Judas, this implied, had been frequenting society, and the conviction that there were "enemies among

us, that the criminal was but the *blind weapon* of some secret machination"
was omnipresent.[20] Seen as a physical extension of some still invisible
other's volition, the body of the tsaricide cast a long shadow towards what
was imagined as the crime's real mastermind—and this mind might well
be pulling the strings of the conspiracy from some swanky salon.

By late April, *Moskovskie Vedomosti* reported that the tension in Petersburg was becoming unbearable. "Terror and indignation" were on the
rise, wrote a correspondent, "now that it has become obvious what terrible consequences there might have been," and then he hinted at the nature of those consequences by repeating rumors of "various chicaneries
done to well-dressed people in the streets."[21] A few days later, a *Golos*
columnist carefully opined that the tight-lipped policy of the Investigative
Commission had hurled society into a state of permanent anxiety: "[The
secrecy had resulted in a] constant unfurling of rumors, gossip, and scandals, one after another, contradicting today what was said yesterday. . . .
[Society] searches with fear and disbelief, asking who its enemies are,
where they come from, what they want, and in whose name they do not
stop even at such a terrible, unheard-of crime?"[22] It was therefore only
with retrospective calm and frankness that Minister of Justice Zamiatnin
could, on September 21, 1866, remind the Supreme Criminal Court of
the anxiety of bygone months: "Who among us does not know the rumors
that . . . arose among the lower classes and threatened all higher orders
with bloody extermination?"[23] The fear at which the newspapers only
dared hint was clearly pronounced behind the court's closed doors: "rumors, gossip, and scandals" had framed the attempted tsaricide as an act
of aristocratic vengeance for Alexander II's 1861 abolition of serfdom.
"They're lucky Karakozov didn't kill the tsar," the police had heard people proclaim. "Otherwise we would have let a fountain of noble blood
flow!"[24] A successful assassination of the "tsar liberator" might well have
unleashed a popular uprising against the gentry, but a failed one was not
without danger.

Though educated society was in fact deeply divided (both against itself
and, in many ways, against the state), April 4 exposed an acute awareness
that in case popular violence was unleashed, the political shadings of the
higher orders would be about as legible to the people as the meaning of
a shorn crinoline. The situation was thus highly precarious: exposed to
"white terror" from above and the threat of "bloody extermination" from
below, society knew itself to be traversed by rifts, but, because the tsaricide was rumored to have come from its midst, had to present a united
front in its loyalty to tsar and people.

That society succeeded in projecting such an image of itself is shown
by the fact that the historiography has characterized the post–April 4 atmosphere as jubilant and unanimous in its patriotic support for the gov-

ernment. Of course it is also customary to remark that Karakozov's as-sassination put an end to whatever progressive tendencies still lingered in the mid-sixties (after peasant revolts, student unrest, a Polish rebellion, fires in Petersburg, the arrest and exile of famous members of the intel-ligentsia, etc.), but the literature barely mentions the popular threat to which society found itself exposed and leaves undiscussed the measures it took to protect itself against this threat. In the wake of April 4, however, the media was in fact very effectively engaged in damage control, and do-ing its utmost to prevent the public at large from drawing (what society hoped were) the wrong conclusions.

The easiest way to do this was, as always it is, to identify the criminal as "other." An early bulletin originating in the capital, for example, ac-knowledged that Karakozov belonged to the higher orders ("his move-ment, poses, and manner clearly reveal that he is not a rough worker"), but noted with relief that "his facial features and especially his knowledge of Polish permit us to rejoice that he is not Russian."[25] Given both the dire need for an external enemy and the rebellion but three years back, fixing the identity of the tsaricide as a Polish separatist was practically au-tomatic, and just how natural were such assumptions about the criminal's ethnic background is shown by a standard version one of the tsar's first questions to the detained assassin: "Are you Polish?"[26]

No paper was more active in promoting this idea than *Moskovskie Vedo-mosti*, whose influential publicist and editor Mikhail N. Katkov was vigor-ously antifederalist, and therefore venomously anti-Polish. Based on early clues, one of its correspondents reported on April 7, the criminal was ei-ther a Polish agent or an agent of the "so-called Russian Revolutionary Committee in exile," i.e. Herzen, Ogarev,* and Bakunin—a triumvirate Katkov had always maintained was in league with the Poles.[27] "His name is Olshevsky; he is a Pole," Katkov triumphantly announced the next day.[28] In the months that followed, Katkov never quite abandoned either his hope that April 4 could be pinned on the Poles, or his confidence that he could convince the public thereof.

Unsettling as it was for everyone, Karakozov was not at all Polish. He had been born into an impoverished aristocratic family from Saratov, had attended the law faculties of Kazan and Moscow universities, and report-edly frequented "nihilist spheres." Each time a bit of evidence of this real identity emerged, it exploded the assumptions of cultural traditions, and then the press either rearranged the criminal's image to resemble yet an-other familiar threat or wriggled its way out of old interpretive categories. Upon disclosure of the tsaricide's ethnicity, "Russian" was instantly sliced up to designate distinct juridical and cultural categories.[29] Newspapers reprinted official notification from Saratov's aristocracy that, in truth, the Karakozovs had never quite been officially registered as members of the nobility.[30] And the press also stressed the Tatar origins of his name: "'kara' means 'black,' 'kiuz' means 'eye,' 'koze' means 'mutton.'"[31] Karakozov was thus not really Russian, not really noble, and so on. "Nihilist spheres," however, presented the public with a problem, and for a number of reasons at that.

First, nihilism—whatever it really was—was homegrown, and everyone knew it. Second, it was linked with everything that was, broadly speaking, progressive, and this presented the (primarily liberal) press with a real dilemma. If nihilism was indeed the seat of the crime, then nihilism had of course to be denounced; but if nihilism was denounced too sweepingly, then this might open the last barrier still holding back a reaction that had already swallowed up *Sovremennik* and *Russkoe Slovo*, and, as one writer put it, "half of the literary men I knew."[32] The solution *Golos, Peterburgskii Listok,* and other journals adopted was essentially to lie low, toe the official line, and once in a while whisper that the political climate was stifling society.[33] "What!" the conservative Katkov then bellowed whenever so much as a hint reached Moscow that Petersburgers were worried about reaction:

> Will freedom of thought suffer if the power to plot evil is reduced? What! Freedom of speech [means] leaving society defenseless against instigators and murderers . . . ? Since when does liberal politics mean allowing the *terrorization* of society by evildoers aiming at the destruction of the state?[34]

News of "nihilist spheres" had thus paralyzed progressives: they could save themselves from drowning in the reaction by condemning nihilism, but they could only condemn nihilism by betraying their own principles—by gobbling up and regurgitating whatever they were fed by official newspapers like *Severnaia Pochta*. Mostly, they did. Therefore, for conservatives, the possibility that April 4 had its roots in nihilism presented a unique opportunity to silence the opposition, but—and this is the third reason why "nihilist spheres" presented a problem—it also meant admitting that nihilism had grown teeth, and in the heart of old Russia, no less; Karakozov's "nihilist spheres" were in Moscow, after all. It meant, in other words, admitting that the empire was now on track with its European neighbors: haunted by the specter of revolution. This being inadmissible—"Look around," Katkov commanded his readers, "where, among this people, is there even a shadow of something resembling those social diseases whence grow revolutionary passions?"[35]—it had to be shown that nihilism was a symptom of an altogether different disease, one "foreign" to the Russian social body.

Moskovskie Vedomosti thus launched a campaign that presented nihilism as a tool of foreign intrigue inside of Russia. In doing so, Katkov was swimming against the current of what he perceived to be popular opinion among Petersburg journalists, who blamed nihilism pure and simple for April 4—"even though until recently," Katkov waxed indignant, "they were all nihilists"—and believed it to be part of an international revolutionary conspiracy. Katkov himself dismissed such a network as chimerical: "There's no such thing. . . . Serious revolutionary activists are not cosmopolitans."[36] Conspirators, according to Katkov's logic, were patriots and thus partisan by nature. Always partisan, he insisted, but mostly Polish: Warsaw police, he knew, had documented ideas of world revolution and regicide as early as 1864.[37] After April 4, Katkov's columns show a repetitive pattern that refuses to see nihilism as the culprit, posits the sudden appearance of "a secret *mot d'ordre*," and then repeats rumors of Polish revolutionary networks and societies.[38] All this to prove to the public that April 4 could not have been the result of a Russian conspiracy.

Although Katkov bluntly dismissed the popular belief in an international revolutionary committee as "an Arabian fairytale" and Petersburgers finally joked that, soon enough, the irate Katkov would blame Moscow's bad roads on intrigues originating in the West, it was never so much the conspiratorial structure as the identity of the agents pulling the strings that was in question.[39] This is what is most interesting about all this discourse slanted by talk of *mots d'ordre*, blind weapons, interested parties, strong influences, secret machinations, and hidden forces: it indicates the existence of a second, hidden reality to which *everyone* has rhetorical recourse and which can be colonized by *any* partisan interest. Not the existence of conspiratorial coordinates, only the names assigned to them are in question. These coordinates represent the limits of the era's imagination: it could not think unauthorized politico-historical agency in terms other than as something being manipulated by a big conspiracy.

For four months following April 4, the authorities maintained their ominous silence and Karakozov's identity morphed back and forth between that of a Polish agent; an emissary of revolutionary exiles in Geneva; and a proxy for imprisoned radicals like Chernyshevsky, or for progressive journalism in general, or for ultra-Russian patriotism, or for nihilism, etc. He was always a "blind weapon," a "blind instrument," or a "blind tool," but never a stray, senseless lunatic; the conspirator's mind-body split was universally accepted. When on August 3 *Severnaia Pochta* at long last released a report of the Investigative Commission's findings, it was an ambiguous composite of all these constituents that left ample room for speculation.

The truth according to the government, as it appeared in the report, was as follows:

There existed among Moscow students a secret society called "The Organization," poised to spread socialism, destroy morality and religion, and overthrow the government through revolution. Spreading outward from and back to "The Organization," an education- and labor-based network of interdependent societies was to cover the empire. Two factions existed within "The Organization": one was made up of gradualists, the other intended to speed up the time towards revolution by means of tsaricide. The idea of tsaricide had been imported from abroad: upon returning from Geneva, one "agent" had told "The Organization" of the existence of a European Revolutionary Committee, members of which advocated and practiced regicide, willingly supplied weaponry for the revolution, and recommended establishing a similar committee in Moscow.

Thus "Hell" was founded, secretly, at the core of "The Organization." Its members took an oath to murder whomever obstructed the path—including the disobedient inside "The Organization"—and designated one among them as tsaricide. The tsaricide was obliged to sever all personal ties and delve into an underworld of debauched vagabondage so as to divert attention from his political activities—going so far as to turn agent provocateur if need be. Upon execution of the crime, the tsaricide had to immediately commit suicide by poisoning himself, leaving behind an explanatory proclamation.

And so Karakozov set off for Petersburg, where he contacted other political parties, propagandized, vagabonded, penned his proclamation, supplied himself with poison, and all the while associated with the unidentified "agent," described as a well-known publisher of harmful literature with ties to the socialist circle of a recently deceased extreme nihilist named Nozhin. This same agent was also deeply involved in designs to liberate Chernyshevsky from his Siberian prison and had already provided one member of "Hell" with the necessary supplies for this endeavor: fake passports, poison, and letters of introduction to Polish exiles in Siberia.

Apropos of Poles, they had already freed a number of notorious politicals from prison over the years and been the ones to supply "The Organization" with poison for Chernyshevsky's liberation. In fact, there existed in Moscow a Polish agency, *Narodowa opieka* (*The People's Welfare*), dedicated to the financial support and liberation of political criminals.

Concluding, the report blamed illegal books, revolutionary literature, and illusionary ideas of equality and unlimited personal freedom for an increasing perversion of traditions; all these had culminated in a crime intended to unleash general unrest and revolution.[40]

Now that this version has been repeated in various guises for some 150 years, it is difficult to see that it may at one time have required a certain suspension of disbelief. From the perspective of what we think we know about the emergence and development of terrorism, this presentation of the case makes sense. "Hell's" tsaricide, for example, seems to exhibit qualities not very different from the revolutionary models that emerged three years on either side of Karakozov's failed assassination: like the "extraordinary man" of Chernyshevsky's 1863 *What Is to Be Done?* and the "doomed man" of Nechaev's 1869 "Catechism of a Revolutionary," this tsaricide or *mortus* is characterized by a single-minded devotion to the cause, austere solitude, conspiratorial pragmatism, and a utilitarian disregard of traditional morality. The group's structural model, moreover, should be very familiar to students of the revolutionary movement. This is the network propagated by Nechaev for *Narodnaia Rasprava;* it gained additional notoriety through *Demons* (1872), Dostoevsky's fictionalization of the Nechaev affair; and then reappeared in renditions by *Narodnaia Volia* during the trial against the six 1881 tsaricides. In 1866, however, these ideas could still arouse outright skepticism and indignation, although, given the reactionary political climate in Russia, only the exiled Herzen, safely tucked away in a Swiss canton, could loudly issue protest after protest: "There was no conspiracy!"[41]

Still, responses inside Russia were not uniform or uniformly acquiescent; fueled by surprise about what had been revealed in *Severnaia Pochta,* the debate about the exact nature of the conspiracy raged on. "And who are these people who decided that Russia was on the wrong historical path?" asked *Golos.* "University and Petrovskaia Academy auditors, philosopher-moralist drop-outs, students, and finally, laughable to say, high schoolers!"[42] As if "Hell"—details of drugs, pistols, debauchery, agents, double agents, murder, and revolution notwithstanding—was not bad enough, the press seemed to have expected something worse, and had difficulty taking seriously the threat of an autonomous socialist student network.

August 3's official report thus did not dispel the magnetic charm of conspiracy theory, but notions formerly attached to the body of the tsaricide were now transferred to the whole of his political circle: in the public imagination, all of "The Organization" became the "blind weapon" of a yet larger force at work behind the scenes. "The conspiracy's Polish accomplices exploited those youngster-revolutionaries," concluded *Golos.*[43] "Smells like Polish propaganda," *Peterburgskii Listok* agreed.[44] And Katkov, too, went on as before: whatever the tales of the European Revolutionary Committee and "The Organization's" proclaimed objectives, he insisted, no revolutionary had ever been known to struggle for universalism, and Poles had certainly been "active accomplices" in founding "The Organization."[45] "The name "The Organization" itself testifies that the prototype they followed was a Polish revolutionary organization," he wrote.[46] Thus the dominant image of the conspirator remained static as a double exposure: an executor, and behind him, spectrally, the figure of a secret sovereign.

Secularization Theory, Conspiracy Theory

But what exactly did it mean to call Karakozov, "The Organization," or nihilism a "blind weapon," "blind instrument," or "blind tool," and the presence of what kind of eagle-eyed weapon, instrument, or tool wielder did
these terms imply? Katkov was not at all alone in his insistent recourse to
such expressions, and interestingly enough, they were employed to describe *both* of the unknowns most spectacularly burned into public consciousness by April 4: Komisarov,* who had supposedly saved the tsar from
Karakozov's bullet (see chapter 3), was God's instrument, and therefore
Karakozov extended from *whatever* evil manifestation covered for the intrigues of a demonic force. This discourse framed the event as a battle
between go(o)d and (d)evil taking place beyond the perceptible, and suggests that the politics of April 4 were read as if occurring against a religious—even apocalyptic—backdrop.

Everyone had recourse to this religious grid, though, again, the names
assigned to its coordinates varied. Some Petersburgers, for example,
rooted the Muscovite conspiracy in the old capital's traditions of religious
obscurantism. "Of course we are far from blaming all of Moscow for having a few insane political sectarians among its inhabitants," wrote *Golos,*

> but we don't see at all why in a time-honored refuge for various absurd sects
> there would not be place for a political sect as well, why in an atmosphere
> permeated by the propaganda of schismatic priests and various holy fools,
> the sermons of holy fools on a par with them, albeit of the opposite ten-
> dency, could not have some success.[47]

In this way of thinking, the structural difference between religious and
political fanatics was nil, that is, nihilists were *like* religious zealots. Katkov
concurred: "You can enrage a nihilist with brutal, false socialist doctrine
in the same way that you can enrage a sectarian with brutal, false religious
doctrine."[48] But the use of a nihilist for the crime was therefore absolutely
incidental: *any* sectarian vessel would have done, "some religious sects'
monstrous offspring gone wild, some Flagellant, or some Runner," and
this meant that the *source* of the crime was *not* to be sought among nihilists, for sectarians, according to Katkov, lacked autonomy and their
presence implied another presence behind them.[49]

Upon reading *Severnaia Pochta*'s description of "The Organization,"
Katkov had insisted that its name testified to the fact that its structure had
been modeled on what he called a Polish "prototype." In late August,
Katkov made explicit the workings of the model he had in mind by means
of a review of N. V. Gogel's *Iosafat Ogryzko* and the Petersburg Revolutionary Government During the Late Rebellion.[50] Based on the testimony given by
one Polish rebel, explained Katkov, the book revealed that Polish sepa-

ratists had begun to organize themselves around Russian centers of learning as early as the 1850s. The results of these efforts was a network of secret societies organized as follows: in each city, there was a "so-called elder," whose name was unknown to all but three select individuals, each of whom in turn selected three more, and so on. Because this secret network actively strove to "draw more Russian youths into its nets," Russian secret societies could be said to be rooted in these Polish machinations. Read with this organizational structure, Katkov's early quip that April 4's criminal director and executor may have been unknown to one another reveals that this was the filter through which Katkov had always regarded the case.[51]

It should be noted that, unlike the supposedly really *existing* net of Katkov's Polish agitators, later Russian incarnations have been presented as manipulative figments of the conspiratorial *imagination:* Nechaev, Verkhovensky (in *Demons*), and Zheliabov were all known (or said) to have *invented* vast networks of interconnected small cells and overarching central committees whose authority they cited to ensure that their own will be done. In the literature on the revolutionary movement, this notorious conspiratorial streak has primarily come to be known as Nechaevism, which, in turn, has been characterized as Blanquism, Jacobism, or Machiavellianism, and portrayed (by Western scholars and, more recently, Russian revisionists) as a prototype for a Bolshevik-style seizure of power and revolutionary dictatorship. At times, primarily apropos of Nechaev, it is also called Jesuitical, and it is this name that is of particular interest to this discussion in light of Katkov's Polish "prototype."[52]

Arguably, the "prototype" is nothing more than the imaginary shadow cast by absolutism: its organization is absolutism minus God-given authority, ergo devoid of (Christian) morality. But in contemporary imaginations, the conspiratorial model that undergirded and best captured the nature of this godless prototype was seen as specifically Jesuit. This was true across Europe, but in Russia such a view received additional support via links with the continued battle against Polish separatism. Significantly, the two most prominent figures in this battle had been, as they were for the Karakozov case, Murav'ev and Katkov: the first had led the bloody military campaign against the Polish separatists, the second had waged propaganda on the home front, and both were fiercely anti-Catholic. In Katkov's mind, moreover, there had even long existed a direct link between nihilism and Jesuitism: in an 1862 commentary on Ivan Turgenev's *Fathers and Sons* (1862), he had characterized nihilism as a religion of negation. Complete with dogma, authorities, teachers, fanatics, and idols, nihilism was the shadow side of religion, and its modus operandi was "in complete accord with the Jesuit fathers, and fully accepts their *well-known rule—the end justifies any means.*"[53] Generally, what historians have regarded as notable about the most notorious features of "Hell" and "The Organization" (spectral central agency, net of interdependent cells, anonymous links, death for the disobedient, tsaricide, etc.) is their structural *anticipation* of such revolutionary phenomena as Nechaevism, terrorism, and vanguard politics. What is in fact no less notable, however, is that to contemporaries these features were still legible as part of an older, religion-based type of conspiracy.

The politico-religious link embodied in the figure of the Jesuit also existed in the popular imagination. In an advertisement placed in *Moskovskie Vedomosti* a little over two weeks after April 4, for example, the bookseller I. G. Sobol'ev chose to present the following new titles right next to each other: *Anthology of Count M. N. Murav'ev's Instructions for the Suppression of the Polish Rebellions in the North-western Provinces 1863–64,* and *The Jesuits and Their Relations with Russia: Iu. F. Samarin's Letters to the Jesuit Martynov.*[54] The coupling is interesting, first, because the concept "Jesuits" could apparently cover a triple threat (religious/Catholic; ethnic/Polish; political/separatist-revolutionary). Second, because Alexander I had expelled them from Russia, a particularly odious atmosphere rooted in relative ignorance surrounded the Black Fathers; and yet, because the tsar himself had thrown them out, the Jesuits appeared as figures not only external to Russia, but also vanquished by Christian Orthodoxy. All this explains why Alexander II appointed Murav'ev to head the Investigative Commission into the Karakozov case and why political conflict was dressed as a religious battle, in which victory, moreover, was already assured.

A few months later, after Karakozov had been publicly executed but before the conclusion of the second trial, *Golos* reviewed and recommended *The Jesuits and Their Relations with Russia* on the grounds that since knowledge of the Society of Jesus was so poor, any publication on the subject merited attention. As can be gleaned from the review, suspicions (or superstitions) apparently compensated for direct knowledge: when two years earlier a French abbot arrived in Russia, this had unleashed rumors throughout Moscow that the government might permit the return of the Jesuits. "Notwithstanding the absurdity of such a suggestion," explained the reviewer, panic had ensued, which had prompted one Moscow paper, *Den'* (*The Day*), to publish an essay on the destructive teachings of the order.[55] In the imagination of the Muscovites, this implies, 'Catholic tourism' was an oxymoron; each vacationing abbot potentially wore a scapular with the Jesuit motto I.H.S. (*Jesus Hominum Salvator*) under his cloak. And this imagination had found its echo in the booming voice of Katkov, who at that very time was habitually making such declarations as "every Catholic pretension contains poison in its root."[56] Catholicism, it seems, was considered conspiratorial by nature.

Notably, the Jesuit trope also debuted in an explicit commentary on the summary report on the conspiracy in *Severnaia Pochta*. "And so, what all of us felt but were afraid to say has turned out to be true!" proclaimed *Peterburgskii Listok*. "Karakozov is . . . one of the members of a circle . . . whose basic teaching was fixed by the Jesuit dogma, 'the end justifies the means.'"[57] The report in *Severnaia Pochta* had made no mention of this "Jesuit dogma," nor does this term or the associated maxim occur in Murav'ev's original report to Alexander II. This is *Peterburgskii Listok*'s ascription to the conspiracy of a dogma that historians have seen as a typical revolutionary's *utilitarian* formula, as a recipe concocted from various brands of continental materialism and served up in Chernyshevsky's *What Is to Be Done? Peterburgskii Listok,* however, instantly maps the *counterrevolutionary Jesuit* over that of the *revolutionary socialist,* and this occurred at the very moment that the latter first emerged, violently, in plain view. In other words, no sooner had the new political threat been publicly unveiled than . . . it turned out to be another Jesuit.

Significantly, by the end of the Karakozov trial, the dogma formerly "well-known" as Jesuit would be firmly attached not only to Karakozov and "The Organization," but also to *What Is to Be Done?* To repeat the verdict pronounced by the Supreme Criminal Court on September 24 and released for public consumption in early October, "that criminal's novel, *What Is to Be Done?,* had the most destructive influence on many of the defendants, inspired absurd anti-social ideas, and, finally, invited them to take as a maxim, *the end justifies the means.*"[58] Henceforth—and especially as the international social revolutionary movement outgrew its initial links and associations with the nationalist struggles of the nineteenth century—the maxim sounded purely political, but subliminally reverberated with the religious dread inspired by the Jesuit, a paradigmatic wolf in sheep's clothing, signifier for the demonic threat of *whatever* incognito political agency veiled by a false religious cloak. And obviously, if *What Is to Be Done?* had been the "gospel" for Karakozov's "spoiled" circle, as Katkov and everyone since has proclaimed, then Chernyshevsky was its demonic evangelist; the extraordinary Rakhmetov, its false Christ; and revolutionaries, its rotten progeny.[59] This, then, is the image of the revolutionary after Karakozov—and ever after: a Satanist, secularized.

Mimesis

It bears repeating, though, that conspiratorial worlds once had a lighter side, too. When Katkov commanded that "the roots of evil must be sought out" and "light must penetrate into the deepest of secret recesses," for example, he shared his desire that chaos be rendered intelligible not just with the machinery of power, but also with the readers of pulp fiction:

Petersburg Mysteries
A novel from the life of the inhabitants of Petersburg's dark corners.
In our capital, as in every big city, there exists a whole layer of small,
obscure entrepreneurs, whose mysterious life long remained unclear to
our society;
the above-mentioned novel is connected to that obscure world and fully
explains all of its criminal tricks and activities.
Price 1 ruble.[60]

As for the dismal world of Jesuitism, it also quite simply titillates and
entertains:

Se'kovskii & Co. Bookstore
JESUIT.
A novel by the author of *The Damned* and *The Nun*.
Translated from the French.
Price 2 rubles 50 kopeks.[61]

The thrills of this genre are made especially obvious by Balzac's *History
of the Thirteen*, which describes "a sort of Society of Jesus in favor of the
devil," but in the first half of the nineteenth century the reading public
was enticed by a whole host of "conspiratorial" novels in which disguised
vigilante aristocrats descend into the underworld to battle evil and save
souls, especially those of compromised women with hearts of gold.
Masked avengers and incognitos hardly only hid seriously menacing Jesuits. As an emblem, in fact, the slumming aristocrat was hackneyed
enough to merit entry in Flaubert's sarcastic *Dictionary of Received Ideas*
("Incognito: The dress of princes on their travels") and, significantly, to
be parodied by Balzac fan Dostoevsky in *Notes from Underground* (1864)
in the episode where the educated underground man attempts to oxy-
moronically seduce/reform the prostitute Liza.[62] For our purposes, there
are two very important points worth stressing about this episode in *Notes
from Underground.*

First, Dostoevsky's parody occurs in the midst of a work consciously
composed to criticize the materialist doctrine propagated by *What Is to Be
Done?* and to ridicule the contemporary habit of trying to imitate the lives
of the novel's characters.[63] By highlighting the platitude of kindred
scenes in *What Is to Be Done?*, the parodic structure of *Notes from Underground* alerts readers to the boulevard background of Chernyshevsky's cast
of characters, which of course includes, besides the requisite reformed
prostitute, an incognito. Notwithstanding Chernyshevsky's realist aesthetics (indeed, the author claims to have known his fictional characters
in real life), therefore, the book's "extraordinary man," the revolutionary
conspirator Rakhmetov, the *ex-*aristocratic "rigorist," actually has an absurd literary precursor.

When *What Is to Be Done?* was first published, the lowly literary origins of its characters were still plainly legible. To sophisticates, indeed, the effect of their arrival in a text by Chernyshevsky was as awkward as an unannounced visit from old provincials: "We were beside ourselves with amazement," wrote the poet Afanasy Fet of himself and Katkov, "and the only thing we didn't know was what surprised us most: the cynical silliness of the whole novel or the obvious collusion of the censorship."[64]

In literature on the revolutionary movement, however, because of the status of *What Is to Be Done?* as the socialist gospel, Rakhmetov has generally been interpreted as a hybrid of the early Christian tradition and the radical intelligentsia, not as a descendant of boulevard adventurism. So, while his name echoes that of the legendary revolutionary sympathizer Pavel Alexandrovich Bakhmetev, his hagiography has been shown to mimic *The Life of Aleksei, A Man of God.*[65] The modus operandi of those who imitated Rakhmetov, therefore, is read in this tradition.

But once Rakhmetov's pulp underbelly shows again, imitations of this "extraordinary man" suddenly appear in an altered light: Karakozov and friends did not only play revolutionary-saints, but also, by extension, dandy aristocrats playing conspiratorial vigilantes, i.e. Flaubert's none too incognito incognitos. When Herzen wrote that "Young Russians were almost all out of *What Is to Be Done?* after 1862," he may still have been able to see the humor in all this replication, but after Karakozov's failed attempt on the tsar, this comedic dimension withered in the shadow of incarnations that looked more like clones from hell, children of the revolution's infernal *matreshka.*[66]

The second important point about *Notes from Underground* is this: Dostoevsky's parody serves as a reminder that imitations of *What Is To Be Done?* remain exactly that—imitations—and that something actually *happens* during imitation. This may seem obvious, but the historiography of the revolutionary movement has long been marked by a blurring of the distinction between the revolutionary's literary model and its social type, i.e. between Rakhmetov and the violent vanguard strand of the revolutionary movement. Ultimately, this lack of distinction is rooted in the novel's reception at a time when books still shone with a sacred glow and authors still wore haloes, while realism was already depicting the world with scientific logos.[67]

Russian literary realism, writes Paperno, was characterized by the double intent to replicate and to teach: "literary characters and literary situations were claimed to have been derived from 'life itself' and thereafter, 'returned to reality' and offered to society as examples worthy of imitation in real life."[68] (Hence, incidentally, Chernyshevsky's claim to have known his characters.) Importantly, she also notes that the paradox of realism—realism's reality is not really real—was transcended by introducing the notion of *type:*

In realist aesthetics, the concept of type was a hybrid of the sociological category referring to a representative member of a class ("social type") and
the Hegelian notion of ideal ... type is an individual fact of reality (a social fact) that, having "passed through the imagination of a poet," acquires
a universal significance of mythic proportions.[69]

Another way of thinking about a Russian realist type is to read it as *exemplar*, which not only clarifies its didactic force, but also provides an
opening for thinking about both proper and improper forms of imitation. The problem is as follows: realist writers synthesized the paradox of
realism through the use of the type, but it is not clear that readers of realism encountered the paradox as ingeniously in reverse.

Commentaries on *What Is to Be Done?* always emphasize its readers' religious awe before the text and their effort at rigorous imitation. "It would
not be an exaggeration to say that we read the novel practically on bended
knee, with the kind of piety that does not permit the slightest smile on
the lip, the kind with which sacred books are read," said one contemporary.[70] "We made the novel into a kind of Koran in which we looked for
and found not only a general guide to a correct life, but also exact instructions on how to act in specific situations," wrote another adherent,
while a contemporary critic called it "not only an encyclopedia, a reference book, but a codex for the practical application of the new word."[71]
Sometimes, comments on this mimesis mania are chaperoned by testi-
monials to the effect that attempts to live Chernyshevsky's literature
ended badly.[72] When the new word was actually applied in practice, real
life outstripped literature, and it was the absurdity of the ultimate mis-
match between fiction and reality that Dostoevsky so poignantly satirized
in *Notes from Underground:* the underground man is absurd precisely because he tries to live by the logic of *What Is to Be Done?*

There is no evidence that readers tackled passages on Rakhmetov differently from those containing instructions on how to arrange fictitious
marriages, separate rooms, or cooperative ventures, that is to say, religiously and rigorously. Nevertheless, bizarrely, imitations of the novel's
"extraordinary man" are never presented as having gone awry. No, this
literary model begot real replicas! No one—neither historians, nor revolutionaries, nor imperial authorities—disagrees with this assessment. This
is the root of the lingering sense that *What Is to Be Done?* animated a
phalanx of revolutionary conspirators who marched straight toward the
twentieth century and into the pages of Lenin's famous response to
Chernyshevsky, his 1902 essay, "What Is to Be Done?"

Whether religious readings and rigorous imitations of Rakhmetov altered or contradicted the original model, however, or whether religious

or rigorous imitations of Chernyshevsky's work are even proper at all, has not received equal attention. And therefore, for example, the reaction to April 4 by an acquaintance of Karakozov's that was cited earlier ("it was probably a lunatic, wanting to take up the role of Rakhmetov from the novel *What Is to Be Done?*") perpetuates an impression of equivalence between the fictional model and his social incarnation.[73] If what can be said about Karakozov is that he was a lunatic because he played Rakhmetov too seriously (or maybe because imitation is lunacy per se), the assessment nevertheless assumes that his reading of the role was both right and representative. But this is the point: Rakhmetov was not at all what the ostensible members of "Hell" called a *mortus,* and if Karakozov was really mimicking *What Is to Be Done?,* then his conspiratorial antics are a clear example of mis- and/or rereading what was written. The reading of the authorities, however, was even worse, because they willfully forced the image of the revolutionary. Put plainly, a vital discrepancy existed between Rakhmetov and his followers, and the one-to-one correspondence posited by first readers, authorities, critics, revolutionaries, and historians is wrong.

The Denizens of "Hell"

To render better contrast between Rakhmetov and the dead men from "Hell," it will be useful to restate that, first, according to the Investigative Commission, "Hell" was a secret society whose members were required to kill and be killed for the cause: the designated tsaricide, upon completing his assassination, had to commit suicide. Second, the verdict of the Supreme Criminal Court claimed that it had been Chernyshevsky's novel that had inspired Karakozov and his co-conspirators to adopt the axiom, *the end justifies the means*—the creed justifying all this immorality.

During the trial, although all defendants categorically retracted whatever they had confessed about "Hell" during the investigation and denied its existence, some did admit to conversations about tsaricide in the context of rumors about the existence of a regicidal European Revolutionary Committee. Ermolov, for example, said that "When Ishutin went to Petersburg, he brought back news of the European Committee, and that started various sorts of talks and suggestions, which afterwards were called 'Hell.' [The talks concerned] the extent to which tsaricide was useful and how to commit it."[74] Stranden's memory was similar, albeit with the additional detail that it had in fact been Ermolov who had invented the name "Hell," "as a joke."[75] He further testified that it had also been Ermolov who had first told him about the *mortus.*[76]

Probably, the *mortus* first emerged during a late night chat among Nikolaev, Ishutin, Ermolov, and Shaganov about historical assassinations, "Fieschi,* Orsini,* etc."[77]

> ERMOLOV: As far as [Nikolaev's] words [about tsaricide] are concerned, I
> can remember that when there was talk about *mortusy* he said that *mortusy*
> must be daring people, but that he'd never be someone like that.
> MINISTER OF JUSTICE: What's a *mortus?*
> ERMOLOV: A *mortus* is a person who takes the duty upon himself to kill
> tsars.[78]

Clarifying, Nikolaev cited history and humor:

> As far as *mortusy* are concerned, that was a joke among a few people, friends,
> who were talking about various assassinations that had taken place at some
> point in the past, and we called the people who had made those attempts
> *mortusy.*[79]

"I can't remember who used the word first," Nikolaev reiterated when
given a last chance to address the court. "It was said while we were joking
around, and it could not have entered my mind that such a conversation
would be taken for a serious plot. . . . Maybe it's a subject about which you
can't even joke."[80]

After that late night talk at Nikolaev's, Ermolov had told Motkov about
the *mortus*—either as a threat, as Malinin testified ("I think he was threatened with violence, or anyway, that's what he said") or as a "practical joke,"
as Ishutin claimed—then Motkov had told Malinin, and then Malinin had
told everyone else.[81] Malinin's testimony confirms the meaning of *mortus*
as a traditional regicide, and the term's connection with Ermolov: he had
heard from Motkov that Ermolov was a *mortus,* and this was "someone
who would try to do something like that [tsaricide]."[82]

Testimonies from what were construed as "Hell's" outer rings include
some interesting, embellished, or altered details. Dmitry Ivanov's testimony, for example, moves the time of the assassination forward to "when
the revolution comes" and mentions serial assassination ("shooting at a
tsar, and if the heir does not comply, then shoot again, maybe two or more
times").[83] Kichin, a student of mathematics who was barely involved in
"The Organization," bent "Hell" into a shape that can barely be called
proto-terrorist anymore: "a society that was supposed to bring about a social revolution by means of systematic tsaricide."[84] The details Kichin provided about the "candidate," as he named the designated tsaricide, are
familiar: vagabondage, the severance—"for a while"—of all ties with his
friends so as not to endanger them, the requirement that he "change and
deform his face with various poisons so that he won't be recognizable,"
and a proclamation listing demands from the tsar.[85] But his conclusion is

more consequent: "So, "Hell" is nothing but the desire to demand a social revolution from the government by means of a threat."[86]

All of the above citations keep the meaning of the *mortus* and the scope
of his activities more or less level as an assassin, and none mentions suicide—not even Kichin's testimony, which explicitly includes the "candidate's" disappearance "for a while" and "various poisons" to disguise him.
This *mortus* need not die. Later during the trial, however, this very Kichin
gave testimony that placed the assassination under the sign of the assassin's own death. Almost as an afterthought, Kichin told the court that he
did not know whether "Hell" existed, or whether April 4 was Karakozov's
own affair or that of "the society," but that some time after April 4, Malinin had told him about Karakozov and his roommates that

> It's nothing other than a society, or, I daresay, you can't even call it a soci-
> ety, a gathering of some people, wishing, as he expressed himself, not to
> lose their lives in vain, people who thought that they would die soon and,
> anxious not to quit the scene in vain, wished to do something like that [i.e.
> tsaricide].[87]

Gone are Kichin's tales of systematic tsaricide and the unleashing of a social revolution. The professionalism of the European Revolutionary Committee has disappeared, as have all possible echoes of the Jacobins (whose
bloodshed Nikolaev had found justifiable), the Carbonari (who had once
impressed Shaganov), and whatever else.[88] This "gathering" is not "Hell"
in whatever guise. Because of the contrast with other definitions given
during trial, across the various degrees of separation that distance Kichin
from the core group, there resounds a reinterpretation of the *mortus* from
daring to desperate on the basis of Karakozov.

When the Muscovites started talking about *mortusy* it was January 1866.
Indeed Khudiakov had come and gone with news of the European Revolutionary Committee, but that was not all: after two months of hospitalization, Karakozov had also reemerged from the Moscow University Clinic
(see Chapter 6). From the clinic, he had written a note to his friends that
included mention of his inevitable death, the tortures of illness, and a request for opium with which to kill himself.[89] According to one acquaintance, Dmitry Ivanov, Karakozov had worsened upon his release from the
clinic: "for days he sat silently in a separate room, hiding his face in his
hands."[90] Another, Ermolov, wrote that "he complained about his illness
and slept almost constantly."[91] There are multiple attestations, furthermore, that Karakozov wrote another suicide note in February that read:
"I'm so sick that I feel incapable of doing anything. Work by yourselves.
Leave me my fate."[92] Reintroducing the tsaricide's suicidal body while he
and his friends were trying to be Rakhmetov and first heard about the

European Revolutionary Committee illuminates the transformation of the idea of the revolutionary conspirator.

According to the written testimony of Ermolov, it was at the beginning of Lent, in early February, that Karakozov began to tell his roommates (those who would come to be known as members of "Hell") that he wanted to make an attempt on the life of the tsar; he considered this "useful, like stirring up fear and unrest among the people, and said that for him, as a sick and wrecked individual, this was the only way out."[93] They had protested, wrote Ermolov, telling him that he would ruin them all, destroy their cooperative ventures and schools, and most certainly provoke his own death.[94] Nevertheless, Karakozov seems to have sparked some ideas: "Ermolov was already pretty drunk," testified Malinin before the court, "and started to ask me questions like, what do I think of exchanging one life for another?"[95]

This, indeed, is Karakozov's idea: a death for a death to stir up fear among the upper classes and revolt from below, to unleash a revolution by means of an act of political assassination. This is what structures the content of his proclamation, "To My Worker Friends": having described an endless cycle of death among the people, the nameless author concludes his political proclamation cum suicide note as follows:

> I decided to terminate the tsar-villain and to die for my beloved people. If I succeed, I will die with the idea that my death will be of use to my dear friend, the Russian peasant. If I don't succeed, I nevertheless believe that there will be people who will follow my path. If I don't succeed, they will. My death will be an example and inspiration for them. Let the Russian people recognize its main and mightiest enemy, be he Alexander II or III and so forth, that's all the same.[96]

This double death was what Karakozov called "a singular fact" or "factual propaganda" (see chapter 6), but not much of it survived the authorities' cuts and rewrites.

When Karakozov's approach to death resurfaced in the *Severnaia Pochta* article, it had been stripped of exemplariness and tangled up with all the meanings ascribed—in earnest, in jest, and under pressure—to the *mortus*. Thus, officially, the tsaricide had emerged from a political organization that required of its members that they kill and be killed for the cause, a modus operandi the Supreme Criminal Court then summed up as the means-end calculus inspired by *What Is to Be Done?*

Revisions

Perhaps because Dostoevsky's brilliant parody of *What Is to Be Done?* places the defense of free will so centrally, there lingers an impression that Chernyshevsky was incapable of seeing or facing the deterministic consequences of his own utilitarianism, i.e. that *What Is to Be Done?* needed *Notes from Underground* to draw out the internal contradictions of the false, socialist gospel. For example, in their introduction to *What Is to Be Done?*, Michael Katz and William Wagner (endorsing Joseph Frank, who in turn followed the Soviet scholars V. L. Komarovich and A. Skaftymov) write, "Frank argues that the underground man is really a parodistic persona whose life exemplifies the tragicomic impasses resulting from his acceptance of all the implications of reason in its then-current Russian incarnation, *especially those that Chernyshevsky chose to disregard.*"[97] Unlike the rest of humanity, this is the implication, Chernyshevsky was almost satanically at ease with becoming either animal or automaton, with being free of will and free from conscience: for this utilitarian, the end justifies the means, after all. The results of Chernyshevsky's disregard seem no less hellish on a suprapersonal level: the novel's scientific utopianism being but a thinly veiled rewrite of Christian teleology, Chernyshevsky's history looks like a clock tick-tocking toward the time for which a bomb has been set, and there is no escaping this hour—a vision that seems to eerily foreshadow the Bolsheviks' terroristic, vulgar Marxist interpretation of history. But the truth is otherwise: *What Is to Be Done?* outmaneuvers determinism, dares do more than simply secularize the gospels, and—anticipating a conservative critique such as Dostoevsky's—offers a radically alternative reading of revolutionary ethics.

On the one hand, *What Is to Be Done?* seems to promote historical inevitability. The novel boldly asserts the recent genesis of a new human type, whose main traits are "cold-blooded practicality, measured and calculated activity, and active common sense," and whose incarnations look historically comparable to a past century's revolutionaries:

> In a few years, a very few, people will call out to them, "Save us!" What this type says will be done by all. A few years later, perhaps not even years, but a few months later, they'll be cursed, driven from the stage, hissed at, and insulted. So what? Hiss and hurl insults, drive them away and curse them; you got your use out of them, and that's enough for them. And amidst the noise of hissing and the thunder of curses they'll leave the stage, proud and humble, stern and kind, just as they always were.[98]

In accordance with the laws of history, it seems, the future revolution will be performed as scripted by the past. The new type will have been useful for the machinery of History, and, rather than being a figure who decides historical change, therefore, Rakhmetov is someone who will be "on time" for the revolution; near novel's end, others speculate on his whereabouts and the hour of his return: "High time he came back."[99]

On the other hand, Rakhmetov may not come back at all. Since it is his return that will signal the inauguration of the revolution, his failure to arrive obviously has no uncertain consequences for the future. But high time or not, Rakhmetov will return only if it is necessary, and the necessary is in fact utterly impossible to determine. Writes Chernyshevsky, "I don't know where Rakhmetov is now, what he's doing, or whether I'll ever see him again. I have neither facts nor guesses, except for those that all his acquaintances share."[100] This shared knowledge is the stuff of legends, namely rumors and reports from distant travelers: "Absolute certainty was impossible, but in all probability it was Rakhmetov. On the other hand, who knows? Perhaps not."[101] Of Rakhmetov's absence, Chernyshevsky quips that it will last, "perhaps forever. . . . But it was much more likely that in three years or so he'd return to Russia because it seemed that there—not now, but then, in three or four years—it would be 'necessary' for him to be in Russia."[102] "Perhaps . . . likely"; "seemed . . . necessary"; "absolute certainty was impossible, but"; "in all probability . . . On the other hand, who knows?" Such are the convictions of the great positivist pedant. It turns out that the backdoor of his utopia—techno-phalansteries wrapped in a glass-iron edifice about which Dostoevsky's underground man says, "Well, and maybe I'm afraid of this edifice precisely because it is crystal and forever indestructible and it will be impossible to put out one's tongue at it even on the sly"—is left ajar.[103] Nothing must be as written, and least of all must some Rakhmetov come back to sacrifice his life for the revolution.

Rakhmetov may have mortified himself, but he is possessed of no inclinations towards becoming either a *mortus* or subject to rigor mortis. *What Is to Be Done?* includes no killing clause for the extraordinary man; and there is no singular, suicidal scapegoat in this book.[104] The original revolutionary has been obscured, like a palimpsest's first text, by historical doxa—and precisely what is extraordinary about people like Rakhmetov, though in plain view, was buried underneath Rakhmetov's "special sin": his rigorism.

Tellingly, however, "rigorism" was first applied to Rakhmetov at a time of play. During a philosophical "argument" spliced between the dances, games, food, and drinks of a picnic, the term is used to describe Rakhmetov while the two other participants in the debate are jocularly accused of "schematism" and "romanticism."[105] The second time the term appears when Vera Pavlovna says, "Rakhmetov, the rigorist, as they refer to him in jest."[106] The third time, "rigorist" is identified as the first of two "nicknames" given to Rakhmetov: "He accepted it with his usual slight smile of grim satisfaction. But when people started calling him Nikitushka or Lomov, or by the full form, Nikitushka Lomov, he beamed broadly and sweetly."[107] How did this joke among a few friends come to be interpreted so *rigorously*? And how did "the rigorist" come to exemplify morbid asceticism and thoroughgoing "Machiavellianism"?[108] Rakhmetov, after all, is a figure of whom Chernyshevsky writes that he is "living proof that a proviso needs to be added to the discussion of the properties of soil."[109]

This may seem like an incomprehensible statement, but the line is a reference to a dialogue in the second of Vera Pavlovna's four prophetic dreams. In order to scientize ideas of transformation, this dream maps Baron Justus von Liebig's (1803–73) theories on soil chemistry (the nature of the fruit is determined by the nature of the root, the soil in which the root grows can be chemically changed, ergo the fruit can improve) onto the Christian parable of the sower:

> A sower went out to sow his seed; and as he sowed, some fell on the path and was trampled on, and the birds of the air ate it up. Some fell on the rock; and as it grew up, it withered for lack of moisture. Some fell among thorns, and the thorns grew with it and choked it. Some fell into good soil, and when it grew, it produced a hundredfold. (Luke 8:5–8)

So far, straightforward secularization. But then, defiant of determinism, and as if it were nothing for an ex-seminary student to amend the gospels in order to accommodate a literary life of his own invention, Chernyshevsky daringly proclaims his proviso apropos of Rakhmetov: "whatever the quality of the soil, one can still come across tiny plots capable of producing healthy ears of grain."[110] Again, nothing must be as written (exceptions are always possible).

The unprecedented influence of *What Is to Be Done?* created an impression that the way it was read (religiously) and imitated (rigorously) were the proper, best, or even most useful approaches to this work. Paradoxically, *What Is to Be Done?* is a book—one of those rare books—that actually comes with instructions on how to read it, and it can be stated with fair certainty that whoever read this novel religiously did not follow the example of its hero (and author), whose approach to texts can only be described as radical, iconoclastic, and sacrilegious. Because Rakhmetov reads in order to extract the fundamental paradigms of all branches of human knowledge, he reads "only original works, and only enough to grasp their originality."[111] This approach has been misread and ridiculed as an expression of utilitarian dogma.[112] But it is not the case that Rakhmetov restricts himself to an established canon; instead, he must discover and extract (if not impose) originality. "Ah, now here's something I'm glad to find," Rakhmetov exclaims upon spotting Newton's *Observations on the Prophecies of Daniel and the Apocalypse of St. John* alongside titles by Ranke, Macaulay, and others he has dismissed as "unoriginal":

> Newton wrote this commentary in his old age, when he was half in his right mind and half insane. It's the classical treatise on the connection between intellect and insanity. The question is one of universal, historical import: this particular combination occurs without exception in all events, in almost all books, in almost all brains. But here this question must appear in perfect form.[113]

What Is to Be Done? may or may not contain within its pages a recipe for social revolution, but it is certainly a manual for critical reading, an invitation to turn words upside down and read texts against the grain.

Perhaps *Notes from Underground* should not at all be read as a book about the absurdity of imitating books per se, but rather about the trappings of imitations predicated on a *type* of reading. Perhaps these *Notes* reveal nothing about the original book (regardless of the widespread conviction that they draw out its internal contradictions). Perhaps they are just the *Notes* of a man with bad reading skills, of an imagination that fails to stretch beyond a literal interpretation and replication of the letter. That kind of reading of Chernyshevsky would indeed be absurd. After all, *What Is to Be Done?* is an ethics; it should not be interpreted too rigorously. A too strictly orthodox approach to the interpretation of doctrine—thus spoke an author who was first and foremost a critic—is a *sin* ("rigorism," he says, was Rakhmetov's "special sin"). In the end, Dostoevsky's hyperbolic reductio ad absurdum of the tendency to literally live by Chernyshevsky's book only means that the underground man is the consequence of a *rigorous* approach to Chernyshevsky's philosophy—*not* of Chernyshevsky's philosophy itself. If this is so, then the parody not so much critiques as fulfills something Chernyshevsky himself had already warned against by *explicitly* naming the extraordinary man's extraordinary sin.

Rigorism, though, need not at all be a permanent condition; it is only the sin of a novice, the sign of a recent conversion, a telltale mark that a newly adopted code of conduct has been somewhat artificially imposed, and does not come quite naturally yet. The tension that exists between what is and what should be, the evidence of a gap despite the best efforts to bridge the distance to the ideal, can sometimes produce laughter—which is of capital significance given Chernyshevsky's estimate of extraordinary people:

> They had nothing in common except for one trait, but this trait united them into a single breed and distinguished them from all others. I used to laugh at those particular individuals, my intimate friends, when I was alone with

them. They either got angry or didn't, but they also used to laugh at themselves. In fact, there was a great deal that was very amusing about them: everything of importance about them was amusing, everything that characterized them as a breed apart. I love to laugh at such people. . . . Yes, people like Rakhmetov are funny, very amusing indeed.[114]

In response to jokes about his yet to be sublimated shortcomings (smoking, love), Rakhmetov finally replies: "'Yes, do pity me. You're right. Pity me. For I too am not an abstract idea, but a human being, one who longs to live life. Never mind. It will pass,' he would add. And he was right—it did."[115] Once it passed, presumably, Rakhmetov shed his sin, transcended being "but a human," and was newly born, divine.

Strange phrases though. Truly, the road to Golgotha is hard, but this revolutionary, we know, is not bound by any death clause, be it suicidal or sacrificial. If indeed being "but a human" passed, Rakhmetov must have transformed into the absolutely extraordinary—not just "an exemplar of a very rare breed," but a rare breed even among exemplars: a nonsuicidal immortal.

But revolutionary life according to Karakozov reads very differently: "my death," he insists, "will be an example and inspiration." Why? What is the source of this difference between Rakhmetov and Karakozov? Precisely being funny: through laughter, Rakhmetov transcends his sufferings; Karakozov cannot.

Optical Illusion

April 4, 1866, revealed something exceptional: the political challenge of a sovereign subject ("no matter the quality of the soil . . ."). To make sense of this impossibility ("Where, among this people, do you see even the shadow of those diseases whence emerge revolutionary passions?"), information about April 4's perpetrator was filtered through existent cultural knowledge (political, religious, literary). The resulting image—a husk of a human who righteously kills and is killed for the sake of ideology—was then mapped onto what was retroactively posited as its source, *What Is to Be Done?* Hereafter, Rakhmetov—shrunk down to nothing but his "sin"—looked like *the* paradigmatic revolutionary, and any paradigmatic revolutionary thereafter looked like him. Save Karakozov: though once upon a time "a lot like Nikitushka Lomov," Karakozov no longer looked like much at all, except of course like something odd. So, oddly enough, like an extraordinary man, after all: a real Rakhmetov.

CHAPTER 3

"A Life for the Tsar"

Tsaricide in the Age of Mechanical Reproduction

"Did you hear that they shot at the Russian Tsar in Petersburg?"
"Yes, I heard. You know who did it?"
"A noble."
"And who saved him?"
"A peasant."
"How did they reward him for that?"
"They made him a noble."

Joke in *Kladderdatsch* (1866)

Among scholars of Russian revolutionary history, it is well known that Karakozov's failure to assassinate Alexander II unleashed a wave of patriotic jubilation (which, so they say, proves that the empire was still too traditional to embrace progressive politics). That the wave's mighty crest carried to hallowed heights the figure of some Osip Ivanovich Komisarov, however, is barely remembered. And of all the memorabilia that once upon a time flooded Russia's developing markets, a sole survivor now hangs in Moscow's erstwhile Museum of the Revolution, accompanied by a brief caption: "Medal in memory of Tsar Alexander II's deliverance by O. I. Komisarov" (see figure 3). This coin-shaped relic, which bears Komisarov's image, already reveals something of the condensation of capital in the myth used to fill the hole left by Karakozov's shot, but nothing as yet about the burlesque biography of the forgotten savior. Here then is his tale, which, as tall as it is, is very telling of its time.

The Rule

On April 4, 1866, the temperature peaked just above the freezing point, Saint Petersburg's roof remained clad in clouds, death took another sixty-

Fig. 3. Medal in Honor of Osip Ivanovich Komisarov-Kostromskoi. With permission from the Museum of Contemporary History, Moscow.

eight lives, and when Osip Ivanovich Komisarov, going home, "[approached] the Neva near the Marble Palace, he saw that the gangways had been disassembled and that crossing to the other side of the river there was no longer possible," so that he was forced to backtrack along the riverbank, past the Summer Garden.[1] At its northern gate, he noticed carriages and a crowd, which meant the emperor was about to stroll onto the boulevard after his regularly scheduled afternoon turn in the park, and so Komisarov halted to see. Of all the above, nothing was in the least exceptional, and not much at all could have indicated to this twenty-five-year-old hat-making apprentice of peasant stock that this day would disconnect him from his former life forever, or at least so long as he could give expression to the eternal unity of tsar and people.

Among the Rulers

Four days later, the Mariinsky Theater resounded with deafening, incessant shouting of his name: "KOMISAROV! OSIP IVANOVICH! KOMISAROV!" Someone said he had been heard begging—"I feel faint! I can't, can't!"—but his "trembling voice" was drowned out, again he climbed out of his box, joined the artists on stage, received the applause, and heard, for what must have been the hundredth time in a few days, the hymn "Bozhe, Tsaria khrani" ("God Save the Tsar"). "He has to forgive us [our enthusiasm]," a man told *Peterburgskii Listok*. "Our love and thankfulness to him for saving the tsar are so great."[2]

Mo(ve)ment

Just as Karakozov shot, it was said, Komisarov struck his hand, causing the bullet to just miss the head of the tsar.

Retrospective (Theory)

Before and after separates but a single movement of the hand. Waved away by this motion is the groundlessness of the most glaring constants— death, disease, delay—and then the exceptions that are the rule appear as the real that is reasonable. In this story, all the world's coincidences vengefully aligned to thwart the tsaricide's historical intentions and transform some anonymous peasant into the tool and weapon of the almighty. Yet once aligned, to unveil its primacy as that on the basis of which rests the order of things, sovereignty requires no more than a reflex. Or maybe not even that. Maybe no more was required of this Kostroma province peasant than to have happened to be there and then to agree with officialdom's narrative of how it really was. And being before otherwise meaningless, perhaps, he embraces fate's clutches, so that after, *Peterburgskii Listok* can report what Komisarov had confessed to his brother: "From that very morning, there was something unusual in my heart."[3]

Retrospective (Historiography)

If Komisarov appears in the annals of the Russian revolutionary movement at all, it is only for the few lines required to summarize his story, question its verity, and rate its propaganda value. Among Western historians, for example, Venturi grants the tsar's "alleged" savior half a paragraph; Ulam reserves one for the politics behind (dis)believing the story and one for the story itself; and Gleason offers a brief summary and declares that "the whole thing was a fake."[4] Among the Soviets, tellingly, the only scholar to exceed the standard summary was the literary critic turned children's poet turned literary scholar Kornei Chukovsky, and this in a work only tangentially related to revolutionary history. In a small book on the poet N. A. Nekrasov, Chukovsky provides a quick, colorful sketch of the Komisarov affair, which he clearly considered a politically motivated fabrication.[5]

Many contemporaries scoffed at the official truth about Komisarov no less than historians would later, though no one openly said so at the time. "The 'savior' Osip Ivanovich Komisarov-Kostromskoi quickly became the hero of the day, but with us he did not have much success," confessed the realist painter Ilya Repin*—though only in his early twentieth-century memoirs.[6] In the actual aftermath of April 4, when he was a student at Saint Petersburg's Art Academy, Repin was careful to hide his politics; "us" in "with us he did not have much success" referred strictly to his close circle of artist friends. Not that skepticism was restricted to the radical intelligentsia. Member of the Investigative Commission Cherevin, for example, filled a sheet of retrospective notes with suspicions.[7] Certainly privy to the details of the affair, he supposed that it was not Komisarov's gesture of deliverance, which had ostensibly been witnessed by the celebrated Crimean War veteran Count Totleben, but rather a distracting, anonymous cry from the crowd that had caused Karakozov to miss his mark. Esipovich, who as secretary of the Supreme Criminal Court was also more than familiar with the facts of the case, shared his fellow official's skepticism, and claimed not to have been alone in this: "I'll mention in passing that even then almost no one in high society believed the fairy tale invented by Totleben that Komisarov had saved the emperor; but at the time everyone tried to show this personage the greatest respect."[8] Everyone tried, because no one had a choice. It was absolutely of the essence that society demonstratively celebrate the miraculous fact that the very tsar who had delivered the people had now been delivered by one of them: to the tsar, this conveyed loyalty at a time of unparalleled political challenge; to the people, it showed support for the abolition of serfdom at a time when April 4 was rumored to be an act of aristocratic vengeance for 1861. During the dark days that followed April 4, fêting Komisarov seemed like society's sole defense against the threat of violence—political and/or physical—from above (state) and below (people).

Whether Komisarov did or did not save Alexander II from Karakozov, however, will not be of concern here. Nor will there be an attempt to prove that imperial authorities, through sly discursive maneuvers, used Komisarov to maintain the traditional balance of power in the wake of a modern political shock. Of course they did. Komisarov was exhibited precisely to preserve the myth of timeless unity between tsar and people, and with this myth to suppress the history Karakozov was trying to make. Much like the possibility that the story itself was a lie, this substitution strategy was not lost on contemporaries. One anonymous correspondent, for example, addressed himself as follows to Katkov: "There is a rather probable supposition that they raise the frightful, colossal noise surrounding Komisarov . . . to divert attention from the criminal."[9] But exactly because he so obviously substituted for Karakozov (about whom it was impossible to write due to both the severity of the reaction and a sheer lack of information), because he was so obviously used to regulate Russia's emotional temperature after April 4, Komisarov serves as a very good gauge for reading a range of reactions to this unprecedented political event.

Take for example the fact that, as was shown in the previous chapter, it was Karakozov's crime that, for the first time, exposed the threat contained by the crowd. Not only did Komisarov neutralize this threat (a man of the crowd attacked the tsar, but a man of the crowd saved the tsar), but he also put on this anonymity a legible mask: "[Komisarov's] biography . . . will be the biography of thousands of people . . . it presents a true and detailed sketch of the life of a whole environment, and acquaints with that life many who only know it from novels and essays."[10] Simultaneously, though, while Komisarov was being held up as exemplary representative of the people, a radical operation cut him off from his material conditions, dressed him up as one of power's own, and, in this guise, distributed him throughout the empire. Komisarov thus fulfilled functions that were multiple, and at times mutually exclusive. Should we succeed in sorting these out, it should break the spell of that other myth about Komisarov: not the one in which he saved the tsar, but the one in which he represents irrefutable evidence of the Russian people's rejection of Karakozov's historical program.

The best way to understand the function of the double myth of Komisarov will be to develop some stills from the spectacular production involving what was arguably Russia's first modern mass media star, and to read these for expressions of the time's reaction to April 4. Analysis of the orchestration of this "frightful, colossal noise" will show that the speed with which new technologies, waxing media, and speculation saturated Russia with an official truth is no less interesting than the intentions animating this truth. How effectively Russia's nascent capitalism launched into orbit a counterrevolutionary myth reveals much about the Russian empire's capacity to withstand and consume the shock of an unprecedented, modern political crisis. But because the means of production, distribution, and consumption also have their own, nonpartisan logic, they can trigger unpredictable effects: the reception of the savior indicates that this product possessed the potential to dialectically undermine the state's ideological intentions. A last point: reading the story of Komisarov primarily means reading the history of an image. The sources—advertisements, newspaper articles, police reports, rumors, legends, memoirs, and jokes— refuse direct access to Komisarov; they are spun, filtered, and overproduced. And yet, behind all of them, the force of Komisarov's historical presence can be felt, and it is in fact this that finally destroys the image.

The First Fifteen Minutes or So

On April 14, *Peterburgskii Listok* carried Alexander II's official notice that Osip Ivanovich Komisarov had been elevated to the nobility.[11] His sensational rise in value was expressed in the doubling of his name: "Kostrom-skoi" was added to "Komisarov." This added appellation canonized what had already been proclaimed in the streets, where Komisarov had almost instantly become known as "the new Susanin."[12] A legendary peasant-hero poeticized in Mikhail Glinka's* patriotic opera, *Zhizn' za Tsaria* (*A Life for the Tsar*), Ivan Susanin supposedly sacrificed himself to save the first Romanov from Polish invaders. Given the historically recent sepa-ratist insurrections in the Kingdom of Poland, not only did Russians ini-tially suspect that April 4's assassin had been an ethnic Pole, but also, as fate would have it, Komisarov happened to have been born in the Kos-troma province, whence too stemmed his legendary prototype, Susasin. After April 4, therefore, *A Life for the Tsar* was everywhere performed ad nauseam:

> Today the Bolshoi Theater once again performed the opera, *A Life for the Tsar*, and once again those same manifestations repeated themselves. The public greeted the sounds of the national hymn [*God Save the Tsar*] with a deafening "Hurray!" and demanded 11 encores.[13]

These performances must have been very effective normalizers after the shock of April 4: again and again, the tsar's life is endangered, saved, and the curtains go down. The fact that audiences repeatedly refused to allow the performance of the second act, in which Poles take the stage, more-over, evidences a strong desire to exert control over the historical event, and to nurture the illusion that its outcome was either preordained or could otherwise be summoned, reenacted, and redirected at will. "Skip it! Skip it! Third act!" came orders from audiences, among whom, one night, sat the young Peter Tchaikovsky: "As soon as the Poles appeared on the stage, shouts began, `Down, down with the Poles,' the chorus was confused and stopped singing, and the audience demanded the anthem, which was sung about twenty times. At the end the Sovereign's portrait was brought out, and the ensuing madness cannot be described."[14]

Via the recently installed telegraphs, meanwhile, countless messages crisscrossed and shrank the vast empire.[15] For months, *Severnaia Pochta* crammed its pages with telegrams and letters unanimously celebrating Komisarov:

> Osip Ivanovich!
> It pleased Almighty God to use you as his tool for the deliverance of the life of the Tsar-Liberator and Russia's benefactor. Seventy million inhabi-tants of the Russian land bless your name and will not forget it so long as Russia lives.
> Allow us, the dwellers in distant Tiflis, to add to the general voice of grat-itude an expression of our feelings. May it serve you as a reminder of that minute of your life in which you saved Russia's happiness.[16]

Other newspapers only bothered to print in full the most impressive letters and listed the remainder in column after column: "Kursk—from citizen S. Ryl'sk; Novgorod—from the priests and parishioners of the
Novgorod churches . . ."[17] As if Karakozov's shot had been a photograph
followed by a mighty flash, the whole of the Russian empire had suddenly
become visible to literate eyes, and was seen to be glowing with gratitude.

Donations poured in on the heels of the thank-you notes. Russia's
"readiness to make sacrifices in commemoration of the glorious event"
meant thousands and thousands of rubles collected to set up stipends,
schools, memorials, and the like.[18] In commemoration of his role in the
glorious event, Komisarov received a fair share of these donations. Housing, large sums of money, an education, and a career were placed at his
feet.[19] Instantly a desired guest in the beau monde, Komisarov was feasted
at a specially prepared banquet hosted by Saint Petersburg's exclusive English Club; Moscow's Nobility Club extended its membership to him; and
Kostroma province declared him its first citizen.[20] His bust was sculpted.[21]
That medal was cast in his honor. Nekrasov, Maikov,* and a slew of lesser
poets waxed lyrical over him.[22] The shoemaker Sitnov, who had won a
prize at the previous year's World Exhibition in London, expressed the
wish to make a pair of new boots for him.[23] Someone composed a "Komisarov Polka" for piano.[24]

These deeds of artists and aristocrats, however, were accompanied
by reactions of an altogether different order. As soon as Komisarov's
value had been artificially inflated, manufacturers began selling him off
to the public: consumers could eat Komisarov pies, candies, and chocolates, drink specially re-issued Kostromskoi beer, and smoke "Komisarov-Kostromskoi Cigarettes."[25] Paraphernalia of this type may function
as proof that April 4 transformed the entire empire into a united state
of tradition-bound patriots, but not without also exposing market
mechanisms sophisticated enough to produce, distribute, and consume
a phenomenon like Komisarov. Launched by the tsar and company, the
savior had indeed landed softly in the arms of Russia's developing capitalism, whose embrace soon had him eagerly engaged in an orgiastic
reproduction.

Ad(vantage)

Within weeks, the market already offered at least five publications relating the details of the event: *The Fourth of April; The Attempted Assassination
on the Life of His Imperial Majesty Emperor Alexander II; April Fourth and Its
Patriotic Meaning for Rus; God Saved the Tsar;* and finally, on April 15, the
third (!) edition of a large-format, twenty-four-page brochure entitled

Thanks to the Almighty for the Tsar's Salvation.[26] Outpacing the official biography of Komisarov to the market stands, these brochures, although "but a medley, not always believable, and not nearly as complete as what was printed in newspapers," according to one *Golos* correspondent (who evidently felt his own journalistic privileges to have come under threat), were devoured by the lower ranks of society and the people.[27] Among other things, the last of the above-listed publications included a transcript of Alexander II's April 4 speech at the Winter Palace; poetry by Nekrasov and Maikov; and, importantly, Osip Ivanovich Komisarov-Kostromskoi's portrait, which it can fairly be said was *everywhere.*

Notwithstanding the considerable contributions of more traditional media (poetry, sculpture, music, theater, and even the press) to shaping Komisarov's image, its production was primarily the work of the still youthful technologies of lithography and photography. Etchings taken from Komisarov's photograph were dispersed by relatively new and increasingly popular illustrated news organs like *Illiustrirovannaia Gazeta* (*Illustrated Newspaper*) and *Modnyi Magazin* (*Fashion Shop*), but his likeness also appeared on the brooches, medallions, and rings offered by one I. P. Sazekov, and probably on the wrappings of the candies, chocolates, cigarettes, and other items (see figure 4).[28]

Within a week of April 4, a first advertisement for Komisarov's actual photograph appeared in Petersburg newspapers. On April 9, three days after Komisarov had had his photograph taken in a studio on Nevsky Prospect identified in the press as having "formerly belonged to Levitsky*" (by far the most famous photographer at the time), *Golos* printed the studio's announcement of what it claimed was its *exclusive* product.[29] To organize what was evidently expected to be a high demand, the shop ordered potential buyers to mail in a deposit: one silver ruble guaranteed a spot on the wait-list. Curiously enough, though, on April 12, *Peterburgskii Listok* carried an offer by A. Eikhov's photography shop for portraits in all sizes for five to ten rubles apiece.[30] And the next day, although *Golos* advertised a certain Nikolaev's pretensions to exclusive rights for lithographs with a price tag of one ruble, a notice in *Peterburgskii Listok* announced that *all* bookstores now had fifty-kopek, two-tone lithographs in stock. Moreover, this last notice shared the page with yet another ad, placed by I. V. Junker & Co.:

> Photographs of O.I. Komisarov-Kostromskoi in various poses by the artist Den'er. To make portraits of Komisarov-Kostromskoi available for the entire public, prices start at 15 silver kopeks.[31]

These ads indicate that the autocracy could rely on a robust market for the distribution of official ideology. On the other hand, obviously they

Fig. 4. Osip Ivanovich Komisarov-Kostromskoi. *Modnyi Magazin,* no. 77 (1866), 162.

also reveal competition and class tensions below the surface of the social harmony embodied in the image of Komisarov.

The increase in availability and the decrease in price, in fact, may have occurred in direct response to the outrage of the public, whose demand was soon outstripped by both the quality and the quantity of the supply. One columnist for *Golos,* for example, scolded all photographers who "dare exploit [Komisarov's photo] as exclusive property"; such greed, he fumed, "gets rich at the expense of the Russian people's patriotism and limitless love for the Tsar."[32] And after seeing the initial advertisement in *Golos* by the studio formerly belonging to the famous Levitsky, one disgruntled reader had sent off a protest to *Peterburgskii Listok.* He wondered why, given everyone's overwhelming desire to possess Komisarov's portrait, the (re)production rights should belong to Levitsky only, and he contested both the long wait necessitated by the studio's slow system of distribution and the notion that its single photograph would satisfy the public's demand.[33]

Evidently, this issue was sensitive enough to provoke a response from Levitsky, which was published in the next issue of *Peterburgskii Listok.* Claiming no further connections with the studio on Nevsky Prospect, its former owner agreed that "the portrait of a personality like Komisarov should be in everyone's possession—and the duty of photography [studios] consists in lowering its price and making it available to all classes."[34] He concluded his letter with an endorsement of the artist Den'er, who, as seen in the above-cited advertisement, offered his portraits for as little as fifteen kopeks.

Nikolaev's pretensions to lithographic exclusivity, meanwhile, compelled a contestation from Komisarov himself. Across the rented space of *Golos*'s back page, the savior's announcement explained that he had indeed granted Nikolaev publication rights, but that these rights were no different from the rights he had granted to many others: "Mr. Nikolaev has no basis whatsoever to consider the right given to him as exclusive."[35] Whether ignorant or negligent of property rights, by concluding contract upon contract with photographer upon photographer, Komisarov had in any case been actively exerting personal force on the proliferation of his own image. Soon enough, though, Komisarov would discover that in fact it was he who held no exclusive rights to his own face.

Time is Money

A letter signed only with the initials "I. S." and intercepted by the Third Section brought the political event and the market into direct collision when its author speculated that "If stories like [April 4] happened more often, well, they'd sell countless newspapers, no? . . . Profitable for photographers, too. Here in Kazan we've already received 2,000 photos of Osip Ivanovich Komisarov."[36] *Golos,* indeed, freely admitted that it had never sold as many copies as during the days after April 4.[37] And just how profitable April 4 was for photographers can actually be shown with some exactitude.

Sometimes in the company of his wife, Komisarov mostly appeared on three-by-five-centimeter *fotograf“cheskie kartochki,* the Russian term for the *cartes de visite* that were widely in circulation across the continent at this time (see figure 5). *Kartochki* could function as business or social calling cards, but were also simply exchanged among family and friends, or collected in case they depicted the (in)famous. In the mid-1860s, to run a successful business, a photographer might charge a customer an average of fifty kopeks per card order, a price that presumably covered the costs of a session, processing, and printing.[38] But given that Komisarov posed only once and thereafter Levitsky, Eikhov, Junker, or whoever could and did run off prints ad infinitum, the costs were obviously reduced. Not that this fact, any more than did either the special circumstances or public grumbling, occasioned a real marking down of the usual charge toward a price reflective of labor invested: studios continued to charge fifty kopeks, Levitsky's successor one ruble, and Eikhov a startling five to ten rubles per portrait.[39]

Even Den'er's exceptional and generous offer of fifteen kopeks per portrait ensured him a fair profit. Assuming the costs of printing to be 10 kopeks, if Den'er sells 2,000 *kartochki* to the merchants of Kazan at 15

Fig. 5. Osip Ivanovich Komisarov-Kostromskoi (*Fotograficheskaia kartochka*). With permission from the State Museum of Political History of Russia, Saint Petersburg.

kopeks each, he still makes 100 rubles.[40] Should the new owner of Levitsky's old studio get the same order from Kazan, however, he rakes in 1,800 rubles. Or Eikhov: 10,000 rubles at the very least. Komisarov's glitz added mountains in ruble value to objects produced by technologies with the potential to minimize the costs of and equalize access to the otherwise entirely unattainable. Small wonder that when (what had appeared as) exclusive rights to the famous countenance were violated, its original owner was dragged into court.

In late October, a clerk of the secret police filed the following report:

After April 4, Osip Ivanovich Komisarov-Kostromskoi first had his portrait taken by the photographer Levitsky, with whom, as they say, he concluded an agreement stating that if [Komisarov] had other photographs taken, he would pay Levitsky a fine. Probably Komisarov somehow forgot about this and ordered his photographs from a different photographer. Levitsky got angry and filed a lawsuit. Yesterday, the Civil Chamber's First Department began to process the case.[41]

Neither *Peterburgskii Listok,* nor the official news organ of the Ministry of Justice, *Sudebnyi Vestnik* (the *Judicial Herald*), nor *Glasnyi Sud* (*Open Court*), a newspaper that went into circulation that very October with the express purpose of reporting on court-related news, however, discuss or even list the case revealed by this report. Possibly a decision was made to keep the financial battles surrounding the national hero out of the press, and it thus remains mysterious whether Levitsky himself or the second-generation owner of the studio faced Komisarov in court and, more interestingly, how the case was resolved.

Of further interest in the letter from Kazan is its date: April 18. In the mid-1860s, no direct railway line covered the more than one thousand kilometers that separated this city from the capital. From Petersburg, Komisarov *kartochki* would have first gone by rail on the new Nikolaevskaia Line to Moscow, where they became available on April 12, and then two thousand of them would have traveled onward by other means to become accessible to the residents of Kazan no later than April 18.

Less than two weeks, that is, for Komisarov to get a makeover and rush to Levitsky's old studio for his first photo shoot on April 6, onwards to the studios of Eikhov, Junker, Den'er, Nikolaev, and who knows where else throughout the following days, and then for thousands of prints to be developed, reproduced, packaged, carted off, and dispersed throughout the empire to hundreds of photography studios, bookstores, and vendors. About two weeks also for the appearance of publications like *God Saved the Tsar.* More complicated commodities like Komisarov jewelry or Komisarov Cigarettes took slightly longer, but two weeks seems an accurate assessment of the time it took Russia's nascent capitalism to turn Komisarov into product, icon, and fetish, and hence deliver him to his fate in the public sphere. And so within two weeks, also, the Third Section could record the following incident:

Yesterday, around 6 o'clock, some young fellow in a Slavic costume bought a photograph of Komisarov-Kostromskoi at Demidov's on the corner of Nevsky and Malaia Sadovaia. Saying "Here's your Komisarov," he then tore it up into little pieces. The public that witnessed the incident immediately scolded the young man, loudly expressed its indignation, and intended to take him to the police. The noise of the crowd attracted two police officers, and the whole thing ended with the crowd's dispersal. Three days ago, they say, a similar incident took place on Nevsky. At that time, some man tore up 4 photographs of Komisarov. No one noticed him, however, and he calmly walked off."[42]

Two weeks, that is, for Komisarov not only to be ennobled, celebrated, toasted, applauded, and gifted, but also worn, played, drunk, eaten, smoked, reproduced, distributed, sold, bought, and, finally, available for symbolic gestures in the marketplace of free ideas, to have his face torn up.

Exposure

This violence done to Komisarov's image should be distinguished from the danger to which his living body was exposed almost instantly upon becoming famous. From across the political spectrum came a number of death threats that were addressed to Komisarov and quickly secured for him the permanent company of a bodyguard. A group calling itself the Russian Revolutionary Committee, for example, sent Komisarov notice that he had better watch himself, "for his hours were numbered."[43] After April 4, this group sent a series of such notes—identifiable by the hand-writing—the content of which leaves no doubt as to its left-wing political sympathies. The following message, however, clearly came from the pen of an altogether different type of author:

> Hereby notifying Osip Ivanovich that from April 5 on his life is in danger, just as is [the life] of the one who escaped his fate for the time being [Alexander II]. The first will be poisoned and the second strangled. There are new Palens and Talyzins [Paul I's tsaricides] who will save the Russian nobles from the petit-bourgeois Tsar. It won't be long . . .[44]

Written as if by nobles—though hardly in a noble hand—the note plays on the deepest fear of the upper classes: by threatening Alexander II and Komisarov with tsaricides of the old type—courtiers capable of getting close enough to strangle victims in their beds or poison their carefully concocted meals—the note indicates that April 4 had been an act of aris-tocratic vengeance for the 1861 abolition of serfdom. Irrespective of con-tent, however, neither note is a purely political gesture; whether written in earnest or in jest, they tried to reach Komisarov privately, not to "go public" with their threat.

The saturation of Russian culture with Komisarov's image, however, eventually made it altogether unavoidable to encounter the savior pub-licly: he not only stared out at readers from the pages of newspapers, but also looked down at people from city walls; he shone as an exemplar of civic duty in courts, welcomed customers in stores, and greeted guests in restaurants; he was held up by merchants at markets and vendors at street corners; and worst of all, at least so later it seemed, one could meet him on the boulevard: "All sorts of idiots seemed to be carrying portraits of Komisarov about the city in order to ensnare those who did not remove their hats, and to inflict blows upon them."[45] In a flash, Komisarov's eye could size up degrees of political separation; his look was a loyalist yardstick, and it was everywhere.

Sometimes, Komisarov's gaze triggered effects that ultimately launched full-scale investigations. One day in late May of 1866, for example, some Sergei Kudriavtsev and a few others showed up at a party in the provinces and asked what was new. When the host handed over a paper with Komisarov's portrait, Kudriavtsev said, "Yes, that's the one who saved the tsar, but I'm going to drink to Karakozov anyway." Gulping down his vodka, he added, "Long live the revolution! Long live the guillotine!"[46] So someone said, in any case, after someone else had told local authorities. Likewise, in 1867, when one Danil Sorokin, a soldier of peasant origin, appeared before a district board hearing, it was a portrait of Komisarov that got him caught in a conversation about the latest failed tsaricide, this time by Polish nationalist Anton Berezovsky, whom Sorokin insulted with this incriminating phrase: "What a fool, that son of a bitch, that he didn't kill the Emperor. He deserved to die."[47] Shredded photos, death threats, and insults alike, though, were all reactions to the *idea* of Komisarov. Now for the effect of the real Komisarov on this idea—and vice versa.

The Return of the Real

Not yet a month after April 4, a secret police report claimed that among "all levels of society—even in Kostroma—doubt has increased that Komisarov was really the savior of the Emperor's life."[48] Komisarov's self-confidence, on the other hand, had only grown, and soon his affected behavior began to place additional strain on people's faith in him. Sources suggest, in fact, that few analogies are more appropriate for Komisarov than that of a genie escaped from a bottle and run amuck.

The first sign of alarm concerning Komisarov's excesses appeared among the files of the Third Section a mere month after April 4. On May 8, one of the clerks charged with tracking the urban rumor mill jotted down a first, single sentence: "They say that Komisarov was in a tavern, got drunk, and got into a brawl."[49] Hardly evaluative, this is a description of only the vaguest sort: the "they" is left unidentified, so is the place of the incident, the grounds for the fight, as well as the alleged opponent/s.

The report does not even betray whether the tone of the rumor portrayed Komisarov's drunkenness and belligerence in a negative or positive light.

Two weeks later, however, rumor had it that Komisarov, escorted by a guard named Plaksin and some other officials, had ended up in a restaurant, "where, of course, champagne played the leading role," and this report leaves no doubt as to the implications:

> After some glasses of wine, Komisarov became so ecstatic that he began to force Plaksin to dance the *trepak* [a Ukrainian dance]. Plaksin began to explain to him that he was assigned not to amuse him, but rather to protect him from any possible harm that might befall him. "Well, here's what I say to you," Komisarov replied. "If you value your job, then dance right now." Nothing was to be done: Plaksin thought and thought, and then performed the *trepak*.[50]

The reporting agent saw fit to add a warning regarding the veracity of this rumor: "That Komisarov boozes may be the case; not once has it been said that he [behaves indecently] at whatever occasion; but that Plaksin decided to dance for him, and in a restaurant at that, is improbable: Plaksin well knows how to behave himself."[51] The truth of this report consists not in its details, but in its force to produce an effect: the clerk reporting on Plaksin's dancing the *trepak* obviously felt compelled to insert himself into what should have been a neutral report. This discursive disturbance in the clerk's work is evidence that he at least feared that people might have believed Komisarov to possess enough power to order the likes of Plaksin around.

Half a year later, another report indicates that Komisarov's behavior had begun to be regularly monitored:

> For the third day in a row, Komisarov attended a dancing party at Gebhardt's. He was with some colonel and his bodyguard Raevsky. Drinking himself into a champagne stupor, Komisarov behaved himself very unpleasantly, used the shallowest expressions, and boasted of his power. On this occasion, Komisarov's cynicism was so great that he even attracted the attention of prostitutes."[52]

And Komisarov bothered not just the police: multiple attestations prove that his "cynicism" sent shock waves through several layers of the population. For example, the landlord/surveillance agent at Komisarov's erstwhile residence on Apraksin Lane—located in the slums of the capital near the Haymarket—sent a letter of complaint to the authorities: one night, Komisarov had shown up with a drunken entourage of friends from his hat-making days—including one who was now calling himself his "secretary." The group had allowed itself all sorts of familiarities and jokes at the expense of the agent, and Komisarov himself had forced him to drink champagne with them. "What are you, too good for us? Drink—we're equals after all, although actually I'm even better: a noble!"[53]

Meanwhile, Komisarov's wife was faring no better. Initially, observers reserved their disapproving looks for her curious appearance: at a banquet held in her husband's honor, she had been seen wearing "a shawl with unusually bright, bizarre flowers," and at a theater, "clumsy, shockingly tasteless peasant headgear."[54] Notoriety, however, she gained for her greed, gluttony, and gracelessness: "his wife wanders from morning till night through the Gostiny Dvor bazaar avidly buying silk and diamonds," Chukovsky noted, "everywhere introducing herself as the "wife of the savior.""[55] Ilya Repin, too, remembered her shopping habits, plus one additional detail: "it was rumored that at the height of his glory, his wife was demanding big discounts from merchants as 'the wife of the savior.'"[56]

Finally there was the trouble with Komisarov's father, Ivan Alekseevich, a convicted arsonist and consequently a Siberian denizen.[57] In May of 1866, by special orders of the tsar, Komisarov the elder had received permission to return from exile. En route to join his son in the capital, Ivan Alekseevich was welcomed and fêted everywhere by villagers both rich and poor.[58] Not yet half a year later—at the very time that society's tongues were really beginning to wag about the savior and his wife—Ivan Alekseevich was sent back into exile, this time to Narva, and placed under strict police surveillance.[59] The archives are silent on the official grounds for this second exile, but rumor had it, thus scribbled a scribe, that old Komisarov had been stirring up the people, telling stories of his suffering and poverty, painting the power of the landowning classes in the darkest of hues, and badmouthing the state.[60]

By late November, Komisarov's (or the Komisarovs') exceptional behavior had officially become the rule and the situation turned critical. "Since [Komisarov] was, as if by the will of fate, made famous to the entire world," reported a clerk, "[fame] has completely turned his head upside down and, so to say, knocked the sense out of him." Incessant scandals, the report continued, "humiliate him more and more in the eyes of society"; he had been christened "the accidental man" (*chelovek-sluchaia*), and to this epithet some added *khaluia* (slave, servant; also sponger, freeloader)—"and sometimes worse." His wife, meanwhile, had shamelessly graduated to announcing herself as "the wife of the savior" even in high society. Skepticism about the affair, so the memo, was gaining ground: society had had enough of the Komisarovs' presumptuousness and "the donations for their benefit"; many were beginning to voice the opinion that it might be useful "to allot them a different place of residence."[61]

Thus, a report on April 4's first anniversary noted that Komisarov had taken part in a peacefully observed commemorative procession and, as rumors had it, would become an officer.[62] When next Komisarov appeared in the files of the secret police, yet another year had gone and he was far removed from the capital, whose residents had begun to theorize about his absence:

> Yesterday, in the well-known Restaurant Tsaritsyn, some man related that, supposedly, Komisarov was killed on January 27 in Novgorod, that the government, fearing agitation among the people, forbade publication, and is trying to hide it by all means.[63]

A few months later, another Third Section memo recorded that someone had shared a train compartment with Komisarov and reported that, even though his fellow officers all held him in high esteem and his behavior was good, Komisarov was "not entirely satisfied that he had ended up in the military." He recognized, however, that he had only himself to blame: upon being asked by the tsar what he would like to be, Komisarov, always having wanted to be closer to the court, intended to say *Kammer-Junker,* a chamberlain, but "forgot the first half of the word," and ended up saying *Junker,* that is, an officer.[64] Obviously, this report contains no truth about Komisarov's whereabouts and the reasons for it. More likely, as had the report on the rumors doing the rounds in the Restaurant Tsaritsyn, it caught the echoes of popular wisdom/humor making sense of the savior's mysterious disappearance. But even this "dead," i.e. having died in the media, Komisarov had not died his last death just yet . . .

Return to the Rule

An entire decade of archival silence shrouds Komisarov's life until, on June 11, 1877, a confidential memorandum, originating from Konstantinograd's head of the nobility and having already passed through the hands of Poltava province's governor, appeared in the chancellery of the Ministry of Interior. The memo reports that Staff Captain Komisarov-Kostromskoi had "of late begun to lead a perpetually drunken life, and consequently fell into such a state that he shot at both himself and his wife, although, by the way, the shot missed his wife and [he] only lightly wounded himself."[65] The writer then relates that he has been approached to ascertain whether "special measures should be taken to extract Komisarov-Kostromskoi from such an indecent life," but replied that "Komisarov-Kostromskoi should not consider himself beyond the law and, as such, in the event that he commits crimes worthy of prosecution, he should be treated like anyone else."[66]

Apparently, the information was forwarded to the Third Section. One month later, the agency replied to the minister that his report had been brought to the emperor by the head of the Third Section, Adjutant General Mezentsev,* who "completely shares your opinion that Komisarov-Kostromskoi need not consider himself beyond the law."[67] He would not be resurrected. The archives contain no further files detailing the life of Osip Ivanovich Komisarov-Kostromskoi.

The Virtual

What remains of Komisarov first seems but an image revealed by the spotlight of power in 1866. Precisely as an emanation of that power, the medal cast "in honor of the tsar's deliverance" was hung right next to Karakozov's police photograph in the Museum of the Revolution, and told viewers that Russia's first modern tsaricide had misread the times, that, objectively, 1866 was too early for revolution. What this framing of the figures misses, though, is that as the tsaricide's substitute, the savior shares his form, and that Russia's embrace of Komisarov, therefore, was not without danger to the order of things at all. Hence the additional and actual concern of the anonymous correspondent who had confessed to Katkov his suspicions about "the frightful, colossal noise" surrounding Komisarov: shopkeepers displaying Komisarov *kartochki* to the eager public, he wrote, were promoting their ware as "next in line for Emperor."[68] With this, the chapter comes full circle to its epigraph: ennobling a peasant, the tsar had virtually created another potential tsaricide.

Timeline

The typical revolutionary timeline has thus been challenged. Historiographically, the Komisarov craze signified that Russia was still too traditional to condone terrorism: historically, it was "too early" for Karakozov. But there is nothing traditional about Komisarov: he would have been impossible had Russia not been permeated by the forces of modernity such as capitalism, the railway, the telegraph, and new media. The unity in unison that crystallized in Komisarov, moreover, was a special side effect of these forces—not the persistent presence of people's devotion to the eternity of empire. Nor, therefore, can it be maintained that Karakozov was out of sync with the time, for there no longer was but "one time." And if anything, arguably, the times were ripe: even if Russia was not, its media were ready for the revolution.

Another Time

After April 4, modern media were mobilized to catapult a counterrevolutionary message into the streams of contemporary consciousness. Consequently, clearly, these media were equally available to distribute a
revolutionary message. And indeed, albeit through less official channels,
the fetishes of the underground circulated right alongside those of the
official world: besides illegal literature, these were for the most part
"illicit photographs of 'politicals.'"[69] Growing up right alongside photography, after all, generations of radicals had been pictured: the Decembrists in Siberia (1820s), Herzen & Co. abroad (1840s), Mikhailov* in jail
(1860s).[70] In 1866, Karakozov found exposure among their ranks:

> There are portraits of Karakozov among the public. It is unknown by what
> means they were obtained and they are not the ones taken by the Third
> Section, but his profile. A passenger arriving here on the Nikolaevskaia Line
> had one such portrait.[71]

Two orchestrated weeks, as noted, were needed for Komisarov to give em-
pire-wide visual expression to the eternity of tsarism. Just three weeks
thereafter and despite being locked up in the Peter-Paul Fortress, Karakozov, bearing a temporal alternative, rolled into the northern capital on
the Nikolaevskaia . . .

CHAPTER 4

RASKOLNIKOV, KARAKOZOV, AND THE ETIOLOGY OF A "NEW WORD"

"A new step, their own new word, that's what they're most
afraid of all . . .
I babble too much, however."

RASKOLNIKOV, in *Crime and Punishment*

PRINCE OLDENBURGSKY: A sharp, decisive fact! What did [Karakozov]
understand by that word?
ISHUTIN: Some decisive step or other. He didn't say anything specific.
PRINCE OLDENBURGSKY: A decisive, sharp step? And why did he buy
the pistol?

Trial of Nikolai Ishutin

Because the stories produced by April 4 have always obstinately refused
to agree with one another, the event hurls the historian straight into the
chaotic heart of history's homonymic nature. The date marks not only
the original act of revolutionary terrorism, but also an as yet unsolved
crime: did Karakozov act alone or as part of a conspiracy? Unless the case
is closed, it seems, discovering the proper narrative for this event will remain as elusive as its motive is mysterious, and therefore April 4 always
tempts the historian to search for the source of the crime, to locate the
clue that will disclose, once and for all, the cause of the Karakozov case.

But this temptation is a trap. April 4 can never be brought back to its
source, unless this means that April 4 be brought back to itself: the event
was its own source, for the challenge that it constituted was a hitherto unthinkable puncturing of the political. The reason that the cause of April
4 is difficult to determine, in other words, is that the event was unprecedented, and the unprecedented cannot be traced to its precedents: there

always exists a gap—however small—between the new and all that came before it. And so the real question is: if the event April 4 was unprecedented, then how should one narrate its history?

Fortunately, and scarcely coincidentally, at this very time in history, in 1866, there appeared a novel addressing precisely such problems as outlined above: Dostoevsky's *Crime and Punishment*. *Crime and Punishment* is notoriously many things to many people, but it is undeniably (1) a detective story centered on the enigma of the criminal's motive; (2) a philosophical meditation on the first of Dostoevsky's man-god characters, Raskolnikov; and (3) the literary debut of Dostoevsky's new narrative technique, the omniscient third-person chronicler. Placing the events *Crime and Punishment* and April 4—or Raskolnikov and Karakozov—side by side, we can inquire into the etiology of a form of politico-philosophical violence that first emerged in Russia in the year 1866.

Why 1866? Or rather, why *this* violence in 1866? It is highly noteworthy that the year provides two very similar examples—one real, the other fictional—of the individual use of violence to *force* the birth of an idea that, at its core, crowns the subject sovereign: Karakozov's decision to inaugurate the reign of the people through tsaricide ("a decisive fact," "a decisive step") and Raskolnikov's to "become a Napoleon" through homicide ("a new word," "a new step"). What does it mean, this coincidence? On the one hand, that in 1866 it was not antichronistic to imagine, as Karakozov did, that violence was the way toward the new subject: not once, but twice at once it was imagined that murder was the means to this end. On the other hand, the fact that both perpetrators were thought to have been (more or less) "temporarily insane" suggests that the new subject was, nevertheless, still somehow unthinkable. At this time in history, therefore, this violence was possible, and yet exceptional: it appeared as a rupture on the outermost edge of 1866's horizon of possibilities.

How perilous the path can be leading to and from such a rupture Dostoevsky knew better than most: *Crime and Punishment* is entirely devoted to chronicling the painful process through which Raskolnikov comes to pronounce and then comprehend his "new word." Karakozov, on the other hand, historians have always narrated as acting out some already existing word—only to discover that something in his story still does not quite make sense. Ultimately, therefore, this is the lesson to be learned from *Crime and Punishment:* the history of April 4—and with it, the genesis of terrorism—becomes thinkable only through a poetic intervention that stages Karakozov as the subject of his own "new word."

Prospectus

Below appears part of a letter Dostoevsky wrote in September 1865 to Katkov, who besides being editor of *Moskovskie Vedomosti* was also the publicist of the literary journal, *Russkii Vestnik*. Composed to convince Katkov to publish *Crime and Punishment,* this prospectus lucidly introduces Dostoevsky's initial conception of the novel's plot and problematic; in addition it contains a phrase (printed in bold) that will turn out to be of distinct interest for this chapter's argument.

To Mikhail Katkov
September 10/22–15/27, 1865. Wiesbaden.
Draft
D[ear] M[ikhail] N[ikiforovich],
Can I hope to publish my story in your journal, *The R[ussian] H[erald]*?
I have been writing it here, in Wiesbaden, for two months now and am now finishing it. There will be from five to six signatures in it. There are two weeks of work left on it, perhaps even more. In any case, I can say for certain that in a month and absolutely no later it could be delivered to the editorial offices of *The R[ussian] H[erald]*.[1]
The story's idea, as far as I can assume, could not in any way contradict your journal—to the contrary even. It is the psychological account of a crime.
The action is contemporary, this year. A young man, expelled from the university, petit-bourgeois by social origin, and living in extreme poverty, **after yielding to some strange, "unfinished" ideas floating in the air, has decided, out of light-mindedness and out of the instability of his ideas** (*po legkomysliiu, po shatkosti v poniatiiakh, poddavshis' nekotorym strannym "nedokonchennym" ideiam, kotorye nosiatsia v vozdukhe, reshilsia*), to get out of his foul situation at one go. He has resolved to murder an old woman, a titular counselor who lends money at interest. The old woman is stupid, deaf, sick, greedy, charges Jewish interest, is malicious and preying on someone's else's life by tormenting her younger sister, whom she keeps as a servant. "She's worthless. Why is she alive? Is she of any use to anyone at all?" And so on. These questions confuse the young man. He decides to murder her and rob her in order to make his mother, who lives in the provinces, happy; to deliver his sister, who lives as a hired companion for certain landowners, from the lascivious attentions of the head of the landowner household— attentions that threaten her with ruin; and to finish the university, go abroad, and then for his whole life long to be honest, firm, unswerving in fulfilling his "humanitarian duty to humanity," whereby, of course, "the crime will be expiated," if in fact crime is the term for that action against a deaf, stupid, malicious, and sick old woman who does not know why she is alive herself and who perhaps would have died on her own in a month.
In spite of the fact that such crimes are terribly difficult to commit— that is, people almost always leave threads crudely sticking out, clues and so forth, and leave terribly much to chance, which almost always gives away

the guilty parties—he manages in an absolutely accidental way to accomplish his undertaking both quickly and successfully.

He spends almost a month after that until the ultimate catastrophe. No suspicion lies on him, nor can it. At this point the whole psychological process of crime is unfolded. Insoluble questions arise before the murderer; unsuspected and unexpected feelings torment his heart. God's justice, earthly law, comes into its own, and he finishes by being compelled to denounce himself. Compelled, so as to become linked to people again, even at the price of perishing at penal servitude; the feeling of separation and alienation from humanity that came over him immediately after committing the crime has worn him out with torment. The law of justice and human nature have come into their own, inner persuasion even without resistance. The criminal himself decides to accept suffering in order to expiate his deed. It is difficult for me to explain my idea completely, however. I want now to give it the art[istic] form in which it took shape. About the form. [Unfinished in the original.]

In my story there is, in addition, a hint at the idea that the legal punishment imposed for a crime frightens the criminal much less than lawmakers think, in part because he himself psychologically demands it.

I have seen that even in the most backward people, in the crudest instance of chance. I wanted to express this precisely through an intelligent person, one of the new generation, so that the idea can be seen more vividly and tangibly. Several incidents that have occurred recently have persuaded me that my *plot* is not at all eccentric. Specifically, that the murderer is an intelligent y[oung] man and even one of good incli[nations]. I was told last year in Moscow (reliably) about a student who was expelled from the university after a Moscow student incident—that he resolved to smash a post office and kill the postman. There is still much evidence in our newspapers of the extraordinary instability of the notions that impel people to horrible deeds. (That seminarian who murdered the girl in the shed by arrangement with her and who was arrested an hour later at break[fast], and so on.) In a word, I am convinced that my plot is partially justified by contemporaneousness . . .[2]

All that need be noted for now is that in this early conception of the novel: (1) the young man will kill out of utilitarian humanism, i.e. killing one will be useful for many; (2) there is no mention of the "Napoleonic Idea"; and (3) the "artistic form" is not yet settled. In September 1865, therefore, *Crime and Punishment* was hardly yet what it would become within but a few months' time: a detective story narrated by an omniscient third-person chronicler that will reveal Raskolnikov's "new word" as the cause of the crime.

Interruption

Between the publication of the second and the third installment of *Crime and Punishment* in Katkov's journal, Dostoevsky stormed into the Petersburg home of his dear friend, the poet Apollon N. Maikov, exclaimed, "They shot at the Tsar!", nearly collapsed into an epileptic fit, and then rushed back out onto the streets to mingle and talk with the curious crowd.[3] When a long week later *Russkii Vestnik*'s third issue came out in print, it carried an apology instead of Part Three of Dostoevsky's "psychological account of a crime": "Since illness did not permit the author to revise the manuscript as he wished before it went to the press, the continuation of *Crime and Punishment* has been postponed until the next issue."[4]

One Dostoevsky scholar has suggested that this postponement was in fact forced by the political impact of April 4, that it should be attributed to an executive decision of Katkov's that fell quite independently of Dostoevsky's illness and editorial wishes.[5] However, as noted in the meticulous research presented in the *Annals of Dostoevsky's Life and Works,* this suggestion remains speculative: there exists evidence that Dostoevsky indeed only managed to submit all six chapters of Part Three after *Russkii Vestnik*'s third issue was published on April 14.[6] In a letter of April 25 to Katkov, Dostoevsky reported having sent "three chapters a week ago. I'll try not to be late with the rest. It's very hard for me to work here—bad health and domestic circumstances."[7] Dostoevsky scholarship takes these "three chapters" to refer to Part Three of the novel. Part Three was thus, if not composed, nevertheless at least revised in the context of what were in all likelihood the after effects of one of the author's many epileptic fits and the anxious atmosphere of the "white terror."[8] Given Dostoevsky's status as both a man of letters and a convicted conspirator, how could April 4 and its aftermath—whose harshest reprisals were reserved for literary and revolutionary elements—have failed to decisively impress his psyche and affect his creative process?

Below follows a fuller discussion of *Crime and Punishment*'s publication history. At present, it is simply important to note that the delayed chapters were precisely those in which Dostoevsky first thoroughly explicated the novel's "Napoleonic Idea." A quick sketch should suggest why the formulation of this idea at precisely this time in history might have made an explosive impression, or at least led Dostoevsky to think that it would. A discussion of his logic, however, will show why he may nevertheless have thought that his artistic expression should be able to proceed without trepidation and without impediments from politics.

Hints

The exegesis of the novel's "new word," as Raskolnikov (like his creator) calls any truly novel thought, happens in Part Three, Chapter 5, in the

course of a conversation among Raskolnikov, his friend Razumikhin, and
the psychologically gifted investigator, Porfiry Petrovich.[9] The discussion
takes off from Porfiry's mention to Raskolnikov of "an article of yours:
`Concerning Crime' . . . or some such title," the argument of which the
examining magistrate sums up as follows:

> Yes, sir, and you maintain that the act of carrying out a crime is always ac-
> companied by illness. Very, very original, but . . . as a matter of fact, what
> interested me was not that part of your article, but a certain thought tossed
> in at the end, which unfortunately you present only vaguely, by way of a hint
> . . . In short, if you recall, a certain hint is presented that there supposedly
> exist in the world certain persons who can . . . that is, who not only can but
> are fully entitled to commit all sorts of crimes and excesses and to whom
> the law supposedly does not apply.[10]

"Raskolnikov smiled at this forced and deliberate distortion of his idea,"
writes Dostoevsky. "'That isn't quite how I had it,' he began, simply and
modestly."[11] Then follows a discussion that determines how Raskolnikov
did quite have it, after which he confirms Porfiry's introductory remarks,
"Not all of that's in the article; there are only hints there."[12] The "new
word," that is, had not yet been spelled out.

The fictional article does not appear in the novel; its content is only
reconstituted through a set of references and dialogues dispersed throughout *Crime and Punishment*. Clearly, however, there is a sense in which Raskolnikov's survey of "the psychological condition of the criminal throughout
the commission of the crime" presents in microcosmic form Dostoevsky's
own "psychological account of a crime." Or rather: *Crime and Punishment*
draws out the implications of what "Concerning Crime" "tossed in at the
end" and presented "only vaguely, by way of a hint," namely the right to
kill. Limited to "extraordinary" people ("lawgivers and founders of mankind" such as Lycurgus, Solon, Muhammad, and Napoleon, but also the
likes of Kepler and Newton, i.e. those who shift epistemological paradigms
precisely by pronouncing a "new word"), and in strict "proportion" to the
merit and relevance of novel thought, Raskolnikov's own "new word" pronounces not simply the *right* to transgress the first commandment—something that would still register as an expression, however "criminal," of
Christian free will—but a *moral sanction* to do so.[13]

Razumikhin—whose name derives from *razum*, the Russian for "reason"—intuitively grasps that this moral sanction to kill is both "what is
really original" in Raskolnikov's thought and "more terrible than official,
legal, license to do so . . ."[14] This "more terrible" resounds as the voice of
reason not because Raskolnikov's "new word" professes amorality as the
motor of history ("nothing especially new here," says Raskolnikov, and
Razumikhin confirms, "you are right . . . similar to what we have heard

and read thousands of times"), but because it conflates historical reality with truth, with that order generally identified as "eternal," "universal," or even "divine."[15] Prescribing an order whose first principle is the *absence* of the proscriptive principle by means of which there exists *any human order,* this "new word" names the negation of the *logos.* Claiming for this theory the status of truth ("This law is, of course, unknown at present, but I believe that it exists, and consequently that it may be known"),[16] Raskolnikov achieves what Dostoevsky presents as a disastrous Copernican turn: to exchange the ideal notion of divine justice for the narrow reality of human decision reduces truth to a pale reflection of historical habit and, finally, robs humans of a possibility for transcendence.

As Raskolnikov remarked about his "new word," however, "Not all of that's in the article; there are only hints there"; "all of that," instead, only emerges over the course of the novel. Precisely the same should be said of what Dostoevsky's letter to Katkov presents as "strange, 'unfinished' ideas floating in the air": their implications, too, only emerge over the course of the novel. Both the "hints" of Raskolnikov's article and this cluster of "unfinished" ideas of Dostoevsky's letter—these are ontologically level: they exist as excess, as a certain charge of thought. And it is specifically to this charge that we must turn in order to find the key to writing the history of a "new word."

The letter's cluster of ideas, as is well known, refers to nihilism.[17] And yet, if the referent was so obvious, then why did Dostoevsky call these ideas "unfinished" in scare quotes? Possibly, the quotes signify his attitude toward a specific author's text (say a recent article by the fiery young critic writing for *Russkoe Slovo,* Dmitry Pisarev*), or perhaps they refer to what was at that time a stock phrase of radical criticism, or maybe even to some nondescript but ideologically charged discursive tic.[18] Possibly. More likely, however, Dostoevsky's use of the term "unfinished" means that he thought the implications of its referent, however ostensibly obvious, had not yet been drawn out.

There exists a shift of emphasis in presenting these referents as a *charge of thought* and the manner in which Bakhtin designates *prototypes* for what he calls the idea-images of Dostoevsky's novels: the former suggest something yet to be done, the latter something already made. Aware of Dostoevsky's conviction that reality includes its potentialities ("Reality in its entirety is not to be exhausted by what is immediately at hand," Dostoevsky once wrote, "for an overwhelming part of this reality is contained in the form of a still *latent, unuttered future Word*"), Bakhtin insists that "precisely this potential is of the utmost importance for the artistic image":

As an artist, Dostoevsky did not create his ideas in the same way philosophers or scholars create theirs—he created images of ideas found, heard,

sometimes divined by him *in reality itself.* . . . Dostoevsky possessed an extraordinary gift for hearing . . . voices still weak, ideas not yet fully emerged,
latent ideas heard as yet by no one but himself, and ideas that were just beginning to ripen, embryos of future worldviews.[19]

Here, though, the emphasis should shift away from the artistic nature of
what Bakhtin construes as a divinatory gift and toward the philosophical
or scholarly crux of Dostoevsky's encounter with thought.

If Dostoevsky is able to "divine ideas in reality itself," this is because he
is very skillful at locating—and locking in—the junctures of any existent
idea's unthought element. Aligning this element with what Bakhtin called
reality's "potentialities" makes plain why Dostoevsky's gift for artistic creation was simultaneously his devastating skill for waging philosophical
war: any posited system's "unfinished" element is not only the thinkable
genius loci of an artistic event, but also its Achilles heel or blind spot, that
unseen, silent, or empty remainder where the wedge of dialectics can be
inserted and thus whence an assault from within can be launched. Dostoevsky is a master artisan of the ideological Trojan horse, and terms like
"unfinished," "hint," "latent," and "unuttered" are thus not only always
telltale signs of vital activity in Dostoevsky's thought as an artist, but also
can mark the seeds of "new words" that the author as critic insists are false
prophesy and intends to unmask as such. For Dostoevsky, to engage an
"unfinished" idea means he intends to finish it off.

Freedom of Speech

Arguably, April 4 finished off in its own way whatever ideas were "floating
in the air" in 1866. Presented by the administration and press as an inevitable consequence of radical thought, the event inaugurated a devastating political reaction that spelled the end of all open, public dialogue.
Against this backdrop, Dostoevsky the writer and convicted conspirator
must have proceeded with exceeding care while he was crafting for public consumption a philosophico-literary dialogue concerning the right of
certain persons to kill for the sake of a "new word"—a philosophico-literary dialogue concerning the moral sanction of the maxim that *the end
justifies the means.* Given Dostoevsky's logic, though, it becomes clear why
in his letter to Katkov in which he cites "bad health and domestic circumstances" to explain his delays, this notoriously conservative novelist
advocated what looks like a peculiarly progressive ploy to ensnare nihilism. In sharp contrast to the administration's policy of censorship, op-
pression, and secrecy (and Katkov's support thereof), Dostoevsky wrote:

But how can you fight nihilism without freedom of speech? If even they, the nihilists, were given freedom of speech, that might even be more advantageous then: they would amuse all Russia with the *positive* explanations of their teachings. But now people attribute to them the form of sphinxes, enigmas, wisdom, mystery, and that entices the inexperienced.[20]

Paradoxically, his weapon of choice to battle the "strange, 'unfinished' ideas floating in the air" is the same as Porfiry Petrovich's recommended cure for Raskolnikov: "Now you need only air, air, air!"[21]

Zeitgeist, Its Groundlessness

If what was intimated above about Dostoevsky's method is correct, then the origin and originality of this writer's "new words" should never be located anywhere outside of his own thought—outside of whatever evidence we have of its creative logic. And rather than their sources, it is the process by means of which "new words" come to be pronounced that is of real interest for historical studies concerned with causality. This should be emphasized: nothing truly novel will ever be reducible to the elements making up the situation whence it emerged; the new is *excess*, excessive to the order of things, and the history of its emergence can only be written by recognizing and retaining the distance that separates it from what came before and after. This also applies—and this is the real point of placing side by side the events *Crime and Punishment* and April 4—to Karakozov's "new word," his "decisive fact" or "decisive step": revolutionary tsaricide.

Note, once more, that peculiar phrase of Dostoevsky's in his September 1865 letter to Katkov: "A young man . . . after yielding to certain strange, 'unfinished' ideas in the air . . . decided . . . " Interestingly, the trope "in the air" has also long been used to narrate the historical emergence of terrorism: to explain the etiology of Karakozov's 1866 introduction of political assassination, scholars of the revolutionary movement have suggested that the idea of tsaricide was already "in the air." There is, however, a crucial difference between the two uses of the phrase: whereas the thoughts and actions of Dostoevsky's young man embody the implications of as yet "unfinished" ideas, Karakozov's tsaricide is presented as the simple execution of an always already and readily available idea. Upon inspection of whatever was "in the air" prior to April 4, however, it immediately becomes clear that no such idea existed at all, and that most narratives of revolutionary terrorism thus sidestep by means of a zeitgeist trope the complexities of writing the history of its genesis.

To illustrate, one example will suffice: Petr G. Zaichnevsky's* 1862 manifesto, "Young Russia," which is the most frequently cited "word" (propaganda) preparing the ground for the "act" (terrorism):

> We studied the history of the West, and that lesson was not wasted on us; not only will we be more consistent than the pitiful revolutionaries of [18]48, but even than the great terrorists of [17]92, we will not be afraid if we see that to overthrow the present order we will have to shed twice as much blood as did the Jacobins during the [17]90s. . . .
>   Soon, soon the day will arrive when we raise the great Red Banner of the future and, with loud cries of "Long live the social-democratic republic of Russia," move on the Winter Palace to exterminate its inhabitants.[22]

Zaichnevsky's use of the term "terrorists," however, is very traditional: "Young Russia" implies a concept of violence whose habitat is *la Terreur* of 1793–94. Indeed, this proclamation brims with historical examples of rebellion—from the Cossack and peasant revolts led by Stepan "Stenka" Razin* (1670–71) and Emelian Pugachev (1773–75) to the failed European revolutions of 1848—but the sheer fact that this discourse was fluttering about the capital in no way accounts for its coagulation into terrorism, a phenomenon of an altogether different order. It is not possible to draw a direct line from the discourse of "Young Russia" to the action of April 4, 1866, without glossing over a very real difference between the violence of French *terreur*, be it Red or White, and Russian revolutionary terrorism. For one, once a chanting mass, banners aloft, has made its way through the streets of the capital and into the imperial residence, the killing of the imperial family simply signifies that a revolution is naturally culminating in a violent transfer of power. The violence of terrorism, however, is of a very different temporal order: rather than a culmination of, it is an impetus toward the revolution.

The Fallacy of Source Study

Few historical phenomena illustrate the operational logic of such intellectual short-circuiting better than does the reception of *Crime and Punishment*, a work that spawned a truly unusual and absolutely zealous effort to track its most minute and remote sources. Of Raskolnikov's "new word," Joseph Frank writes that academics have "ransacked the culture of past and present in pursuit of 'sources' for Raskolnikov's division of mankind into 'ordinary' and 'extraordinary' people, and searched high and low for precedents anticipating his theory that the second category possessed the *right* to disregard the injunctions of the moral law prohibiting murder."[23]

Fig. 6. Dostoevsky Caricature. *Iskra*, no. 14, 1867.

This search, moreover, has animated readers and critics alike since *Crime and Punishment*'s very appearance. Although often affably astonished by what Dostoevsky saw as his plot's "contemporaneousness," his contemporaries could also strike decidedly strident or mocking poses whenever their encyclopedic scrutiny bore fruit. In its April 1867 issue, for example, the satirical magazine *Iskra* (*Spark*) carried a caricature reflecting a widespread perception of Dostoevsky's creative method (see figure 6).

> Quickly telegraph Mikhail Nikiforovich [Katkov] that I'll send him the fifth part of *Crime and Punishment* tomorrow. Please take the *Gazette des Tribunaux*, cut out the case of that fiend Lemer who killed his father's bride, etc., and write everywhere Raskolnikov instead of Lemer, and Petersburg instead of Paris. Do you understand? That will be the fifth part of my novel. After all, those lighthearted French will not be able to draw a general conclusion from an individual case.[24]

There may or may not have been a real "fiend Lemer." That is beside the point. What matters is that, since the beginning, commentators have unearthed "Lemer" after "Lemer" in order to explain how Dostoevsky came up with Raskolnikov. Thus the *Annals of Dostoevsky's Life and Works* underlines the relevance for *Crime and Punishment*'s plot formation of A. E. Nikichenko's August 1865 attempt to assassinate the secretary of the Russian embassy in Paris—in addition to the September 1865 robbery-murder of two elderly people in Moscow by Gerasim Chistov, and then yet another murder in Saint Petersburg committed by someone from the "new generation."[25] To these and more one may readily add the potentially postal student, the seminarian shed murderer, and all other "incidents that have occurred recently" mentioned in Dostoevsky's own prospectus. All of these cases went into *Crime and Punishment*—and yet *Crime and Punishment* is none of these. In exemplary fashion, *Iskra*'s caricature illustrates an approach the great literary scholar Leo Spitzer called "the fallacy of 'source study.' "[26] Originality, when truly there is some, always exceeds its origins.

"We Have Predicted Facts"

Among all criminal cases contemporaneous with Raskolnikov's fictional homicides, however, one in particular has conquered a privileged place in the scholarly literature and merits a brief discussion here. This is because the case stands out not as a source for the novel, but as testimony to what Dostoevsky insisted was his *realism,* "only deeper" or "just in a higher sense."[27] In December 1868, in response to Maikov's report that the reading public's "chief criticism is in the fantasticality of [*The Idiot*'s] characters," Dostoevsky, as Frank writes, "sets down the famous declaration of his aesthetic credo of 'fantastic realism' ":

> Oh, my friend, I have a totally different conception of reality and realism than our novelists and critics. My idealism—is more real than their realism. God! Just to narrate sensibly what we Russians have lived through in the last ten years of our spiritual development—yes, would not the realists shout that this is fantasy! And yet this is genuine, existing realism. This is realism, only deeper; while they swim in the shallow waters . . . Their realism—cannot illuminate a hundredth part of the facts that are real and actually occurring. And with our idealism, we have predicted facts. It's happened.[28]

These "predicted facts," as has often been noted, referred to an 1866 criminal case whose occurrence, the author held, was plain testimony to the fact that he was no idealist—at least not in the ordinary sense.

On January 15, 1866, that is, when Dostoevsky had already submitted Part One of *Crime and Punishment,* but it had not yet appeared in print, the Russian press reported the double homicide, presumably motivated by robbery, of moneylender Captain Konstantin Fedorov Popov and his assistant Maria Nordman.[29] After *Russkii Vestnik*'s January 30 issue (carrying Part One) came out, and especially after the murders of Popov and Nordman had been attributed to Moscow University student Aleksei Mikhailovich Danilov*, contemporaries began to compare real life and fiction.[30]

When the transcripts of the Danilov trial appeared in print a year later, however, comparisons made way for contrasts.[31] The defendant, so the prosecution, had simply murdered Popov and Nordman to gather the requisite funds for his wedding; philosophical questions were not apropos here, and were never raised during the trial. And so, one month after both the novel and the Danilov trial had been concluded, a review of *Crime and Punishment* argued against the notion of a structural correspondence between the two cases:

> The murderer of Popov and Nordman did not behave himself at all as did Raskolnikov, neither after the crime, nor during the trial. . . . Popov and Nordman's murderer weaves unbelievable tales, is notable for his cold-bloodedness, and lies. Here there were no reflexes, and no idée fixe; just a case as dark as all cases of this kind . . ."[32]

The trial also quieted any suspicions as to whether Dostoevsky had simply lifted his plot from the Danilov case; the author had clearly begun to compose *Crime and Punishment* months before Popov's murder had even been conceived.[33] Ultimately, beyond the fact that the intended victims were moneylenders and that the unintended murders of Lizaveta and Nordman were occasioned by a door left ajar, Raskolnikov and Danilov had little in common. A very real congruence did exist, however, between Raskolnikov and another contemporary of his: Dmitry Vladimirovich Karakozov.

Correspondence

Practically the same age, Raskolnikov (twenty-four) and Karakozov (twenty-five) are dirt-poor dropouts of the law faculties at Petersburg's and Moscow's premier universities, whose fees exceeded their provincial means. Both are given to *molchanie* (silence) or spleen, both are misanthropic, and both are monomaniacal "hypochondriacs." Furthermore, importantly, after committing their ideological meditations to paper (the article "On Crime" and the proclamation "To My Worker Friends") and coincidentally intercepting "idle talk" (Raskolnikov hears a dialogue between a student and an officer, Karakozov a rumor from his doctor), both proceed to carry out their respective crimes in a state bordering on delirium, as a result of which both forget to erase a set of conspicuous clues. Lastly, in that each, as Dostoevsky put it in his September 1865 letter to Katkov, "decides to break out of his disgusting position at one stroke" after months of being idle and monomaniacally marinating in his own thoughts, Raskolnikov and Karakozov share a very specific all-or-nothing temporality.

The correspondence between Raskolnikov and Karakozov, with but very few, little known, and cursory exceptions, has remained undiscussed among both contemporaries and scholars of Dostoevsky and the Russian revolutionary movement. At the time, only Katkov and Pisarev presented this comparison between real life and literature, and even then only implicitly. First, Katkov once indirectly compared Karakozov and Danilov, and thus, arguably, *eo ipso* Karakozov and Raskolnikov: in a column devoted to deconstructing the Investigative Commission report published in *Severnaia Pochta*, Katkov contrasted the Karakozov case with an unidentified, upcoming trial in Moscow that was clearly Danilov's ("a young fellow who killed a man and his servant"); but while both cases were criminal, he argued, only the Karakozov crime was political.[34] Second, in 1867 Pisarev wrote a long response to *Crime and Punishment*, "Bor'ba za zhizn'" ("Struggle for Life"), and the secondary literature offers one article by A. Volodin, "Raskolnikov and Karakozov: The Compositional History of Pisarev's Essay, 'The Struggle for Life,'" which presents Pisarev's essay as an "answer" to April 4, i.e. as a critical thinking through "Karakozovshchina." "We do not have enough evidence to show that Pisarev responded precisely to Karakozov's act in 'The Struggle for Life,'" writes Volodin, "But here he discerned the same problems with which this event [April 4] confronted Russian society. Therefore, objectively speaking, it was precisely an answer to the shooting of April 4."[35] Its suggestive title aside, however, Volodin's piece is not at all comparative in the sense meant here.

Otherwise among scholars, only Frank has remarked that the "shattering event" of April 4 "increased the impact made by Dostoevsky's portrayal of the crime committed by *his* ex-student, and certainly affected the mood in which the final sections of the book were composed."[36] Although Frank provides no evidence for this claim, it is reasonable enough. Karakozov, after all, did not just coexist with *Crime and Punishment*, but tore a hole right through the fabric of its continuity: April 4 literally interrupted and delayed the regularly scheduled intervals of the as yet unfinished serialized novel. But there is more: the Karakozov case found its way into the novel—and in such a way as to show the limits, or blind spot, of Dostoevsky's "realism."

History into Art

When Karakozov compelled Dostoevsky to join the crowd on April 4, the author had not yet completed Part Three. Quite possibly, April 4 provoked the illness that would force Katkov to print an apology for the delay over the blank space left by the absentee chapters. Likewise, Part Four suffered a delay and did not appear in print until June, but a first version had certainly been completed by May and perhaps even earlier. Here censorship played a part: *Russkii Vestnik*'s editorial board thought it recognized traces of nihilism and a definitive threat to morality in the episode where Raskolnikov and Sonya read "The Raising of Lazarus" together; the corrections were submitted by July 8 and Part Four was published on July 20.[37] Conceivably, therefore, anything after Part Two could have been affected by Karakozov's attempt, but direct influence on the formation of *Crime and Punishment* is more likely for Chapters 5 and 6 of Part Four, all of Part Five and Part Six, and the two Epilogues.[38]

By the summer of 1866, however, most of the novel had long been worked out in Dostoevsky's head. Source studies have tracked down *Crime and Punishment*'s composition stage to as early as the late summer of 1865. Ideas had probably been coalescing since that year's February, when the author read the introduction to Napoleon III's *History of Julius Caesar* in *Sankt-Peterburgskie Vedomosti* (the *Saint Petersburg News*), though they had then yet to merge with another story Dostoevsky had been writing, "The Drunkards," and with the "recent incidents" mentioned in his September 1865 letter to Katkov. By November 1865, in any case, Dostoevsky had already burned an entire early draft. On the other hand, as late as June 1866 he confessed that "so far I have only written perhaps half for *Russkii Vestnik*," and in July he was still drawing up character sketches for Porfiry Petrovich.[39] Lastly, and legendarily, Dostoevsky interrupted work on the novel for the whole month of October in order to dictate to his future wife the novella, *The Gambler* (1866).

Formally, therefore, *Crime and Punishment* was still open-ended enough to be able to absorb the unforeseen influence of April 4. Adaptation of the Karakozov case, however, has only been suggested for Dostoevsky's later works. For example, scholars point to Ishutin's October 4 public pardon as a prototype for Myshkin's famous relating of the execution scene in *The Idiot*. Though the novelist was in fact in Saint Petersburg on this date, the comparison must be modified. Even contemporaries noticed the more obvious parallel between Ishutin's mock execution and those of the Petrashevtsy, and of course the young Dostoevsky was a Petrashevets; having himself been arrested on conspiracy charges, condemned to death, and pardoned at the very last minute, the author wrote his own experience into *The Idiot*.[40]

With respect to *Demons*, obviously the main source of inspiration for the plot of this most polemical of Dostoevsky's novels was Narodnaia Rasprava's 1869 murder of one of its own members, Ivan Ivanovich Ivanov. Nevertheless, certain characters have been seen as having their roots in the events of the 1866 Karakozov case. P. E. Shchegolev suggested that a fusion of Nikolai A. Speshnev, the "leader" of Dostoevsky's own conspiratorial group in 1848, and Ishutin, the "leader" of "The Organization" and

"Hell," served as prototypes for Stavrogin, and that the relationship between Ishutin and Karakozov stood as model for that between Stavrogin and Petr Verkhovensky.[41] Speculations such as these seem to garner support from Dostoevsky's *Notebooks,* where Karakozov's name appears no less than five times, though a careful reading of these entries shows the real connection to have been between Karakozov and Kirilov.

Finally, one must wonder—and it is rather a wonder that no one has—about the nominal link between Karakozov and the Karamazov brothers. No doubt, had Dostoevsky lived to carry out his intention to transform his monkish Alyosha into a revolutionary tsaricide, the (possibly subconscious) allusion would not have been lost on readers.

But there are, as a matter of fact, passages where details from the Karakozov case were written into *Crime and Punishment,* and these passages are extremely revealing of the impact April 4 had on Dostoevsky. The most suggestive of all occurs when a long-confounded Razumikhin has his last meeting with Raskolnikov, and finally decides:

> He's a political conspirator! For sure! And he's about to take some decisive step—for sure! It can't be otherwise. . . . And all the earlier things are explained now! That illness of his then, all that strange behavior, even before, before, still at the university, he was always so gloomy . . . [42]

Those lines were written in September 1866, that is, after Karakozov's trial had been concluded (August 31) and long after details of his case such as the following had been reported (early April):

> The criminal, according to the testimonies of some of his friends, suffered from fits of melancholy and hypochondria, and was hospitalized in Moscow University's clinic for more than a month. . . . Acquaintances and relatives said that Karakozov constantly complained that life was a burden to him, that he had already had enough of it, and that he hates people. Additionally, Karakozov held ideas of the most extreme type of socialism.[43]

Only after Karakozov had publicly rendered intelligible the possible connection between illness, ideologically inspired crime, and revolutionary politics could Dostoevsky have Razumikhin's healthy reason draw such an obvious conclusion: "It can't be otherwise . . . And all the earlier things are explained now!" After all, even the more basic version of this link—Raskolnikov's idea that "the act of committing a crime is always accompanied by some morbid condition"—is qualified by Porfiry as "very, very original," i.e. not at all yet part of any assumed or self-evident cultural backdrop. Additional evidence comes from the fact that in all of Dostoevsky's notebooks and drafts, which contain quite a few versions of dialogues between Raskolnikov and Razumikhin on the topic of crime and illness, there is nothing to suggest that "political conspirator" is ever an option in terms of thinking about Raskolnikov. Therefore, it is Karakozov who stands between crime and illness in a way unthought by the novel when first conceived, Karakozov who allows for later on imagining the link "illness-crime-politics" as natural and logical.

Karakozov thus reveals the limit of Dostoevsky's imagination, a place where, evidently, the link between illness and crime did not extend into the realm of politics. Indeed, retrospectively, it is remarkable how free of politics is *Crime and Punishment,* a work whose original intent, after all, was to expose the fruit of nihilism as rotten. Perhaps the only logical conclusion is that the very link between nihilism and political violence was unimaginable before April 4, but that they became so intimately linked afterwards that now it is almost unimaginable that they ever were not. In their stark self-evidence, in any case, Razumikhin's phrases highlight how strangely absent is politics in *Crime and Punishment,* and strongly suggest that it is Karakozov who injects the political into Dostoevsky's writing.

One last example in support of this idea. This one comes from the chapter interrupted by Karakozov's shot on April 4: Part Three, Chapter 5. Specifically, it concerns a set of arguments advanced by Raskolnikov to dismantle the threat of his own theory. The first of these Raskolnikov himself volunteers in order to show that, apropos of "extraordinary" people, there is "not much cause for alarm: the masses hardly ever acknowledge this right [to crime] in ["extraordinary" people]; they punish them and hang them (more or less)."[44] This is an odd passage, for although arguably "true," generally speaking, who, in fact, of those Raskolnikov has mentioned—Kepler, Newton, Lycurgus, Solon, Muhammad, and Napoleon—were "punished and hanged (more or less)"? No draft for this passage appears in the notebooks, and the same goes for the follow-up phrases that, "Some . . . triumph during their lifetime . . . and start doing their own punishing."[45] The most likely reference of this "some," it seems, are the Jacobins, but what seems more relevant than the identity of the referent is the fact that the discussion, in so far as it relates to the possibility of public death, has narrowed to the realm of the political—and this in a passage expressly intended to show that Raskolnikov's theory is "not much cause for alarm," i.e. that the theory may seem threatening, but has no political consequences.

Next, Porfiry asks two questions about the implications of Raskolnikov's theory, and the latter assures him once more that there is "nothing for you to be alarmed about."[46] First he tells Porfiry that "ordinary" people who fancy themselves "extraordinary" and start acting accordingly "never go far" and, second, that there are not so many "extraordinary" people around.[47] What Porfiry's questions reveal is that the potential threat posed by Raskolnikov's theory is not so much the theory itself, but rather a mix-up or excess of the "extraordinary." And this is logical enough, in fact; for where is the threat in a theory containing a "law of nature" that rediscovers human inequality at the very moment of historically constituted equality (i.e. Russia in the 1860s)?

I would argue strongly that Razumikhin's reasonable idea of Raskolnikov as a political conspirator was directly influenced by the Karakozov case. The narrowing of the discussion to the political plane during Raskolnikov's conversation with Porfiry in Part Three, Chapter 5, seems very suggestive of such an influence. Especially in light of the two pages that defuse the political threat of Raskolnikov's theory, it seems not unreasonable to suppose that these two pages were a caveat added after April 4; one should not confuse so great a criminal as a tsaricide, after all, with an "extraordinary" man—at least, not so long as he fails.

Art into History

Raskolnikov did not affect Karakozov in the way that Karakozov affected Raskolnikov, and this for the simple reason that *Crime and Punishment* did not interrupt, delay, and then change what happened on April 4 in the way that April 4 interrupted, delayed, and then changed what happened in *Crime and Punishment.* Nevertheless, courtesy of the correspondence between Karakozov and Raskolnikov, Dostoevsky's novel can change how we conceive of the history of April 4. We need only agree that a "new word" is an event in every field—i.e. that authoring a political event is no less complicated than authoring a work of art—and then learn from Dostoevsky some lessons in narrating the history of the new in 1866.

So let us return to the beginning. *Crime and Punishment* is (1) a detective story centered on the enigma of the criminal's motive; (2) a philosophical meditation on the first of Dostoevsky's man-god characters, Raskolnikov; and (3) the literary debut of Dostoevsky's new narrative technique, the omniscient third-person chronicler. It should be underlined that these three points are directly related: it is the new narrative technique that allows the reader to take up residence in Raskolnikov's mind and watch him discover that the cause of his crime was his desire to "become a Napoleon." Without this technique, knowledge of Raskolnikov's "new word" would be nil, and without this knowledge, Raskolnikov would appear to the reader as he does to the court that judges him at the end of the novel: either as a conventional criminal (an impoverished student robber) or an unthinkable mystery ("temporarily insane"). Only the omniscient third-person chronicler, because he has access to Raskolnikov's psychology, can prove the complex, causal relationship between "certain strange, 'unfinished' ideas in the air," Raskolnikov's "new word," and his crime. Only *Crime and Punishment*'s artistic form, which shows Raskolnikov as a subject constituted by his own "new word," allows his violence to appear as something novel. And this is the wisdom of *Crime and Punishment* to be applied to April 4: its historically unprecedented violence requires a narration that allows Karakozov to be seen as the subject of his own word.

For as with Raskolnikov, so with Karakozov: it has always been clear that Karakozov was the criminal, but never—at least not conclusively—why he committed the crime, and this has considerably complicated determining the narrative arc of its history. No matter the tale told about Karakozov, part of it always sticks out conspicuously; no matter the sentence written about his motive, a qualifying clause undermines its truth. And so it will be as long as the cause of his crime continues to be sought outside of Karakozov, as long as Karakozov is seen as acting out someone else's already existing word. The history of April 4 will only find its final form when it is no longer presented as prologue or epilogue to a history we already know, and when instead Karakozov's "new word" comes to be clearly heard.

Of course all this does not mean that a novel history of the Karakozov case must somehow mimic the narrative mode of *Crime and Punishment*. Raskolnikov is a useful reference, but he is a fictional character; the historian cannot do with Karakozov what Dostoevsky did to Raskolnikov (spy on his mind, "objectively" observe his psychological processes, move him towards foregone conclusions, etc.). Still, via a variety of other methods, the second half of this book does explore Karakozov's inner world: based on evidence about his clothes, his body, and his psyche, the next three chapters show Karakozov becoming the subject of his own "new word" and, thus, April 4 as the unprecedented historical phenomenon that it was.

CHAPTER 5

ARMIAK; OR, "SO MANY THINGS IN AN OVERCOAT!"

[An official] warned me not to touch the clothes Karakozov had worn at the time of the crime and that were now lying in this cell; in his words, they were covered by the most disgusting insects.

SENATOR IAKOV G. ESIPOVICH

This chapter analyzes the meaning of Karakozov's appearance on April 4, 1866, where "appearance" means both historical emergence and physical looks. For reasons that have been discussed in the first half of this book, Karakozov is the odd man out of the revolutionary movement; he does not quite fit in with the other figures in this tradition. The symbol I have chosen to represent this fact is Karakozov's peasant *armiak*, a garment much more complicated than would seem from its simple cut. Karakozov's *armiak*, however, has more than symbolic value: its material reality had consequences for Karakozov himself, for the execution of his crime, for his alleged co-conspirators, and for revolutionary politics. Karakozov's *armiak*, in fact, contains the alpha and omega not just of his case, but also of the strategic dimension of the type of political struggle of which April 4 was but the first example: terrorism. Because of all this and more, the chapter begins with an overture on Nikolai Gogol's "The Overcoat" (1836), the paradigmatic tale about an odd man in an odd coat.*

---

*Synopsis of "The Overcoat": Among the fashionable young men at the office, Akaky Akakyevich, a clerk, stands out—with all the usual consequences: "It must be mentioned here that Akaky's overcoat, too, had been the butt of the departmental wits; it had been even deprived of the honorable name of overcoat (*shinel'*) and had been called a capote (*kapot*). And indeed it was of a most peculiar cut." More than just peculiar, the "capote" was becoming dangerous: after years of faithful service, it had grown too old to offer protection

The Original Overcoat

When Akaky Akakyevich died, writes Gogol in "The Overcoat," the poor civil servant did not have any heirs, and left behind nothing beyond the following set of articles: "a bundle of quills, a quire of white Government paper, three pairs of socks, a few buttons that had come off his trousers, and the capote [overcoat] . . . A human being just disappeared and left no trace."[1] But because Gogol took this capote and spun a tale from its tattered yarn, something appeared that left its prints all across Russian literature: "We have all come out from Gogol's 'Overcoat,'" it is said (some say, first by Dostoevsky), and therefore Akaky's heirs and inheritance were not none and little, but infinite and invaluable.

Of course even inside the tale, actually, Akaky no less disappears without a trace; twice, at least, he marks an event.

The first happens to the heart of a fellow clerk who once heard Akaky defend himself against the office's fashionable young men with an outcry—"Leave me alone, gentlemen. Why do you pester me?"—that made of him, this fellow clerk, a changed man:

> [He] stopped abruptly . . . as though stabbed through the heart; and since then everything seemed to have changed in him and he saw everything in quite a different light. A kind of unseen power made him keep away from his colleagues whom at first he had taken for decent, well-bred men . . . [in] those pathetic words he seemed to hear others: "I am your brother."[2]

Rewriting the paradigmatic Pauline *Augenblick* ("Saul, Saul, why do you persecute me?" Acts 9:4), Gogol names Akaky as the cornerstone of a modern ethics.

The second event occurs after Akaky's death. Roving the streets for overcoats, Akaky's ghost fills the hearts of his victims with fear and leaves their bodies exposed to face "everyone's great enemy," Saint Petersburg's northern frost.[3] In just this way, the ghost also attacks the "Very Important Person," the personage not solely, but most immediately responsible for Akaky's death: "In this emergency [the VIP] was seized with such terror that he began, not without reason, to apprehend a heart attack. . . . [After that] it was not so frequently that his subordinates heard him say, 'How dare you, sir?'," the very phrase with which the VIP had mortified Akaky. No less than the living Akaky's pacific protest, therefore, his ghost's

---

against the cold. Nothing was to be done but save up, scrape by, and replace the "capote." The new garment, however, kills Akaky: thieves rob him of the coat; then the frost attacks his unprotected body; and finally a verbal assault from his superior, the "Very Important Person," hurls Akaky into delirium. He dies, but is "resurrected" as a ghost haunting the capital in search of overcoats.

strategically targeted vengeance has the potential to democratize. So long as his specter haunted the capital, indeed, "the police were in such terror of the dead that they were even afraid to arrest the living . . ."[4]

A vanishing personality and an irremovable paradox: irrespective of Akaky's personal will, social position, and even ontological status, via antithetical means—a desperate "why?" and unpunishable terror—his "spirit" animates a universalist ethics of fraternity that is excessive to the order of things.

Odd Man Out

It was Karakozov who introduced for the Russian revolutionary movement a new type of irregular political struggle and—in the triadic form of the crowd, costume, and violence—a new type of enemy. On April 4, as Alexander II exited the gates of Saint Petersburg's Summer Garden, etc., Karakozov, indistinguishable from other spectators, suddenly pulled a pistol out of his abject *armiak* and shot at the crown. This shot sounded the death knell of the reform era and forced a complete revaluation of the politico-juridical order of things; for what April 4 paradoxically brought to light was an invisible enemy—indiscernible precisely since he was in plain view. Henceforth, the world looked a little more like one of those old double exposures in which every body has a ghostly double hovering behind its back—and no aspect of civil life could remain outside the political.

Theoretically, the problem might be conceptualized as follows. On April 4, 1866, Karakozov introduced a set of elements constitutive of the spatial dimension of terrorism. Given the presence of this dimension, at any moment, otherwise familiar territory can be estranged when, suddenly, an undetected (disguised, camouflaged) enemy appears out of nowhere, acts, and disappears again. Faced with such a foe, the world is forever lined with the terrible potential to transform, at all times, into its opposite: the uncanny. So long as these spectral enemies virtually traverse space, essence and appearance are like mischievous twins—and the old world is suspended. Here and now, nothing is as it seems, all must be doubted, and most things are up for redefinition: the situation has been electrified into a permanent anticipation of what some see as the "high points of politics," namely, that moment when the enemy is recognized as enemy, i.e. that instant when an other becomes visible and calls for a decision to distinguish between friend and foe, life and death, war and peace.[5]

Although in the narrow sense Karakozov's attempt "failed," it succeeded in politicizing all of Russian life. The scholarly literature has hardly reflected this: basically because Karakozov was fifteen years "too early" to be anything but a proto-terrorist, he has mostly been seen as an anomalous antichronism. And yet, once again, it is odd Karakozov "who bears within himself the heart of the whole." To try to capture this heart, this chapter will proceed via the above-mentioned Gogolian tactic: by taking up the odd man's overcoat and spinning a tale from its tattered yarn. A careful look at Karakozov's careless appearance exposes its saturation with issues directly relevant to the new type of political struggle, and to the socio-cultural norms making up the reform era's political climate. Ultimately, such an exposure hopes to suggest the good that might come of a more sweeping brush through the long history of the Russian revolutionary movement to tease out the tangles of politics and fashion. Via a small parenthesis illustrating just such a snarl, let us turn to Karakozov's revolutionary out/look.

Next Season's Fashion

In the midst of the spectacular serial assassinations flanking *Narodnaia Volia*'s "emperor hunt," an anonymous artist penciled a political cartoon depicting the boulevard *flânerie* of two elegant ladies and one gentleman— their fashionable fabrics entirely woven out of a knight's metal armor: "Next Season's Fashion" (see figure 7). In its defense against the violent onslaught of the present political, the beau monde is shown to have turned toward the faded summer of its youth, brushed the dust off its old battle dress, ordered it remade and remodeled, and now struts about, flaunting feigned nonchalance, as if to convince onlookers that everything is normal, that there is nothing exceptional going on, that its estate is not at all besieged, exposed to mortal danger, and in fact already geared up for combat.

This cartoon marks a moment in political time when fashion has become both explicitly *evident* and *available* as an instrument of political struggle. Via dress or disguise, it knows, a new political enemy has surfaced, and yet remains invisible. To the beholder of the Russian revolutionary movement, therefore, "Next Season's Fashion" pronounces this moment—1880—as one when fashion, as a dimension of social history, already refers not only to the discernible, triumphal forms of life, but also offers itself as reference to deeper historical movements, including those of the lower strata and the underground. As in the beginning, the dawn of this reformed epoch saw humanity (re)dressing itself, and so this chapter takes up quite literally the idea that in order to enter through the gates of history, revolutionaries had first to (learn how to) get dressed. The first figure to make explicit use of fashion for revolutionary political violence

Fig. 7. "Next Season's Fashion" (1880).
Unknown artist. With permission from the
Museum of Contemporary History, Moscow.

was Karakozov—and it is precisely for this reason that he ended up looking odd.

Faux Pas

While terrorism had thus become fashionable by 1880, the political climate was much hazier still in 1866, when the present in fact seemed to be under attack by nothing so much as the past. Saint Petersburg's *Illiustrirovannaia Gazeta* reported

> such chaos in fashion that it is impossible to say *what* exactly to wear, or *what* is new, for one meets fashions from the Directory and the First Empire, the epoch of Louis XVI and Marie Antoinette, and Greek and Roman hairdressings, Egyptian friseurs, and Asian adornments besides, and all this has to be multicolored, bright, and brilliant from head to toe.[6]

At this time, although all of Russia was being overhauled by the Great Reforms and ostensibly had fixed its gaze on the future, the present nevertheless appeared to be weighed down by an excess of history. What presented itself as the eerie recurrence of an improperly buried past entirely obstructed any vision that could have discerned the forms proper to time and place.[7] The times are out of joint, society, oh, just doesn't know *what* to wear, worries about not appearing comme il faut, about being out of date, anachronistic, and, eventually, obsolete, the equivalent of a pharaonic friseur . . . Society, in other words, knows not what to do; it only knows that whatever it is, it has to be spectacular ("multicolored, bright, and brilliant from head to toe").

Down below, the currents of appearance were generally still regulated by more discernible and harsher patterns: weather, poverty, tradition, labor, and law. The people does what it always has done; and it is first of all the overcoat—announcing as it does estate, rank, and occupation—that tells the environment what that might suitably be. The fate of whatever body is circumscribed by its coat, and without one that is proper to whatever body's station in life, a subject is no less exposed than a nude in winter.

On April 4, 1866, the high and the humble came face to face at the northern gate of Saint Petersburg's Summer Garden. And, no, there was nothing unusual about this. Lined up with the Marble and the Winter Palaces along the riverbanks of the Neva, the Summer Garden's northern gate opened onto what was at that time not only a stretch of boulevard, i.e. a gathering ground for fashionable society, but also the city's main street for accessing the multiple bridges stretching across the water and towards Petersburg's poorer boroughs. It was custom for commoners to gather at the gate and gaze at the tsar as he walked the Garden, and until the moment Karakozov pulled a gun out of his overcoat, there was nothing noteworthy about the looks of April 4's crowd. Yet upon arrest, the tsaricide's appearance presented an immediate problem: up close, it looked not so simple at all.

Right after the failed attempt, one of the officers who had halted Karakozov testified that the would-be assassin had been "dressed in foreign style, in a coat, hatless, and his pants tucked into big boots."[8] But newspapers claimed otherwise: some simply noted the criminal's "long coat," others his "simple dress," and still others insisted he had been "dressed like a peasant."[9] Readers were alternatively told that the assassin had claimed to be a *meshchanin* (petit-bourgeois), but was suspected to be a "disguised revolutionary emissary"; that he had identified himself as the son of a peasant; and finally that he did not come from the lower classes at all.[10] In estimating the style of the criminal's clothing, *Moskovskie Vedomosti* summed up a few days after April 4, witnesses had been divided in their opinions: "some say [he was] in an *armiak*, others, in foreign dress—but with a red shirt."[11]

Most readers would have been no less puzzled after reading that phrase, which indicated that Karakozov had donned something either quintessentially Russian, or quintessentially not Russian, or both, or neither. But when Ishutin read it, he knew right away that the police in Saint Petersburg had arrested for attempted tsaricide his runaway cousin, Mi-

Fig. 8. V. Kozlinkskii, *Armiak.* Ryndin, *Russkii Kostium,* 147.

tia.[12] And their mutual acquaintances knew it too: "Ishutin said that the newspapers said that [the criminal] was dressed as a *meshchanin.* We got terribly scared," testified Ermolov. Then he added specifics: "the newspapers said that the murderer had on a thin, white shirt underneath a red one. Ishutin told us that he had seen Karakozov wear two shirts."[13] Red shirt, white shirt, two shirts—and one or both with what overcoat was odd? What here was custom, what costume?

Armiaki, which lack waists, are tied with sashes, sometimes lined with fur, and were traditionally worn by the poor, could not reasonably have been mistaken for "foreign dress" (see figure 8).[14] As will be shown, moreover, Karakozov's overcoat seems to have been a particularly poor *armiak,* and therefore even less like anything foreign and fancy, but what is important here is that the mention of the *armiak* may have been no less

Fig. 9. V. Kozlinkskii, The Urban Poor in Winter Wear. Ryndin, *Russkii Kostium*, 153.

tellingly qualified by the clause, "but in a red shirt," than was the phrase "in foreign dress." Police photos of Karakozov are of course black and white, but do show the top collar of what was probably this red shirt, which seems to have been either a *pestriad'* or an *aleksandriika*, both of which were typically worn by poorer craftsmen, shop assistants, and the like.[15] So note how *Moskovskie Vedomosti* immediately threw doubt on the unidentified tsaricide's claim, "I am a *meshchanin*," with the following information, "It turned out that underneath his red shirt (*rubakha*) there was an ordinary white shirt (*sorochka*)."[16] The red *rubakha*, that is, was part of a disguise—and the criminal was not at all a *meshchanin*, nor necessarily anything else his appearance suggested. But what in fact did it suggest?

It may at first seem a curious fact that Karakozov's modest looks both could cause a stir and make him conspicuous. In retrospect, witnesses—

Fig. 10. Ilya Repin, *The Propagandist's Arrest* (1880–92). With permission from the State Tretyakov Gallery, Moscow.

from the weapons dealer who sold him five bullets, to an apothecary's assistant who filled his prescription for morphine and codeine, to officers
and bystanders in April 4's crowd—all remembered Karakozov: they recalled a long, dark, peasant *armiak,* fastened with a red sash, high boots
worn over dark, tattered pants, a red shirt, and a cap with a patent-leather
brim.[17] Essentially, though, these details reveal that Karakozov simply resembled the urban poor in winter wear; in any given crowd, these clothes
could hardly have attracted much attention, not to mention aroused suspicion (see figure 9).[18] It is well known, besides, that less than ten years
later, youth across Russia would dress much like this to "go to the people," and that another fifteen to twenty years after that, as plainly shown
by Ilya Repin's painting, *Arest Propagandista* (*The Propagandist's Arrest;*
1880–92), this look was quite proper to, if not emblematic of, the revolutionary (see figure 10).[19] But when Karakozov donned the plain attire
in 1866, often enough, he still stood out as a curiosity.

  Indeed, Saint Petersburg appears to have reacted to Karakozov's outfit much as Raskolnikov feared it might do to his soiled but originally ex-
pensive top hat from Zimmerman's famous shop:

  It is funny, and therefore conspicuous . . . (*smeshnaia, potomu i primetnaia*)
  I must get a cap, any sort of old cap to go with my rags, not this mon-

strosity. Nobody wears this sort of thing. It would be noticed a mile off, and
remembered . . . that's the point: it would be remembered afterwards, and
it would be evidence . . . [20]

The problem is not just that the hat in itself is, as Raskolnikov says, "a
monstrosity," nor that "nobody wears this sort of thing," but also that Zimmerman's fashion does not "go with my rags." Elsewhere, besides, the
reader gets a glance at another conspicuous incongruity, namely, that the
rags do not go with Raskolnikov: "[the lieutenant] looked askance and
with some displeasure at Raskolnikov; his dress was really too disgraceful
and yet his bearing, in spite of its humility, was not in harmony with it."[21]
Something about Raskolnikov sticks out, seems disordered. In just the
same way, the real clue that gives Karakozov away consists in his being mis-
matched. Said one hospital orderly in Dr. Botkin's* Therapeutic Clinic,
where Karakozov had been treated by one of his alleged accomplices,
Alexander Alexandrovich Kobylin: "He caught my attention because of
his strange attire, and because the mark of his speech did not match his
simple dress."[22] Somehow, Karakozov seemed odd.

The nature of the odd bears significant implications for history, as can
readily be shown by means of the curious position of Raskolnikov's hat.
It is precisely at the moment when somebody publicly ridicules him—"Hi,
you in the German hat!"—that Raskolnikov recognizes the danger. Being
funny, thinks Raskolnikov, "[the hat] would be remembered afterwards,
and it would be evidence."[23] In its own time, an appearance divided
against itself or at odds with its surroundings may seem amusing, but retrospectively it is precisely the malapropos that contains the possibility of
bringing back a memory, bridging time, and fetching a fact from the past;
the faux pas is an instant mnemonic cue to something that happened.
For this reason, too, and because the funny reveals a limit precisely by vi-
olating it, Dostoevsky insisted that the strange, eccentric, or odd man
sometimes contains "the heart of the whole."

This brings us back to Karakozov, whose inability to blend in also made
him look odd, to contemporaries and historians alike. Across the ideo-
logico-temporal divide, Russia's first tsaricide has largely been footnoted
as a rather absurd anomaly, his name clad in adjectives like "strange," "suicidal," "infantile," "insane," "fanatical," "impatient," "too early," "too fast,"
"untimely," etc. As an oddity, Karakozov usually stands out as something
other than what he was supposed to have been in a given place and at a
given time—and this is precisely why it is he who can contain a past that
includes both the norm and the challenge of the exception.

To the very extent that Karakozov's appearance was easy to remember
as image, however, it was—and remains—difficult to read as text. For even
if he looked like the folksy students who went "to the people" in the early

1870s or like the revolutionaries populating Repin's canvases during the 1880s, Karakozov was obviously neither of these. Moreover, the whole problem of his appearance was that it obfuscated consistent social commentary. In this respect, it is highly noteworthy that while "nihilist" was among the most popular labels to slap onto the body of the tsaricide, no single witness to the crime actually said that Karakozov looked like a nihilist. Why not, exactly? What does this reveal about nihilism and its relationship to the revolutionary movement?

Aestheticism and Asceticism: Nihilism

Originally infamous and historically far better known than the fashion delirium cited at the beginning of the previous section, the appearance of the 1860s nihilist in texts has long been a common sight: simple dress; long hair for young men and short for young women; informal address, brusque manners, dirty fingernails and walking sticks; sometimes wide-brimmed, flattened, black Fra Diavolo hats or otherwise Polish caps, and dark blue tinted glasses. The meaning of these emblems, too, is more or less clear. The headgear, for example, was "political": it showed sympathy for Italian risorgimentists and Polish separatists. In *Chernyshevsky and the Age of Realism,* Paperno notes that nihilist fingernails sharply contrasted with their manicured predecessors belonging to the title character of Pushkin's *Eugene Onegin* (1833), which were "canonized . . . as the mark of an aristocratic dandy," and she also explicates nihilist rudeness:

> The awkwardness and lack of social skills characteristic of the original *raznochintsy,* who came from lower social strata and had not received instruction in manners (an important part of the upbringing of the gentry), were deliberately cultivated, both by those who were naturally ungracious and by those trained in the social graces.[24]

With its modus vivendi, therefore, nihilism blurred the traditional divisions among estates and narrowed the gap of social difference. Progressive implications for the redefinition of gender relations are obvious from the exchange of hair length standards among men and women, just as tossing out the delicately carved and elegantly swung canes of cavaliers only to pick up the rough wooden sticks carried by peasants cried out for the real. "*Sans-crinolines* advancing to replace *sans-culottes,*" Herzen summed up.[25] Only why—this remains forever mysterious—does the world of the nihilists look blue?

As if a move from aestheticism to asceticism were not also but a turn of fashion, nihilism's stripping off of decorum presented itself as having occurred solely from historical modesty, shame, and sincerity. But nihilist asceticism was still aesthetics and, as Simmel once remarked, "Fashions are always class fashions."[26] In confronting nihilist style, however, some scholars seem at times to have suspended disbelief, to have simply taken a historical phenomenon at its word, and accepted the nihilists' own conviction that the rude is real and the ascetic a bare truth.

As a trope, of course, a suspicion of appearances—such as animated the nihilists of the 1860s—had led an active life since at least the official dawn of Russia's modern age. Once he had hurled the ship of state onto a Western course, after all, one of the first things Peter the Great insisted on was that everybody change their clothes; "the beard tax" still resounds as a symbolic echo of this devastating makeover. By the late eighteenth-century reign of Catherine the Great, the inner/outer split had become chronic, that is to say, natural—at least in society. In addition to dividing society against itself, pretty/Western masks and mannerisms signified the distance between lives lived out at court and years spent on Russia's black earth. By the mid-nineteenth century, discourses across the political spectrum curved around the turns of suggested routes returning Russians to what was really Russian.

It is for this reason that nihilism insisted on being rude: shedding *politesse* and *civilité*, nihilists broke with the nobility and united with the *narod* in a single gesture. The reader will recall the scene from Turgenev's *Fathers and Sons* in which Bazarov, the original literary nihilist, hesitates before offering his bare red hand to Arkady's father, but also—in an illustration of the falseness of the mask—that Arkady's well-groomed uncle, Pavel Petrovich, demonstratively stuck his "beautiful hand with its long pink nails" back into the pocket of his dark English suit rather than offer it to Bazarov.[27] For the nihilist, the rude signifies a permanent being in truth with one's interior; the slovenly, a becoming real of human relations.

Of course, precisely by so brazenly parading its truth and authenticity, nihilism betrays its dependence on décor: *larvatus prodeo,* "as I walk forward, I point out my mask." Turgenev must have had this in mind when he had Bazarov don a long, tasseled *balakhon* (a coarse, woolen, formless coat, sometimes hooded) that is obviously bad form on a country estate, and that its wearer provocatively refers to as his "little garment" (*odezhenka*) when he requests that it be taken up to his guest room by a servant. "Certainly," replies Arkady's father and, using a euphemism, calls out the order: "Prokofich, take the gentleman's overcoat (*shinel'*)."[28] The conspicuousness of Bazarovian dress exemplifies the use of fashion for the purpose of differentiation at its most blatant.

At that moment when praxis turned toward the politically clandestine, contrarily, it was forced to adopt the fashionista's modus operandi for exactly the opposite reasons: to *mask* difference. In the mid-nineteenth century, this not only meant going provincial ("to the people"), but also being of and blending in with the new urban crowds—a skill the Russian revolutionaries acquired slowly, and at a high cost. What sets Karakozov apart is that he was a first figure to try to go under cover of the crowd. And this means, in fact, that Karakozov was *not* simply a nihilist—if only because nihilist dress was quite inappropriate for an active revolutionary life.

The nihilist look left no doubt at all as to the politics and identity of its wearer. For example, note the following excerpt from the memoirs of V. K. Debogory-Mokrievich cited by Paperno: "After returning from the university to his hometown, he paraded in his new attire under the windows of his old schoolteacher. The 'elder,' writes Debogory-Mokrievich, 'looked at my long hair, spectacles, and thick walking stick, and said: "I can see you've drunk the whole fill of nihilist wisdom".'"[29] Lev Tikhomirov*—writing at a time when he was still a few years shy of becoming the revolutionary movement's most infamous apostate—also underlined the hyperbolic conspicuity of the look:

> The tendency towards democratic ideas manifested itself occasionally by the most exaggerated aversion from everything that was aristocratic, from everything that smacked of the nobility, and consequently from all the formalities of superficial civilization. Uncleanly faces, disheveled hair, dirty and fantastic clothes were to be seen.[30]

Tikhomirov stressed that, "the very facts which had called forth the nickname [nihilist] naturally disappeared very rapidly . . . soon all these childish things—women cutting their hair short, or exaggerated rudeness of manner—became discredited."[31]

Tikhomirov does not date what he retrospectively saw as the natural extinction of nihilism, and of course maturity must have been one reason why "these childish things" became discredited and then disappeared, but unarguably April 4 was another. Following Karakozov's failed assassination bid, for example, one secret agent reported to his superiors that, "lately, nihilists are barely noticeable in the capital."[32] Until the time before "lately," in other words, nihilists *had* still been a recognizable, regular, and (therefore) regulated or at least regulatable part of urban fauna.

After April 4, intolerance of the nihilist look resurfaced, surged, and finally reached juridical heights. Summing up in a small article written a year later, Herzen characterized Karakozov's shot as an administrative godsend:

> "There it is, Your Majesty," they began to whisper to him, "that is what not dressing in uniform means . . . all these spectacles and shock-heads." After this the Privy Council, the Synod and the Senate gave orders that within

twenty-four hours the girls were to grow their cropped hair, to remove their spectacles and to give a written undertaking to have sound eyes and to wear crinolines.[33]

Herzen's prose bears the mark of hyperbole, but in fact April 4 did trigger an official crackdown on the nihilist look.

Besides hauling in for questioning anyone looking like a nihilist, authorities took steps to stamp out the look from the city's décor, particularly, it seems, among women. "In Petersburg, Murav'ev gave nihilists 'yellow cards' [usually reserved for prostitutes]," wrote the author of the "The White Terror,"

> and in Moscow [the police had been ordered] to obtain signed agreements from all female nihilists to stop cutting their hair, put on hairpieces and crinolines, and wear neither blue glasses, nor little round hats. Should the female nihilist refuse to sign or, having signed, continue to wear glasses, a round hat, short hair, and not change into a crinoline, then expel her from Moscow by administrative order within a period of twenty-four hours.[34]

Following similar threats issued in the fall of 1866 by Saint Petersburg's governor to exile wearers of illegal nihilist gear, a French paper quipped that forcing the culprits to don the ugly look for life might have achieved the administration's goal much sooner. "Really," wrote a columnist in *Petersburgskii Listok,* "the French paper is right: society has long scorned those pranksters, and the suggested punishment would be the best penalty for them."[35] Though he was not so cynical as to equate social and political exile, Herzen agreed that there was something advantageous about erasing the look:

> These extreme measures were of enormous benefit, and this I say without the slightest irony: but to whom? To our Nihilist girls. . . . It is terribly hard for one who is used to a uniform to cast it off of himself. The garment grows to the wearer. . . . Our girl-students and *Burschen* would have been a long time taking off their spectacles and their other emblems. They had them taken off at the expense of the government, which added to this good turn the aureole of a *toilette* martyrdom.[36]

April 4 may have reanimated the political implications of nihilism, but before that, contemporaries had clearly begun to see it as just a fashion, and could recognize a nihilist a mile off. For the purpose of clandestine political activities, therefore, the provocative look was entirely too conspicuous.

Aestheticism and Asceticism: The Folk Look

So, as the 1860s unfolded, the ascetic aesthetic had been standardized, popularized, and therefore looked less alarming. Young women actually flaunted simplified versions of the once elaborately decorated crinoline while young men openly declined to cover their heads with the requisite top hat. Among their own, they opted for slack blouses of dark tones, jackets with folded collars, and loosely knotted Garibaldi ties, but also increasingly wore folk costumes in the form of high boots worn over pants (instead of the usual half-boot hidden under tight, long slacks) and double-breasted Russian or embroidered Ukrainian shirts.[37] A caricature in the satirical *Iskra* declared that high society actually tolerated the folk look—so long as the wearer spoke French.[38] So long as, in other words, nothing more serious was going on here than a bit of leisurely slumming.

Of course such cultural tourism was actually frowned upon by the authorities, however, as shown by the case of Saint Petersburg's Medical-Surgical Academy student and part-time professional photographer Bonifatii Steput, who was arrested in 1862 for reproducing photographs of "criminal content." Besides a copy of a Polish liberation movement proclamation, a search of his establishment dug up negatives, prints, and cards depicting the poet Mikhailov in jail; the revolutionary exiles Herzen and Ogarev; and a group of young people wearing "Polish national costumes."[39] Under investigation, one of Steput's assistants testified that while some of these young people had brought their costumes along, others were already wearing them underneath their overcoats when they entered the studio. The participants in this costume party were promptly hauled in for questioning. "We wanted to see if they looked good on us," confessed one subject, while another protested:

> I can't say these are Polish costumes: some of us were in Hungarian clothes, others in *chemarki* [the customary dress of the Moscow *streltsy* or musketeers], others in *sermenzhki* [the usual clothes of peasants and poor day laborers]; I was dressed in civil attire. True, at present, young nobles in Poland walk around in similar clothing . . . [40]

Given the explosive political situation in secessionist Poland in the early 1860s, no wonder this masquerading was undesirable, against the law, and perpetrated in secret. "[When] we found out it was illegal to take photographs in others' costumes," one young person still tried to defend himself, "each of us tore up the picture."[41]

Around the mid-1860s, other kinds of folk clothing could be worn, though they were no less conspicuous. A self-confessed Ukrainophile during his student days, Ilya Repin got himself a Ukrainian *kireia*, wore it everywhere, and, so he wrote in his memoirs, was often made to blush by all the attention this garment attracted. His route to the Art Academy took him by the Neva right past both the Winter Palace and the Summer Garden—the site of Karakozov's assassination attempt—where, "more than once, the aristocrats, riding along the riverbanks, tracked me with their lorgnettes."[42] After April 4, 1866, when it was widely suspected that the assassin had been a Polish nationalist, Repin knew his *kireia* could be taken for a "demonstratively Polish costume, and I hurried to change into a regular coat (*pal'to*)."[43] The folk look had gone from provocative to dangerous.

Only a few photographs of Karakozov's friends have been preserved, but these openly (in their free time, at least, and possibly in secret) announce their populist tastes. His right hand loosely tucked into his pants pocket and leaning into an engraved pillar—a symbol of education as well as a physical support to enable the subject to stand the long exposure time—Zagibalov, a twenty-two-year-old expelled from Moscow University for disorderly conduct, sports a craftsman's holiday costume.[44] The twenty-year-old aristocrat Ermolov, meanwhile, his left hand folded into a cloak at heart's level, shows off the winter exotica of a garrison soldier.[45] But this is not Karakozov: he does not don other people's clothing on special occasions or to provoke.

A few summary remarks about nihilist and folk fashion. An impediment to action, the daily indecision and disorientation that accompanies the historicist fashion delirium is one reason for nihilism's stripping down to a bare minimum; another is sheer boredom with decorum.[46] Second, given that nihilism manifests Realism as dress—at the crest of historicism's wave, no less—the look is a sign that reality has died. This means, on the one hand, that nihilism mournfully imitates simplicity as if out of respect for a soon to be absolutely inaccessible lost world, and yet on the other brazenly shows off for a little while what the *narod* had been condemned to bear for life, namely, forbearance. Put differently, coming as it does at that time when capital begins to flood the reformed empire, nihilism rejects the brutality of the market, including forms of fashion, and, at the same time, functionally erases the difference between itself and the people. Officially representing a zero degree of ideology to the people, though, nihilism is in fact not necessarily, or in any case not only, the radically universalist factor it fancies itself to be. Erasing apparent difference, nihilism as fashion is also a protective front at the very moment when the people suddenly, dangerously step into the theater of history.

Given their infamy and their associations, in any case, clearly the nihilist as well as the folk look are terribly conspicuous. And Karakozov's careless dress, indeed, should not be confused with either. Even among progressives, as we will see, Karakozov looked out of place. This is because Karakozov's being out of style had already severed itself from the fashionable negation of being comme il faut, because he had transformed what for others had been leisure suits into active wear. Karakozov is not rude, but laconic; with him fashion has found a new function. Unlike Bazarov's "little garment" and Repin's *kireia,* which are emblems of mannerism, Karakozov's *armiak* is camouflage.

"Be dressed for action . . ."

Among the files of the Karakozov case, multiple attestations confirm that those who would later be cast as members of "Hell" discussed and/or jested that, to avoid suspicions of political activism, anyone designated a tsaricide should sever all personal ties and delve into an underworld of vagabondage.[47] Accordingly, perhaps, Karakozov ran off to Petersburg and moved about under cover of the crowd. He adopted a disguise, began to identify himself as "Vladimirov" (a folk form of his real patronymic), and frequently changed his residence, sleeping at friends' places, in cheap hostels, under bridges, and beneath the open sky—"wherever," as he put it in his written testimonies, "the poor, lacking housing and food, shelter themselves."[48]

Rather than just being careless about his appearance, Karakozov strove to divert attention from himself—and did this well enough to sustain residency in the capital for over a month without a shred of legal permission. From a distance, in this incognito Karakozov even effectively eluded old familiars. When his Moscow friends, Stranden and Ermolov, searched the streets of Petersburg for him to intervene in his tsaricidal plans, Karakozov's camouflage hindered his being detected until the moment he chose to identify himself to them. Spotting Stranden near the Neva, Karakozov recalled, "although I was in an outfit not at all like the one in which I went around in Moscow and of course he would not have recognized me, in order to protect myself even more, I covered my face with my gloves," which illustrates well enough, moreover, that he was not dressed down in order to make some sort of politico-cultural fashion statement.[49] But there *were* occasions when Karakozov's presence became conspicuous.

First, those who knew Karakozov were confused by his new appearance. Once he had made himself known to Stranden and Ermolov, they asked, according to Karakozov's written testimony, "What's this outfit you're wearing?" ("Chto eto za kostium na vas?")[50] Thereafter, the fact that Karakozov was roaming the streets of Petersburg "dressed like a meshchanin" ("odet v meshchanskoe plat'e") became common knowledge among his

Moscow friends; evidently, it was a curious enough fact to merit repetition as gossip.[51] So curious, in fact, that when Ishutin told them that the criminal arrested for attempted tsaricide had been "dressed like a *meshchanin*," their reaction of dread was instant: "Ishutin said that the newspapers said he was dressed as a *meshchanin*," the reader will remember Ermolov testifying. "We got terribly scared."

Further, sometimes Karakozov himself was struck by some almost forgotten detail, and became alarmed that he did not match his own disguise. The decision to drop his own name was in fact a consequence of just such a worry. Apparently because it sounded too noble, the name "Karakozov," he presumed, might arouse his landlord's suspicions and cause him to notify the police.[52] His patronymic pseudonym, contrarily, sounded plain enough to make an important lie stick: he had told the landlord that he was a Moscow *meshchanin* and, asserted Karakozov, "the outfit in which I was going around, that is, the *armiak,* didn't conflict with my *meshchanin*-like name at all."[53]

More importantly, sometimes Karakozov was betrayed by his nature, or at least by a chronic case of culture: his speech patterns. Whenever the disguised Karakozov spoke, his interlocutors were instantly alerted to a certain disorder. The clinic orderly cited above testified to this; so did Karakozov's doctor and alleged accomplice, Kobylin, who recalled that a first serious talk with his hypochondriac patient occurred after an initial electro-shock "séance," when Karakozov "surprised me with the tone of his speech, which did not correspond to his clothing."[54] Karakozov's mouth was something like a badly hidden trapdoor, and whenever he spoke, his incognito became a personified *lapsus linguae.*

The fact that Karakozov's clothing had elicited the adjectives "strange" and "simple" in a single utterance from the orderly, it should now be clear, was attributable to "Vladimirov's" conspicuousness against this clinical background. Indeed, for just this reason, because some "Vladimirov" receiving electro-shock treatment made a strange sight, Karakozov attracted the attention and lodged himself in the memory of another patient of Kobylin's, Alexandra Komarova: "Who was that interesting peasant (*muzhichek*) I saw with you?"[55] The doctor had answered her that Karakozov was not a peasant, but a future student, that he came to Petersburg to enroll in the university, and so on.[56]

Essentially, instances of conspicuity occur when "Vladimirov" circulates in what would have been Karakozov's natural habitat, among the educated and professional (see figure 11) or, presumably, vice versa. Walking from Botkin's clinic to the university one morning, for example, Kobylin had reminded "Vladimirov" of a meeting set for the next day with a friend of Kobylin's, Putiata, about a possible job. To this, testified Kobylin, "Karakozov replied rather strangely: 'How can I go in my clothes—look

Fig. 11. V. Kozlinkskii, The Educated and Professional Classes. Ryndin, *Russkii Kostium,* 145.

at the clothes I'm wearing.' I assured him Putiata was not pretentious."[57] Putiata not, perhaps, but Kobylin was: having walked on a bit, Kobylin related, he wanted somehow to get rid of Karakozov because they had approached a place—near the university—where he could run into acquaintances, "and it was embarrassing if they saw me with a fellow so badly dressed."[58] Around other students, the recent dropout's alter ego was undesirable and strange, no matter how educated his discourse might have sounded.

Double Count

The bits of intelligence about Karakozov's appearance exist because the police explicitly and repeatedly asked. As *Moskovskie Vedomosti* reported

Fig. 12. V. Kozlinkskii, Paupers. Ryndin, *Russkii Kostium,* 159.

about a week after the failed assassination, the police had noticed the criminal's disorder: he had identified himself as the peasant Aleksei Petrov, claimed illiteracy, and looked the part, but "his movement, poses, and manner clearly reveal that he is not a rough worker."[59] Indeed, it was because Karakozov's appearance slightly wrinkled the usual discursive flow whenever mentioned that the police suspected that there was a plot behind the camouflage. *And because there was a surplus clue.*

A late, but very clear example of a narrative wrinkle comes from an exchange that took place during the trial between Alexander Alexandrovich Lebedev (Khudiakov's brother-in-law) and Alexander Markelovich Nikolsky (married to Khudiakov's wife's cousin). To contest the prosecution's assertion that he had told Lebedev that the attempt on the tsar would have been successful had more people participated, Nikolsky interrupted the proceedings:

> A conversation of the sort did take place, but not in the sense you [Lebe-
> dev] now mention: remember, I called to your attention that Karakozov shot
> from a flintlock pistol, and that he was badly dressed, and from that I drew
> the conclusion that Karakozov's crime was his own doing, not the result of
> a suggestion by some society; that if Karakozov acted, then he acted alone.[60]

Precisely such comments led the police to suspect that Karakozov had accomplices among the dwellers of Petersburg.

Karakozov himself had given such conflicted testimonies about the
clues collected from his body that in mid-June he was still answering questions about his looks. Because Karakozov had, as Kobylin later put it before the court, appeared at his family's house "dressed a bit more tidily,
not like a pauper [*v prostonarodnom kostiume*, literally "a commoner," but
see figure 12], but more like a mixture between a manager and a peasant," the tsaricide was forced to detail for the police that, before entering Kobylin's brother's study, he had taken off his *armiak* and thus
appeared before him in "a black coat" (*v chernom pal'to*).[61] When asked,
he explicitly stated that he had had nothing else with him upon arrival
in the capital after a brief trip to Moscow around Easter, from which the
police could conclude that Karakozov thus wore two coats: the abject
armiak and a black *pal'to* underneath.

Neither of these, however, accounted for the presence of an additional
garment. Curiously enough, the first entry on a list of abandoned objects
collected in Karakozov's Znamenskaia Hotel room is "a green peasant
armiak of smooth woolen cloth."[62] This *armiak* could not have been the
same as Karakozov's old *armiak* for the simple reason that Karakozov was
arrested in his old *armiak*. But it could not have been his "tidier" outfit,
either, since that was not a green *armiak*, but some black "managerial"
pal'to. How many overcoats were there? Witnesses had mentioned many
types (foreign, simple, managerial, *meshchanin*, peasant, pauper, or just
"old") and all gradations of dark ("black," "brown," "dark gray," "tobacco-
colored," "green") when describing Karakozov's outfit, but once all these
have been shorn of adjectival decorations, the sources still fail to account
for one too many overcoats.

Evidently, even after the trials had been brought to an end, Karakozov
had been hanged, and all other defendants sentenced and exiled, the police remained interested in the issue. A report submitted by tsarist agent
A. Trofimov-Trokhimovich, undercover as a Polish revolutionary in Khudiakov's Siberian prison camp, claimed that when he asked Khudiakov
how he had defended himself against Karakozov's assertions that he had
not only received money from Khudiakov for the purchase of a pistol, but
also "shot in his [Khudiakov's] overcoat," Khudiakov supposedly replied,
"C'mon man, I explained all that as generosity. Unaware of his intentions,

I could hardly refuse a friend a favor."[63] The truth of the matter is that although imperial authorities obviously achieved many convictions, neither they, nor anyone since could conclusively resolve whether Karakozov covered up a conspiracy or not—which arguably makes him a very singular conspirator indeed.

Out of Step, Out of Time

Differentiating terrorism—"revenge against individual personages"—from the partisan warfare that the Bolsheviks came to endorse during the Revolution of 1905–7, Lenin defined the former as an intelligentsia conspiracy, disconnected from the "mood of the masses," and symptomatic of "the absence of the conditions for an uprising."[64] Terrorism, for Lenin, thus embodies impatience with a "not yet" in revolutionary time, and it always arrives "too early." Whether one agrees with him or not, Lenin, in any case, was looking *forward* to the revolution. When this type of thinking looks *backward* from the revolution, however, then the criterion of un/timeliness not only synchronically judges distance from average ways of being in the world, but also—and much more harmfully—diachronically presumes the existence of the "right time," of some objective historical clock that always accurately tells the time that remains (until the revolution). Terrorism, on this scheme, always already appears as being out of time.

Karakozov makes himself available as a new way of approaching the problematic junction of terrorism and temporality precisely because he was so blatantly antichronistic, a fact that found its most palpable expression in his appearance as not at all fashionable. From the vantage point of Karakozov's untimely out/look, the standard trajectory of revolutionary history suddenly stands unmasked as mechanical movement along a preplanned production line: avant-garde, à la mode, au courant, popular, mass appeal, and then revolution. So what comes out from Karakozov's *armiak*, ultimately, is not so much history as it is historicity: revolutionary terrorism's conviction that historical change does not arrive at an appointed, assessable time, but is potentially embedded in every moment. Of course terrorism's capacity to act on this conviction (anytime, anywhere) is directly dependent on its capacity to blend in (whenever, wherever): terrorism must manage to move under cover of whatever crowd. Its relationship with the masses, therefore, is fundamentally different from that of the Bolsheviks: if terrorism is disconnected from the "mood of the masses," this is because it is strategically connected to their looks.

Addendum: Revolutionary Fashion

In the history of revolutionary terrorism, Karakozov took some first, awkward steps toward making effective use of the urban crowd as camouflage. And from the looks of him, we can discern the potential of a sustained focus on the trivialities of fashion, whence emerges an array of new questions about the relations between politics, violence, leisure, dress, desire, consumption, and pleasure.

The annals of revolutionary history are strewn with anecdotal asides about the appearance of revolutionaries: generally incidental to the argument, they decorate their texts like so many tiny trimmings. But these are not trifles: each of them is an index, comes to us dipped in the dyes of its time. Pulling them out and then together, therefore, means weaving the red thread of an altogether different story—one that will lead to reading against itself, and eventually inverting, the chronicles of a history grown tired from repetition.

In the history of terrorism, for example, Nechaev seems to occupy an awkward transitional moment in political style. Leaving Russia for Europe, he wears "untidy, shabby clothes."[65] On September 3, 1869, three years to the day after Karakozov's execution, he returns to Moscow armed with written evidence of his political alliance with Bakunin and Ogarev, and clad in a "European, well-tailored suit"—but he has yet to remove tell-tale dark blue tinted glasses.[66] In December, after the month and a half Nechaev required to organize *Narodnaia Rasprava,* ensure its demise, and flee Russia once more, head of the tsarist secret police P. A. Shuvalov reports to Russia's minister of interior the possible whereabouts and physical description of the refugee, who wore what had evidently become "the usual outfit, coat and so forth, long boots," but "sometimes a woman's dress or an army engineer's uniform."[67] In addition to furthering attempts to use fashion conspiratorially, Nechaev shows a peculiar concern with style, but he neither blends in seamlessly, nor is yet entirely à la mode. He never quite mastered the compulsion to bite his fingernails down to bloody stumps, either.[68]

Now consider the story of Leon Filippovich Mirsky,* a "slim, beautiful young man with elegant aristocratic manners," who in March of 1879 attempted to assassinate head of the Third Section Alexander Romanovich Drentel'n.*[69] Mirsky rented the best horse from Moris Strass's stables on Mokhovaia Street and, both to ensure a successful approach to Drentel'n's carriage and to become a regular and therefore natural feature of the boulevard, practiced maneuvering the animal around Petersburg streets:

> Once, walking on Morskaia Street at the hour when fashionable society gathers, I saw him, dressed up as a young dandy, pass by on a slim, nervous,

English horse. He was very effective in this guise, and all the high society ladies, slowly moving in their open carriages at that hour, admired him through their lorgnettes.[70]

Apparently Mirsky's appearance on Petersburg's surface was a bit too natural: when he approached his target, fired, and missed, Drentel'n recognized him, and promptly had him tracked down and placed under arrest.

By the early twentieth century, however, Head of the St. Petersburg Department of Police Gerasimov* was forced to claim that "To discern terrorists in a crowd of variously dressed people was utterly impossible. . . . After all, terrorists do not wear a uniform."[71] Or rather: terrorists had learned to wear the uniform of a crowd swollen beyond all recognition. Evno Azef,* the infamous provocateur and main strategist of the Socialist-Revolutionary *Boevaia Organizatsiia* (or BO, Combat Division), tells a terrorist girl to be sure to buy a new dress before meeting him at a fancy restaurant. On stakeout, *boeviki* can pose as cabmen or cigarette vendors for weeks at a time; Ivanovskaia* perfectly imitates countryside dialects and mannerisms; and Boris Savinkov,* knowing not a word of English, is said to have successfully operated in Moscow as an Englishman.[72] In 1909, changing Parisian residences to flee his BO colleagues now wise to his double life, Azef first stuffs his bags with various ensembles, including his summer apparel and lawn tennis outfit.[73] The more than a decade-long successful operations of the SRs signal that their *boeviki* are synchronous with the popular crowd.

Among the teeming variety of bourgeois life, the chameleon, changeling, fashionista, or dandy makes for a perfect conspirator. One unmasks the modus operandi of the BO by combining Flaubert's definition of "incognito" as "the dress of princes on their travels" with Baudelaire's understanding of the spectator as "a prince who everywhere rejoices in his incognito": if the spectator everywhere appears in garb that signifies a suspension of responsibility, the best disguise for the producer and star of the terrorist spectacle is a leisure suit.[74]

CHAPTER 6

"FACTUAL PROPAGANDA," AN AUTOPSY; OR, THE MORBID ORIGINS OF APRIL 4, 1866

"And the nerves, the nerves, you seem to have forgotten them. Nowadays, they are all sick, and fine-drawn, and irritable! . . . And everybody is so full of spleen!
And I tell you, in its way that provides a mine of information!"

PORFIRY PETROVICH TO RASKOLNIKOV, in *Crime and Punishment*

When Dostoevsky brought Raskolnikov to trial at the end of *Crime and Punishment*, the author staged the judicial proceedings in such a way that they would hide the complexity of the case. The radical novelty of Raskolnikov's crime goes unmentioned as he is presented to the court in the recognizable guise of a poverty-stricken and mentally affected student. Thus the examining magistrates and presiding judges found that

> the crime itself could have been committed only in a state of temporary mental derangement, so to speak, as the result of homicidal mania. . . . This conclusion coincided happily with the latest fashionable theory of temporary insanity, which our contemporaries so often try to apply to various criminals. Besides, Raskolnikov's long-standing hypochondria was testified to by many witnesses, including Dr. Zosimov . . . [1]

This explanatory strategy sways the fictional court toward a reduced sentence for Raskolnikov's double homicide, but Dostoevsky leaves no doubt in his readers' minds that he considers the judicial narrative both facile and rash. Not only do the hundreds of pages of *Crime and Punishment* evidence its author's conviction that the connections between ideas, illness, and crime merit close scrutiny, but Dostoevsky also has examining magistrate Porfiry Petrovich explicitly pronounce the suspicion that "psychological means of defense" belong to the realm of rhetoric, not truth:

> There is one thing, however, to be said—all these psychological means of defense, these excuses and evasions, are very insubstantial, and they cut both ways: "Illness, delirium," you say, "fancies, illusions, I don't remember"—that is all very well, but then why is it, old chap, that you see just these illusions in your sick delirium, and not others? There could have been others, couldn't there?[2]

Temporary mental derangement and long-standing hypochondria notwithstanding, whence *this* idea, for *this* crime?

The very question Dostoevsky posited as the central deficit of his fictional trial, however, relentlessly drove the real-life investigation into a crime that was no less riddled with psycho-physical illness and involved Raskolnikov's exact contemporary: Karakozov's attempted assassination of Alexander II. In fact, just days before dying, Karakozov was still being urged to elucidate what he had sworn were the inseparable links between his ideas, illness, and crime: "Majesty," reads an unfinished draft of his last appeal for clemency, "You wish to know why exactly that grave, diseased condition pushed me exactly towards the idea of the crime ..."[3] Throughout the inquest and the trial, indeed, officials had searched for the idea-source of Karakozov's crime, and throughout they had resolutely refused to locate it in the clinical realm. Fashionable though "psychological means of defense" may have been in 1866—and they were in any case fashionable enough to be used by all those who spoke in Karakozov's defense—they did not strike the Russian authorities as a legitimate explanation for Karakozov's unprecedented political violence.

In explaining why Karakozov tried to assassinate Alexander II more than a decade prior to the official emergence of terrorism in the late 1870s, the historiography of the Russian revolutionary movement has found his aberrant, suicidal psychology far more plausible than did mid-nineteenth-century Russian jurisprudence: only an afflicted mind could reasonably fail to grasp that 1866 was still "too early" for revolutionary violence. But as with Raskolnikov, so with Karakozov: the consensus on his abnormality has not so much provoked inquiry into his case as excused its neglect; it seems that because Russia's first modern tsaricide was "deranged," he is irrelevant politically and uninteresting historically. Karakozov's sick irrationalism, consequently, has actually never been properly studied—despite multiple and emphatic attestations that it was at the root of his decision to try to kill the tsar.

The present chapter therefore allows Karakozov's maladies to spill onto the pages of history: it takes a scalpel to his afflictions, lances them, and analyzes whatever emerges in relation to the tsaricide's theory and practice. The format is straightforward: it chronicles Karakozov's *historia morbi*, which coincides with the last year of his life, thereby offering some challenges to the conclusions drawn by both contemporaries and the historiography of the revolutionary movement, and thus to the tendency to treat the political and the pathological as mutually exclusive.

Pharmaka

Upon turning out the pockets of Karakozov's peasant *armiak*, the arresting officers discovered, besides extra bullets and gunpowder for the criminal's double-barreled flintlock pistol, the following clues: two powdery substances; a small, pear-shaped vial containing a sticky liquid; a scrap of paper; a letter; and two copies of the proclamation, "To My Worker Friends."

Fatal folds, these pockets: their contents unraveled the entire case, causing the arrest, prosecution, imprisonment, exile, and/or death of Karakozov's closest friends and farthest acquaintances. The letter, for example, only addressed "Nikolai Andreevich" and was written allusively for the protection of its recipient; but it was easily matched to the address on an envelope discovered in the tsaricide's abandoned room at Hotel Znamenskaia in Saint Petersburg: "His Honor Nikolai Andreevich Ishutin, c/o Poliakov, Bolshaia Bronnaia 25, Moscow."[4] Second, despite being obscurely worded, the letter plainly betrayed a motive of which there was not a trace in the proclamation.

"To My Worker Friends" narrated April 4 as the act of a lone martyr-assassin:

> It saddened and burdened me that my beloved people is perishing like this and thus I decided to annihilate the tsar-villain and die for my beloved people. If my intention succeeds, I will die with the idea that my death will be useful to my dear friend the Russian muzhik. If not, then I nonetheless believe that there will be people who will take my path. If I do not succeed, they will. My death will be an example for them and inspire them.[5]

The letter, by contrast, referred to "acquaintances" who were ready "to get the affair started very soon"; indicated Ishutin's knowledge of this affair; and also mentioned a mysterious "K.":

> You know that my acquaintances, whom I told you about, plan to get the affair started very soon, but that it isn't our thing; our road is completely different; we differ in terms of not only the means, but also the end. You

understand that if such an affront occurs, then it's all the same, and K. can ensure for himself a calm state one way or another. That is, the results would be different if we had more money, if our strength were less restricted; but since, at present, this is not the case, definite harm could come from such ways; we must collect strength and postpone such an outcome for a while. Obviously, at present, some singular fact is much more useful for the shareholders of both our firms. And obviously those shareholders interested in the affair—in case of various clashes—should maintain that this affair is not entirely clean, that it is unprofitable for many because it is only being conducted in the interests of one side. Of course, in general, self-restraint is necessary in terms of explanations so as not to disturb the success of their affair; for them it will be a good occasion. And we can gain excellently here. You probably read in the stock exchange reports that a society of landed credit was built, so we must keep it in mind and try to bear the competition. In anticipation of good results, goodbye, friend.[6]

Obviously, the two documents jarred—and neither, we note for now, mentions illness.

Then there was the scrap of paper, which bore but a single word: "Kobylin." This of course was the name of the young man of twenty-five who was not only Karakozov's doctor and alleged accomplice, but also the sole of the principal defendants to be found not guilty. On August 31, the day Karakozov was sentenced to death, Russia's Supreme Criminal Court ruled that Kobylin had neither known about, nor materially supported the tsaricide (the two counts on which he had been indicted). And yet— only of Kobylin did Karakozov maintain, until his dying day, that he had been complicit. According to Karakozov, Kobylin was not only the source of all three suspicious substances found in the pockets of his *armiak*, but also the spark that had ignited the idea of the crime in Karakozov's mind.

As for the powdery and liquid substances, these were immediately sent for analysis to Dr. Julius Karlovich Trapp,* "the father of Russian pharmacology," who quickly identified them as morphine, strychnine, and hydrocyanic acid, "three of the strongest organic poisons, quick and effective, without antidotes, and very difficult to trace post mortem."[7] Trapp, however, did more than just identify the drugs, and this would turn out to be of central importance for the case.

On April 6, after sending his general findings to the investigative commission, Trapp composed a special letter to chief of staff of the Gendarmerie and leading official of the Third Section Nikolai Vladimirovich Mezentsev. He wished to call attention, he wrote, to certain details about the poisons he had identified. To explain himself, Trapp noted having read Pitaval's multivolume criminological collection, which had provided him with the notion of *Fingerzeige* (*ukazanie*), the apparently unimportant, but really revealing detail: "The smallest and most meaningless circumstances are often the key to solving the whole crime."[8] Hence Trapp di-

rected Mezentsev's attention to the pharmaceuticals' packaging peculiarities: there were "traces of a label" (identified as "yellow" during the trial)
on the vial containing the hydrocyanic acid; the strychnine was folded
into a small, round "filter"; and the morphine had been very carefully
prepared and wrapped. All these were tiny hints that told Trapp the drugs
had been professionally prescribed and prepared. "Conclusion," he stated
ceremoniously: "the criminal is acquainted with people who gave him the
above-mentioned things; he is not just anybody, and his terrible plan is
known to others."[9]

Trapp's *Fingerzeigen* were striking clues at a time when Karakozov was
still pretending to be Aleksei Petrov, a peasant whose proclamation read
as if the assassination had been the act of a solitary martyr. And given the
letter's mysterious "K.," the "Kobylin" scrap of paper, and the fact that
Karakozov had, as early as the very day of his arrest, identified this Kobylin
as (1) a former student at the reputedly radical Medical-Surgical Academy, (2) a resident physician at its adjacent clinic, and (3) the one who
had treated him and prescribed the pharmaceuticals found in his pocket,
the commission logically began to suspect this doctor of conspiring with
his patient.[10] The trail leading into the clinical realm that the police then
began to follow, that is, had nothing to do with the tsaricide's health, and
everything to do with his possible co-conspirators.

Mentalité

Within two weeks of April 4, as the reader will recall, it was reported in
the papers that, according to those who knew him, Karakozov suffered
from melancholy and hypochondria, had spent time in a clinic, "had already had enough of [life], and hated people."[11] Though there appeared
some opinion pieces whose authors might have found these psychological troubles credible ("No, we cannot believe that someone of sound mind
could decide to do something like that!"), overwhelmingly the Russian
public could not imagine Karakozov as a patient, mental or otherwise,
but only as the "blind weapon" of some insidious political plot.[12] Once
the official findings of the Investigative Commission were published on
August 3, therefore, *Peterburgskii Listok* could rightly proclaim that everyone had known all along that Karakozov was "not an insane fanatic."[13]
This, broadly speaking, was the cultural standard against which must be
measured the court's decision on Karakozov's mental and physical state:
disease may have been a ready metaphor for thinking about politics—the
dominant discourse often enough described nihilism as an illness that
needed rooting out, or as a swelling on the social body that needed amputating—but one did not seriously root the political in the pathological.

At the pre-trial hearing on August 10, however, Karakozov had made it quite plain that he planned to do just that. He acknowledged the crime as his own, but then formally requested the presence of medical experts from Moscow University Clinic to testify to what he called his "nervous, disturbed condition" (*nervnoe razdrazhitel'noe sostoianie*).[14] As grounds for potentially avoiding responsibility for the commission of a crime, article 92 of the then-current Criminal Code listed—besides accident, adolescence, and self-defense—the following psychological conditions: "madness, insanity, and attacks of an illness leading to delirium or complete amnesia" (*bezumie, sumashchestvie, i pripadki bolezni, privodiashchie v umoizstuplenie ili sovershennoe bezpamiatstvo*).[15] Since this phrasing nowhere included "nervous, disturbed condition"—since "the nerves" had not yet been formally pathologized—the court denied Karakozov's request.[16] Karakozov's objection that his crime was nevertheless really rooted in his "abnormal condition" (*nenormalnoe polozhenie*) was overruled when it was shown that the medical records from Moscow University Clinic plainly characterized his mental capacities as "normal."[17] The point, Chairman of the Court Gagarin therefore concluded, was moot. Not that the psycho-physical background of the case ceased to be an issue after this: throughout the trial, Karakozov continued to stress the morbid origin of his crime, and ultimately all decisive court documents formally addressed his illness.

Minister of Justice Zamiatnin, for example, centered his prosecution speech on dismantling Karakozov's psychological defense. In all of Karakozov's actions, he argued, there was not a shadow of a doubt that the criminal had been aware of his actions at the time of his crime and, moreover, carried out exactly the plan as thought up by his friends. "Such acts are not those of a sick man," Zamiatnin concluded, and asked for the death penalty.[18]

"The accused himself recognizes the complete gravity of the crime," countered Karakozov's defense lawyer, Ostriakov, but whether or not his client was sane or at least cognizant of his actions at the time of the crime was a real issue. Applying the defense identified by Dostoevsky as "fashionable," Ostriakov stated, "I am far from considering [Karakozov] someone completely insane, someone without formal, logical consistency of thought, but I wish only to maintain the idea that in the moment of the crime's commission, he was in an abnormal state (*v nenormal'nom sostoianii*)."[19] Citing his client's alcoholism, hypochondria, and suicidal tendencies (on which more below), Ostriakov declared that "people thus disposed are inclined to temporary fits of delirium [or of "being out of one's mind," *vremennye pripadki umaizstupleniia*]."[20]

"I have nothing further to add," said Karakozov, given a last chance to address the court after his lawyer had spoken, except that the morbid condition (*boleznennoe sostoianie*) in which I found myself was the whole reason. I was not insane, but I was close to insanity (*ia ne byl sumasshedshim, no byl blizok k sumasshestviiu*). Further, from one day to the next I was awaiting death. Such was the atrocious moral condition in which I found myself. Under its influence [I wanted] to definitively disappear.[21]

Close to insanity, close to death, close to suicide. But not close enough.

On September 3, while Karakozov was being publicly hanged, newspapers released the text of the Supreme Criminal Court's guilty verdict on the failed tsaricide. As related in Chapter 1, the verdict listed the two counts of which the tsaricide stood accused and stated at the outset that Karakozov had pled guilty to a crime he himself acknowledged was "so great that not even the ill, nervous condition (*boleznennoe, nervnoe sostoianie*) he suffered at the time could justify it."[22] Nevertheless, the text noted, throughout the proceedings the tsaricide had tried to blame his crime on the "extremely afflicted mood of his soul (*kraine boleznennogo nastroeniia dukha*)."[23] As it had in the pre-trial hearings, so now this claim prompted the court to pull out the Criminal Code and cite article 92 to dismantle Karakozov's explanation. The court—again, as it had earlier—cited the medical files testifying that the criminal's mental capacities had been "normal," and concluded by asserting that at no time before, during, or after the crime had there ever been

> any signs of an illness that would have had him suffer delirium or amnesia. . . . The determination and consistency with which his criminal plan was conceived . . . exclude all possibility of ascribing his activities to an abnormal state of mental capacities (*nenormal'noe sostoianie umstvennykh sposobnostei*).[24]

Karakozov's psyche was not exceptional, therefore his act was criminal, and he was fit to die.

Karakozov, for his part, labeled the medical records on the grounds of which the role of his illness had been dismissed as "careless," and this dismissal itself as "too fast."[25] Taking him at his word, what follows below slows down the text and carefully reads the records again in order to scrutinize the ruling that Karakozov was "normal" before, during, and after April 4. Because even if his "nervous, disturbed condition" was at that time found inadmissible in court (i.e. legally illegitimate and historically unthinkable), accepting this decision now would bypass the possibility that Karakozov's pathology may nevertheless have been the very element that not only made his case, but also makes it historically interesting and politically relevant.

Historia Morbi

The sources testifying to Karakozov's medical history include records from the Moscow University Clinic; depositions by the staff of the Medical-Surgical Academy's clinic in Saint Petersburg; reports written by medical personnel at the Peter-Paul Fortress in Saint Petersburg; testimonies by Karakozov and his friends (both written and orally given during the trial); testimonies by Dr. Kobylin; and notes (some retrospective) by members of the Investigative Commission and professionals affiliated with the Supreme Criminal Court. We will begin with the sources available for the time after the failed attempt, when Karakozov was under direct state supervision, then move backward in time to the fall of 1865, and then move forward again to the time just prior to April 4, 1866.

Spring and Summer 1866: Saint Petersburg

After his arrest, Karakozov 'proved' he was suicidal no less than three times. First, during the early days of the investigation—thus it was reported in "White Terror"—Karakozov tried to bite through the arteries in his wrists.[26] When this failed, he began to starve himself. In *Notes of a Karakozovist*, Khudiakov wrote that Karakozov kept up this "heroic attempt" until, weakened after a week without food, he was finally force-fed.[27] Lastly, according to member of the Investigative Commission Cherevin, a third episode that was at that time interpreted as a suicide attempt took place in the Peter-Paul Fortress in mid to late May. Under the supervision of two gendarmes, Karakozov was taken from his cell and out to the latrine, which apparently sat on the banks of the Neva:

> The criminal quickly approached [the lavatory seat], tore off a plank in a flash, and jumped in the hole, supposing it had enough liquid to drown, or maybe that it was connected with another one to which he could dive and then onwards to the shore. How surprised and disillusioned he was when it turned out that he had jumped into a hole in which the water only reached to his knees. The gendarmes immediately jumped . . . [28]

Everything Karakozov wrote throughout the weeks following his arrest, moreover, bears out his psychological proximity to death, whether this was given expression as resignation ("the only favor I ask of the emperor is a quick retribution"), indifference ("As far as my death is concerned, what will be will be)," or duty/desire ("If I had a hundred lives, and not one, and if the people would demand that I would sacrifice all hundred lives for their well-being, I swear to all that is holy that I would not for a minute hesitate to make such a sacrifice").[29]

During his incarceration, Karakozov also fell ill for at least two weeks. The archives hold a series of notes from physicians stationed at the Peter-Paul Fortress who found that sometime in late May, that is, just after his third suicide attempt, Karakozov began to suffer constipation and a loss of appetite, and that his mental capacities were characterized by a certain *tupost'*, a dullness, vacancy, or lassitude; his answers, it was written, were "vague and slow."[30] On June 1, Peter-Paul Fortress governor general Sorokin reported that the doctors had recommended that Karakozov get some rest for a few days.[31] During the days that followed, Karakozov's pulse was extremely rapid, his tongue dry, and he was very feverish. Before being declared well enough to return to the investigation, he was administered laxatives, drops to strengthen his nerves, and finally wine.[32] On June 7 he was without medicine, and notice was sent to the commission that, according to the physicians, Karakozov was almost in a normal state again.[33]

Before turning back to the fall of 1865, there are two things worth mentioning about these rather unremarkable symptoms recorded by the Peter-Paul Fortress physicians. Retrospectively, first of all, Cherevin wrote that none of the prison doctors, with whom he said he had often talked about Karakozov, had ever dissuaded him from his opinion that Karakozov was seriously ill and, in fact, "in the first phase of insanity."[34] If this was indeed their medical opinion, their reports—of which no mention was made during the trial—certainly belie the truth; the symptoms recorded in their files sooner resemble some incidental illness induced by prison life. On the other hand, and this is the second point, even just these symptoms may have been less innocent than they looked, for they were identical to symptoms detected by Karakozov's friends and by the staff of both clinics where he was intermittently treated from November 1865 to March 1866.

Fall and Winter 1865: Moscow

According to those who knew him best, Karakozov had always been exceedingly taciturn and partial to solitude—"Even at the gymnasium," testified one of his friends, "they called him "Charles XII" for his unusual indifference toward everything in the world"—but during the spring 1865 semester, he did still attend lectures at Moscow University's law faculty.[35] This changed after a summer's foray through the provinces, when Karakozov returned to Moscow with afflictions his friends variously identified as gastritis, melancholy, or hypochondria, that is, as something physical, something psychological, or something entirely imaginary.[36] Unable to afford tuition and thus cut off from student life, Karakozov seems to have made his health his main occupation. According to Zagibalov, the one thing Karakozov seemed to be doing besides nothing was keeping an incessant string of doctors' appointments.[37]

It was November 11, 1865, when Karakozov, complaining of a liver that hurt, checked himself into Moscow University Clinic and was diagnosed with urethritis, gastric-intestinal catarrh, exhaustion, and, eventually, relapsing or louse-born fever.[38] Examination records show that he looked thin and tired, was hurting from front to back (in his stomach as well as his spine), and felt lethargic and depressed (*upadok* or *durnoe raspolozhenie dukha*).[39] The records also note venereal discharge, clarified in his anamnesis by the statement that he had contracted gonorrhea "around Lent of 1864 in Kazan."[40] The gonorrhea had gone untreated since, save through self-medication, which had meant an increase in his already considerable alcohol intake. At age seventeen, Karakozov had told his doctors, he had begun drinking about half a bottle of spirits a day, and he had continued to do so until his arrival in Moscow in 1864. He knew it was bad, note the records, but could not stop. And lastly, despite all the above, and as the court cited, the clinicians deemed Karakozov's mental capacities "normal."[41]

Confirming his friends' testimonies, Karakozov's paperwork shows that he told his doctors that his health had worsened during the summer. His provincial diet had been restricted to fish and sausage, "the freshness of which the patient strongly questions," since by the end of the summer, his stool had become bloody and diarrheic; this he had tried to cure with "foreign pills and meat broth." Ever since, he had consistently suffered constipation, which he had also tried to remedy by himself, principally with castor oil. In late October 1865, he began to detect pain in his stomach and liver regions, hence his trip to the clinic November 11, where he remained until January 13, 1866.[42]

A veritable parade of symptoms, a paragraph of diagnoses, two whole months of hospitalization—and yet if someone should look only at the day-by-day notations of his medical chart, it would appear as if Karakozov suffered nothing more than insomnia and a lack of appetite—*the very symptoms he officially suffered in prison*—for which he was treated with unimpressive remedies like chicken soup, milky seltzer water, more castor oil, and leg rubs with vinegar and mustard plasters.[43] The point is perhaps obvious, but still: the meaning of the daily reports written by the doctors at the Peter-Paul Fortress only becomes legible when read against the background of the medical records of Moscow University Clinic. And even these, clearly enough, are easy to read selectively: all that mattered to the Supreme Criminal Court, after all, was that Karakozov's admission documents had characterized his mental capacities as "normal."

One month after his admission, on December 8—"suddenly, without special reasons," according to the records—Karakozov developed a painful earache along with the first signs of what would turn out to be an intense fever.[44] December 11, his body burned at 40.1 degrees Celsius.[45]

This is the time from which Karakozov's first suicide note dates. It has not been preserved, but his friends' collective memory of its content included mention of an inevitable death, the tortures of illness, and a request for drugs. "For God's sake, bring me opium," Ermolov thought the note had read. "I want to poison myself to end the unbearable sufferings."[46] Dmitry Ivanov recalled the phrase, "if God doesn't help, the devil will," and Iurasov remembered his friend's conviction that "I have to die soon anyway."[47]

Asked about the note, Karakozov told his friends that one of the doctors, Zakharin, had given a lecture to students at the clinic and publicly indicated that Karakozov's disease was "dangerous," that there was a "valvular disease of the heart" and also some sort of "*febris cerebralis.*"[48] Auerbach, a resident at the clinic and the author of Karakozov's *historia morbi*, however, assured Karakozov's friends that Professor Zakharin, who was the director of the clinic, had said nothing of the sort. Under the impression that Karakozov must thus have hallucinated the Zakharin episode, they told Auerbach about the suicide note and asked whether Karakozov could kill himself "as a result of the condition of his stomach," and whether "catarrh can lead to insanity."[49] Their worst fears were confirmed when Auerbach pointed out that, according to experts like Niemeier, the answer was affirmative: "the majority of cases of catarrh of the digestive organs leads to the disorder of reason," Iurasov recalled having heard.[50] (In other testimony, Auerbach was said to have put it as follows: "Such cases happen extremely often, and he pointed to Niemeier, who says that the majority of suicides are the result of gastric catarrh."[51]) If the conclusions Karakozov's friends drew from this information varied— "We feared for Karakozov's mental capacities," testified Ermolov, while Dmitry Ivanov said he had heard from Ishutin that Karakozov was truly very ill, but making things worse with his hypochondria[52]—this was because they were getting mixed messages from the doctors: on the one hand, Karakozov's condition was strictly physical—"the catarrhal state of the stomach, as a result of chronic gonorrhea and bad food"—but on the other hand, this condition could cause serious psychological problems.[53]

Late in the second week of January, once his temperature had finally stabilized, after no less than three relapses into crisis, the clinicians dismissed Karakozov. Karakozov himself, however, remained convinced he was far from cured.

According to Dmitry Ivanov, as a matter of fact, Karakozov's melancholy and hypochondria only worsened upon his release from the clinic:

"for days he sat silently in a separate room, hiding his face with his hands."[54] Karakozov had been extremely reticent and reclusive, Ermolov agreed, and "slept almost all day long."[55] Ishutin confirmed: "It was his sick condition, his sense that the illness was incurable, his nervous condition—this put the idea in his head that he would definitely die; for days he lay by himself in his room and did not participate in any of our discussions."[56] Dmitry Ivanov barely even interacted with Karakozov during this period—their conversation was in fact limited to the following sarcastic exchange: "How's your health?" "Healthy"—but he did once hear him singing a retrospectively telling song about the executed seventeenth-century rebel-hero Stenka Razin.[57]

And then Karakozov was gone.

For late January *Maslenitsa* (Shrovetide) celebrations, the group of friends had gathered at Malaia Bronnaia 25 for a traditional helping of pancakes, but instead spent the afternoon searching for a clue explaining Karakozov's sudden absence. Finding nothing, they considered his condition, his note from the clinic, the fact that some of them had recently seen him with a gun, and then concluded that he had withdrawn to die. Testified Ermolov: "We thought he would kill himself in a fit of madness (*v pripadke sumasshestviia*)."[58] Karakozov had reappeared three days later, but only confirmed their worries: long had he wandered aimlessly, contemplating suicide. Shortly thereafter, sometime in early February, he was gone again, and none of his friends knew where until Khudiakov came to Moscow in early March and told them their friend was in Saint Petersburg. Prompted by this news, they searched for a note once more, and finally found one hidden behind a cupboard: "I am so sick that I feel incapable of doing anything. Work by yourselves. Leave me my fate."[59] (Alternatively, Ermolov remembered it as having read, "'Goodbye, my life is over, *febris cerebralis, caput,*' and so on and so forth."[60] Stranden likewise remembered some disease spelled out in Latin, "then the phrase, 'insanity and death from [illegible],' and then, 'A thinking realist will have no doubts about the causes of death.'")[61]

Thus, around the time of Karakozov's double disappearance, at least according to much of the written and spoken testimonies, his friends all began to characterize his psycho-physical health in new ways. Formerly, for example, Iurasov had dismissed Karakozov's troubles with a statement that his friend's morbid fixation was so extreme that he had begun to diagnose himself with diseases that were not at all there: "It seemed to him he had consumption, hydropsy, a bad liver, a bad spleen, and some other bad organs."[62] But now Dmitry Ivanov recalled having heard the following from Iurasov about Karakozov: "That's not hypochondria, but simply insanity."[63] "Extremely strange" was how Zagibalov characterized Karakozov after coming out of the clinic: "For example, if he was writing something and someone would approach him, he would try to hide the papers. Once, I asked him for some paper to light the firewood, he gave me a few pieces, on one of which I read, 'Notes of a Madman.' I looked at Karakozov; he blushed."[64] Khudiakov, in his written testimonies, slapped adjectives from "sick" to "wild," "strange," and "suspicious" onto Karakozov, but did note that when he had expressed these impressions to Ishutin, the latter had protested that Karakozov was simply "ill" and, in another version, "good."[65] By contrast, Stranden, according to Motkov, had called Karakozov "a lunatic capable of anything."[66]

After his release from Moscow University's clinic, in sum, Karakozov's social relations became strained. He himself said of this period that his mood was "bilious," and that his illness made him relate to his friends and their activities with "impatience": "My nerves at that time were so excited that peaceful work did not satisfy me . . . I wanted to stir up the workers with propaganda."[67] Facing Karakozov, a question started staring back: was this illness, hypochondria, insanity—or something else entirely?

Winter 1866: Saint Petersburg

Karakozov always maintained—before friends, the commission, and the court—that his reasons for going to Petersburg were both political and medical. Throughout the last two weeks of April before the Investigative Commission, for example, alongside propaganda among factory workers and contact with political parties, he repeatedly listed as motivations for traveling west his quest for a cure and the wish to outrun the incessant idea of suicide.[68] According to his own testimony, Karakozov had visited a rich assortment of medical facilities upon arriving in the capital: "many doctors on various streets . . . one was across from Kazan Cathedral . . . some doctors on Nevsky Prospect and adjoining streets, then when I moved to Vyborg Island I was in a clinic, then on Petersburg Island at a doctor's, then in the fortress, and then in the hospital."[69] Finally, at the end of the first week of March, Karakozov walked into Sergei Petrovich Botkin's Therapeutic Clinic at the Medical-Surgical Academy, and met Dr. Kobylin. One month later, on April 6, Kobylin confirmed before the Investigative Commission that the failed tsaricide, whom he knew as "Vladimirov," had been his patient. During the investigation and the trial, he narrated their relations as follows.

A few weeks ago, wrote Kobylin, "a young man, tall, blonde, and dressed in a dark-gray armiak," had come in complaining of pains in the chest and stomach regions, constipation, and—consequently—insomnia. Kobylin had prescribed a diuretic, "pills from silver," and told him to return for a checkup a few days later.[70] Two days passed, Karakozov came back, but he began to embarrass Kobylin: "in a rather sharp expression before the public," Karakozov had complained that the medicine was not working.[71] Kobylin declared himself unqualified, sent the patient to see Dr. Botkin, and returned to work. There is some confusion about whom Karakozov really consulted with on this occasion—Dr. Botkin or a certain Dr. Golovin—but on this day, in any case, someone diagnosed him as a hypochondriac; there would be no change of medication.[72] When the tenacious patient returned a third time, repeated his complaints, and added details about his overall moral and physical indisposition, Kobylin finally prescribed him morphine (eight packages of one-eighth of a gram each).[73] Karakozov's testimonies confirmed this, as did depositions by the pharmacist Schmitt and his assistant Kreis: Karakozov brought in prescriptions signed by Kobylin and dated March 11.[74] (And this, then, was the morphine found in the pocket of Karakozov's armiak upon his arrest and analyzed by Trapp.)[75]

And yet Karakozov returned for a fourth visit, and asked to be looked at again. Before the commission, Kobylin testified that Karakozov had asked to be hospitalized on this occasion; but because Karakozov was not legally registered in the capital, Kobylin "wanted to dodge his request and began to persuade him that his illness was more imaginary."[76] "Even if his sufferings were imaginary," Kobylin quoted Karakozov's protest, "they were none the less torturous."[77] What happened next was shock treatment. According to Karakozov, Kobylin had mused that morphine might be useless in his case: "the stomach pains could be accounted for by the not entirely normal state of the nervous system, and that in the case of such diseases it is all in all better to resort to treatment with electricity."[78] During this electro-therapeutic "séance" (as Kobylin called the treatment), Karakozov and Kobylin became better acquainted.

Karakozov told Kobylin he was a recent arrival in the capital. Originally from the provinces, he had been enrolled at Moscow University, but now wanted either to attend the Medical-Surgical Academy or study natural sciences at Petersburg University. He was also broke, and although sometimes he worked a factory job for thirty kopeks a day, he hoped to find something better. All in all, the patient struck his doctor as "one of those poor provincials who come to Petersburg for an education," and, seeing in Karakozov "a future colleague," Kobylin actually lent him some three rubles, which Karakozov promised to promptly return (as he did). Kobylin added that Karakozov did not strike him as especially liberal at all; his words were "restrained" and their talk "ordinary."[79]

They made another appointment for March 21, but that Monday, Kobylin wrote, Karakozov declined a second "séance." Penniless and on the verge of being thrown out of his apartment, he had decided to go back to Moscow, where at least he had friends who might help him. When he added that he had nowhere to spend the night, the doctor finally offered him shelter in the comfort of his own home. The third night there, it was Wednesday, Karakozov and Kobylin stayed up talking about literature, science, society, and so forth. According to Kobylin, Karakozov was exceedingly negative, called all of literature "rubbish," and behaved "like a melancholic, because he did not smile once during the course of the evening, irrespective of the jokes to which I resorted to draw him into conversation."[80] Karakozov eventually told him something about life on Moscow's squares, about schismatics, students, and simple folk, but that, basically, was all there was to Kobylin's version of the night's talk.

After that night, Karakozov was in Moscow for a week, returned to Petersburg on Wednesday March 30, headed straight for Kobylin's from the train station on Nevsky, but found only his brother at home. On Thursday March 31, the doctor saw Karakozov twice: once in the evening, when he told his patient he would help him find work through a friend, Putiata, and then late at night, when they both slept at the clinic.

Friday morning, April 1, at Kobylin's place, Karakozov was taciturn as usual ("ten words every ten minutes") and Kobylin, "to make conversation," pointed out that he had some strychnine and potassium sulfate lying around in a drawer: "Hm, I forgot to get rid of these; they're terrible poisons."[81] This, according to Kobylin, brought Karakozov to life: "He asked me how they were used, how we do experiments with them, questions along these lines."[82] They took a walk, then saw each other very briefly once more during the course of the next twenty-four hours, when Karakozov came by to tell Kobylin that he would be leaving Petersburg. The next time they met was April 6, when the doctor was dragged into the headquarters of the Third Section for questioning.

April 2–4, 1866: Saint Petersburg

As for Karakozov's state during the days just prior to the crime, on April 2, 3, and early on April 4, the only available sources of information are Karakozov's own testimonies. According to these, Karakozov spent the night of Saturday April 2 drinking vodka to distract himself from the thought of death that chased him wherever he went. "When I lay down to sleep I already thought I would not wake up again," he wrote. "My head burned like fire. I have no words to describe the sick, torturous condition in which I found myself." Monday April 4 was no better than Sunday April 3: "a similarly heavy state of the soul." "Machine-like," he wandered the streets of the capital, possessed of only one thought, "that I have to die, that all attempts, all hopes for the fruition of my efforts to bring good to the people . . . are lost. And under the influence of those ideas I decided to commit the crime, and the idea was executed that same day."[83] Pistol, poisons, and proclamation in his pocket, Karakozov walked past the Winter Palace, waited near the Summer Garden, then shot, missed, ran, and was stopped, but forgot to commit suicide: "the shock, the feeling that came over me at the time of the crime, I forgot about the poison I had in my pocket; having fired, I was stupefied."[84] No sooner had he been detained, however, than Karakozov resumed his suicidal plans described above.

First Causes

When Karakozov was first asked why he had attempted to assassinate the tsar, he said not a word about his illness and insisted that his motive was outlined in his proclamation.[85] Picking up where the beginning of the chapter left off:

> My death will be an example for them and inspire them. Let the Russian people recognize their main, mightiest enemy, be he Alexander II, Alexander III, and so forth, that's all the same. Once the people makes short work of their most important enemy, the petty remainder of his landowners, grandees, officials, and all the rest of the rich folk will become afraid, for their numbers are not at all noteworthy. And then there will be real freedom.[86]

These themes of sacrifice and serial assassination he reiterated on April 10 in a statement directly addressed to Alexander II: "[From] time to time, people will appear—if not in Russia, then in other states of Europe—who, having seen recent examples in [nihilism], will sacrifice their lives in order to show the people that its cause is right.[87] But in testimony composed for the commission that very same day, April 10, Karakozov had already begun to link this abstract notion of sacrifice with his own physical condition:

> that disturbed, heavy mood of the soul, that illness, this spawned the idea that I was no longer capable of doing anything for the cause of the people, and that I did not have much longer to live. All that could have brought me to suicide and, consequently, to the crime I committed; I thought by committing the crime I would sacrifice myself and be useful (*poleznyi*) to the people.[88]

Obviously, Karakozov had been interrogated about his sacrifice, his suicide, and his soul, and then been asked the question Porfiry Petrovich put to Raskolnikov: Why should *this* mood disorder produce *this* crime? And then he began to unfold an ulterior motive.

Kobylin

In *Notes of a Karakozovist,* Khudiakov asserted that Karakozov had simply incriminated Kobylin (and Khudiakov himself) because Ishutin had requested that he do so, "not openly, of course, but by way of a hint."[89] Probably, what Khudiakov had in mind was that sometime in late April, Ishutin—at the urging of Murav'ev—wrote two small notes to Karakozov, the first of which read as follows:

> Mitia!
> If you have not yet openly told the Commission about that party you know about, then do so; this will diminish your role in this crime, clear me and your other acquaintances, and show your love for me.
> In anticipation of relief from you,
> Your brother, Nikolai Ishutin.[90]

Khudiakov's assessment was speculative, but it is true enough that over the course of the investigation, in accounting for the idea-source of tsaricide, Karakozov increasingly stressed the role of "that party you know" and, consequently, increasingly implicated Kobylin. This process may be demonstrated quite empirically by means of the Karakozov's statements about the poisons found in the pockets of his *armiak.*

On April 4, upon his arrest, as mentioned above, Karakozov told the Investigative Commission that the two powdery substances were medicinal, prescribed by Kobylin at Botkin's clinic, and filled at Schmitt's pharmacy on Vyborg Island. The vial, which he said contained arsenic, he kept for self-defense, namely to kill himself in case his travels landed him in an inescapably bad situation.[91] On April 5 and 6, however, Karakozov testified that he had actually acquired all three substances from "an old friend who sold household goods and whose name I cannot remember right now," adding plausibility—or thinking he would, at least—by writing that this old friend had them "just in case someone needed such things for chemical and physiological experiments."[92] But then Trapp's report came in, and Karakozov was interrogated about the nature of his relationship with Kobylin: had not Kobylin supplied the toxins with the express purpose of facilitating the crime? On April 10 Karakozov admitted that all three substances had come from Kobylin, but swore they had been "for physiological experiments."[93] Karakozov had, after all, presented himself to the doctor as a prospective student of the natural sciences, so—naturally—Kobylin had agreed to bring toxins from Botkin's clinic for the two of them to do some experiments together—except then Karakozov had stolen them from Kobylin.[94]

Two months after saying he had stolen the stuff, Karakozov changed his story again. On June 12, shortly after recovering from the illness he suffered from late May to June 7, he wrote that Kobylin had known about his tsaricidal plans and knowingly provided him with strychnine and hydrocyanic acid so that he could poison and disfigure himself after committing his crime.[95] On June 14 and 15, he reaffirmed this testimony, and during the trial maintained it as well.[96] Even after a harrowing cross-examination by Kobylin's lawyer, Iakov Markovich Serebrianyi,* Karakozov still insisted that prior to his Easter trip to Moscow he had already more or less indicated to Kobylin that he planned to commit his crime, but that upon his return to the capital on Wednesday March 30 he had told him explicitly, and explicitly declared that he needed the toxins for this.[97] Confronted with the fact that he had changed his testimony, Karakozov explained: "That was in the beginning, and in the beginning I did not want to expose Kobylin. I had planned—to the extent that it was possible—to keep Kobylin out of it."[98] No sooner had the "Kobylin" scrap of paper been found, though, Karakozov went on, than his plan had proved impossible, and eventually he had been forced to confess Kobylin's complicity—which meant, in effect, Kobylin's responsibility for making it the case that *this* mood disorder had produced *this* crime.

"K."

The decision to assassinate Tsar Alexander II, thus Karakozov, had been made the day he heard about a party whose members were high-ranking, influential at court, and eager for a change in government that would enthrone the tsar's constitutionalist brother, Grand Duke Konstantin Nikolaevich. This party was "that party you know" of Ishutin's prison note—and obviously also the referent of the "K." in Karakozov's letter to Ishutin: not Kobylin, but Konstantin. The source of whatever Karakozov had heard about the Konstantinians, however, *was* Kobylin.

The late-night talks that Kobylin had sketched as noteworthy for nothing more than Karakozov's hypochondria, anti-intellectualism, and melancholy had meant something quite different to Karakozov. According to Karakozov, he and the doctor had taken a conversational track along Russian and European literature, then past the social question, and had finally arrived at revolution. Here the question had not been whether Russia needed a revolution, but whether the revolution that Russia needed should be economic or, given the empire's backwardness, political, that is to say bottom-up or top-down. Concerning this topic, Kobylin had said that the latter—that is, a coup d'état—was probably what animated the Konstantinian party; he had been unable to give Karakozov any specific information, but said he had heard that the party existed, that its members were influential at court, and that he could introduce Karakozov to a friend, Putiata, whose information and connections were better than his own.[99]

Alongside talk of politics and poverty, Karakozov had also confessed to Kobylin how depressed he had been by his illness, and that he had repeatedly considered suicide. It is hard to die, Kobylin understood, when you know not what you leave behind. Then, in this context, Kobylin ostensibly mentioned that the Konstantinians had long awaited someone willing to give up his life for the cause. When Karakozov then asked Kobylin what he, Karakozov, could expect from the course of his illness, Kobylin had sat silent; "so, as a consequence of our talk, when I realized I had not much longer to live, and given my grave condition, I told him of my intention to commit the crime."[100] Needless to say, Kobylin denied that Karakozov had ever told him about any such plans.[101] What matters here, however, is rather to note that *thus* surfaced Karakozov's tripartite plan (still legible in the letter to Ishutin): first, his assassination (a "singular fact") would unleash a revolt ("an affront") and place the Konstantinian party on the throne ("a safe state"); second, his proclamation would rouse youth and workers against the Konstantinian party ("clashes"); and third, Karakozov would end up a nameless, faceless corpse, to be sure, but his last moments would be gladdened by the thought that his death would be *poleznyi* (useful, good).[102]

Pharmakon-Pharmakos

Being *poleznyi* is a recurrent motif in Karakozov's testimonies about his motive. On April 15, for example, Karakozov wrote that he had first thought of tsaricide upon hearing about the Konstantinians, but also underlined the role of his illness, which had pushed him to the verge of suicide: he wanted to die, but not without having been *poleznyi* for the people.[103] For Karakozov, to be *poleznyi* mostly means to be "useful" as a propagandist, to work toward improving the lot of the people by spreading the word. But because this adjective, *poleznyi*, also means "good," as in "good for one's health," "nourishing," the expression can also mean to heal or to remedy whatever is wrong with the people. The recurrence of this motif, in other words, allows for framing Karakozov's vision of Russia's body politic, and his relationship to it, in clinical terms—for understanding, finally, why Karakozov saw "just these illusions" in his "sick delirium."

In thinking politics via pathology, Karakozov is of course well within the range of the age's positivistic horizon of expectations. Where he exceeds the zeitgeist, however, is in taking its metaphors literally—and this precisely on account of his excessive clinical experience. For months,

Karakozov circulates through the clinical realms of the empire, his thoughts fixed on finding a cure, at the back of his mind the hope of being *poleznyi,* and then, at the very moment he becomes convinced that his "nervous, disturbed condition" is not only permanent, but fatal, Dr. Kobylin provides him with the perfect occasion to use his own illness to the benefit of Russia's health.

For someone who understands himself as a propagandist and—probably having taken a cue from Chernyshevsky's Rakhmetov—once stated that calm, deliberate work as a propagandist first of all requires that one be "healthy in body and soul"; disease is an existentially devastating event not only because it may spell death, but also because it marks one as a bad propagandist.[104] But by turning his illness into something *poleznyi* for the perishing people, Karakozov ingeniously transforms his own death into the last possible act proper to the propagandist: "factual propaganda" (*fakticheskaia propaganda*), he writes in a mid-June set of testimonies, "that is, a crime against the Emperor, and I, because of my physical condition, can commit that crime."[105] Crossing the concept of a traditional tsaricide with that of an ancient scapegoat, Karakozov becomes the perfect propagandist: his body is the word become flesh, act, and fact.

And what can be said now of this fact, Karakozov? Or rather, what does it say? What witness did it bear of the origins of factual propaganda—propaganda by the deed, as it is more generally called, or terrorism? Spleen, fevers, fatigue, insomnia, (mono)mania, hypochondria, neurosis, trichinosis, temporary insanity, suicidal tendencies, sexually transmitted disease, delirium, addiction, a liver that hurts—not just one, or two, or even three, but all the diseases of the urban nineteenth century cling to the body of Russia's first modern tsaricide. A perfect sample of the empire's stressed-out social soil, Karakozov's corporality offers itself as a cipher to the revolutionary politics that exceed its roots: terrorism was born of an affected body, not an irrational mind.

Neologism

"Factual propaganda" is Karakozov's concept.[106] The expression was not part of the common parlance of his acquaintances in either Moscow or Saint Petersburg. It seems instead to have emerged as a methodological response to their critique that his assassination of Alexander II would be a "singular fact." Karakozov's neologism, indeed, contains a type of logic that has long served scholars in distinguishing revolutionary terrorism from earlier forms of political assassination, namely, the logic of systematic, rather than singular, violence. Moreover, it can disclose for us the origins of this logic.

Karakozov's testimonies indicate that there are two possible sources of the critique of tsaricide as a "singular fact": Khudiakov and Kobylin, the two people in Petersburg most likely to have known about Karakozov's plan or at least to have abstractly debated tsaricide with him. When Karakozov first claimed on June 12 that he had more or less told both Khudiakov and Kobylin about his plan, he added that neither had approved, and then twice in as many pages attributed very comparable counterclaims to them. First, asked to clarify a statement attributed to Khudiakov that tsaricide would not unleash social revolution, Karakozov explained Khudiakov's position as follows: "it cannot lead to the expected results . . . because it is a singular fact that cannot be repeated (*fakt edinichnyi kotoryi povtorit'sia ne mozhet*)."[107] Second, a page later, when Karakozov rewrote a dialogue on tsaricide he claimed had taken place between himself and Kobylin, he made the doctor's argument appear in the following form: "such a crime will disappear without a trace, like a singular fact" (*prestuplenie eto proidet bessledno kak fakt edinichnyi*).[108]

Because arrestees were at times required to spell out in writing what they had already orally told the commission, it is probable that Karakozov collapsed the counterarguments of Khudiakov with those of Kobylin when he wrote them out. Their language/logic, indeed, looks uncharacteristic of Khudiakov, who, as an ethno-folklorist, tended to think historically (or at least by means of historical example). In one of his testimonies, for example, Khudiakov volunteered this argument against tsaricide: "similar attempts, as history shows, always ended with the complete ruination of whatever party strove, by such means, to rush the movement of progress."[109] Khudiakov is someone who sooner thinks of the peculiarities of historico-political timing; he might judge Karakozov's act as "too early" or too "rushed," but not somehow "too singular."[110] It is more likely that the objections as they were (re)formulated by Karakozov originally emerged from a scientific mind like Kobylin's, a mind that would find that a single experiment proves nothing (no matter how interesting the results) and would also insist on the principle of repetition as the first and foremost criterion for confirming a hypothesis about any phenomenon.

"Factual propaganda" is thus a response to a scientific critique of traditional tsaricide—and it is a response that incorporates this critique. The solution to the irregularity of regicide is to regularize it: to repeat, systematize, or scientize the singular. This principle of repetition marks not only Karakozov's own commitment ("if I had a hundred lives"), but also—and this is crucial, methodologically speaking—his conviction that others will follow his example and assassinate "Alexander II, Alexander III, and so forth." Ultimately, we might say, Karakozov's application of scientific expertise and clinical experience to politics leads to a turning away from treating symptoms and toward a decision to commit to radical and if need be relentlessly repetitious shock treatment designed to eliminate the cause of the disease that is ailing the body politic. Terrorism, therefore, is regicide reproduced in the age of science.

CHAPTER 7

THE HEAD OF THE TSARICIDE

"The first glance tells you [Karakozov] renounced any kind of religion a long time ago."

THE PRIEST I. N. POLISADOV

On September 6, 1866, three days after Karakozov had been hanged on Saint Petersburg's Smolensk Square, one of the clerks of the Third Section reported rumors that students had crossed over to Golodai Island, sought and found the site of the tsaricide's unmarked grave, and covered it with flowers.[1] True in its specifics or not, this would have been but one of many illegal excursions to Karakozov's grave: several reports verified the trend, which neither guards, nor arrests could check.[2] It would also have been but one of the more innocent trips to the island, which served as the city's cemetery for suicides and criminals; more sinister sorties, so the stories went, meant to steal and skin Karakozov's cadaver, and then to keep his skeleton at the Medical Academy, "as a monument."[3] Word on the street was that to prevent this from ever happening, the authorities had rendered the corpse forever unrecognizable by cutting off its head.[4] Now, rather remarkably, while the archives remain silent about the 'who' of these terrible trespassers, one name was reclaimed for the historical record when, in the early twentieth century, an artist working on his memoirs suddenly recalled having gone to Golodai in the late summer of 1866.[5] The artist in question was Ilya Repin, and everything he remembered that day, he remembered because of Karakozov's head.

Fig. 13. Ilya Repin, *The Refusal of the Confession (Before the Execution)* (1879–85). (Tretyakov Gallery) With permission from the State Tretyakov Gallery, Moscow, Russia.

(Before) The Refusal

In 1881, years after he had established himself as one of Russia's foremost realist painters, Repin announced to a friend that he had abandoned all historical subjects and embarked on a project conceived "long ago" to paint a contemporary reality "more disturbing to us than all past events."[6] He was referring to what would become a celebrated set of paintings that included the following titles: *The Meeting; by the Light of a Lamp (Skhodka; pri svete lampy,* 1883); *The Propagandist's Arrest (Arest propagandista,* 1880–92); *Before the Confession (Pered ispovedi, 1879–85); Unexpected (Ne zhdali,* 1884–88); and *Ivan the Terrible and his Son Ivan, November 16, 1581 (Ivan Groznyi i syn ego Ivan 16 noiabria 1581 goda,* 1885).

Concretely, these works picture a selection of emblematic episodes from the lives of late nineteenth-century Russian revolutionaries: conspiratorial gatherings, propaganda, arrest, imprisonment, murder, judgment, exile, death. Courtesy of the scenes' Christian iconographic arrangements, Repin not only captured or solidified a behavioral code proper to revolutionary life (engraving ethics in gesture, gaze, disposition), but also poured mystical content into its forms. For example, the motifs of *The Propagandist's Arrest* allude to Christ's betrayal and the crucifixion; *The Meeting* gathers twelve around an orator; and *Unexpected* shows a "resurrected" exile entering a living room whose walls are graced with a print of Christ at Golgotha. Here, however, I would direct the reader's attention to one painting only: *Before the Confession,* or as it came to be known, *The Refusal of the Confession (Before the Execution)* (*Otkaz ot ispovedi* [*Pered kazn'iu*]). (fig. 13)

Like the rest of the series, *Before the Confession* centers on the manifestation of the Word, the word, or, more mundanely, an act of speech; in this case, obviously, it is religious confession. But because the work invokes Christ before Pilate (Mark 15:5, Matt. 27:14), that is, in essence, the silence of the Word before the Law, there is a strong suggestion that this speech event, confession, may never manifest itself. Literally, of course, this is precisely right: the action on the canvas stays forever arrested in the anterior of its title. Symbolically, though, the scene is rather less settled. Or once was, in any case. Precisely to avoid ambiguity, presumably, the work was renamed *The Refusal of the Confession* sometime in the twentieth century.

Renamed, Repin's painting was perfect for the revolutionary pantheon: "Refuse to testify!" ("Otkazyvaites' ot pokazanii!"), after all, was the golden rule of resistance. Given that priests were legally required to comply with the state, lest revolutionaries betray their cause they could not but refuse confession. Typically, in the days before dying, they dismissed priests, declined to kiss the cross, etc.; thus rejecting religion, they realized revolution. As *Otkaz*, therefore, Repin's work stands as the paradigmatic gesture of a revolutionary death; its silence speaks for the life that refuses to be conformed to this world—and regrets nothing. But Repin, we know now, was less decided. That is, as yet.

(Involuntary) Memory

Although by the end of the 1870s, as a topos of revolutionary life, the confrontation with the cross was evidently discernible enough to emerge as emblem in Repin's work, it is unknown whether the painter actually attended any of the public executions of that time (such as the execution of the 1881 tsaricides), that is, whether he personally witnessed such spectacles and then translated them into his art. What is certain, however, is that he was present at Karakozov's hanging in 1866, and that the event left an indelible impression on his mind.

Fig. 14. Ilya Repin, sketch of Karakozov's head.

Many decades later, in the same autobiography that describes his foray
onto Golodai, *Faraway So Close (Dalekoe blizkoe)*, Repin depicted the effect
of the hanging as follows: "I almost fainted, grasped [his friend]
Murashko, and then nearly jumped at the sight of his face—strikingly
dreadful with its expression of suffering."[7] Further telling of the impact
(or at least of interest provoked) is the fact that Repin, then a twenty-two-
year-old student of the Saint Petersburg Academy of Art, sketched Karakozov's head (see figure 14). It was in fact the rediscovery of this small pencil
drawing, relates Kornei Chukovsky in his foreword to *Faraway So Close,*
that occasioned both Repin's recollection of Karakozov's execution and
then his written narrative of it.[8]

Comparing the sketch, the face of the revolutionary in *The Propagandist's Arrest,* Repin's description of the execution in *Faraway So Close* (on
which more below), Karakozov's police photograph, and other, independent sources detailing the tsaricide's appearance, the temptation rises to
posit that these all signify one and the same subject: the long nose, slight
beard, light, longish hair, red *meshchanin* shirt and the plain white one below, dark peasant coat, pants tucked into long boots, and so forth. Here,
nevertheless, I actually mean to proceed in the opposite direction: neither to locate the possible survival of a youthful impression into mature

artistic work, nor to emphasize an element common to materials otherwise diverse and asynchronous, but rather to focus on a *disappearance*. During the event that so shook Repin, something happened that not only
failed to make its way into both his art and writing, but also actually seems
to have been brushed away and staged anew: Karakozov's religious reconciliation.

The Bow

When Repin summoned his memories to traverse the age, they were embedded in the painterly prose of a seasoned artist. In *Faraway so Close*'s
description of the execution scene, colors, lines, positions, expressions,
movement, and gestures define the trajectory of Repin's story; speech, by
contrast, is reduced to sounds (words spoken from the scaffold are inaudible, there is an indistinct humming from the crowd, some unintelligible cries from shriekers resound, and so forth). Here is Repin's
description of Karakozov's last moments:

> On the scaffold—and where we stood no one obstructed us from seeing—
> they took from him a long-hemmed, black coat, and he, swaying, stood in
> a gray jacket and gray pants. Official figures read something for a fairly long
> time, but none of this was audible. They turned to the "criminal," and the
> gendarmes and some other assistants, taking from him his black prisoner's
> cap, started to shove him toward the center of the scaffold. It seemed he
> either could not walk, or was in a trance; it must have been that his hands
> were tied. But then, untied, devoutly, à la Russe, not hurrying, he bowed to
> the people on all four sides of him. This bow instantly turned the crowd on
> its head; it became kindred and close to this alien, strange creature (*chuzh-
> domu, strannomu sushchestvu*), at which it looked as if at a miracle (*chudo*).[9]

Engulfing people and tsaricide, Karakozov's bows collapse the space that
distances stage from audience and transform the spectacle into a mystical scene; to the exclusion of authority, the crowd and criminal unite in
sympathy, and transcend the partitions of power. "Perhaps only at that
minute," writes Repin, "did the 'criminal' himself vividly feel the significance of the moment—an eternal parting with the world and a universal
connection with it."[10]

Contested Past

Even though invariably somewhat at odds with each other as well, all other
contemporary accounts contest Repin's hallowed memory. Not that those

accounts are devoid of piety; but rather than drench the scene in sacral hues, they record the traditional ceremonials of Orthodox Christian ritual. One secret police agent, for example, mentioned that at the sight of a church passed en route to Smolensk Square, Karakozov took off his cap and crossed himself; and two separate newspaper accounts mentioned the same reverent gestures after Karakozov's cart had come to a halt in front of the scaffold with the gallows.[11] To render the invisible absence of Repin's tale, let us look closer at other narrations of the minutes just prior to Karakozov's dying.

The official whose public announcements Repin dubbed "inaudible" was the man who had also served as secretary of the Supreme Criminal Court, Iakov G. Esipovich. In his recollections, Esipovich writes that his own descent from the scaffold was followed by the ascent of one last authority figure: an Orthodox priest. "In vestments and with a cross in his hands," writes Esipovich, "he approached the condemned man, spoke to him a last parting word, gave him the cross to kiss, and removed himself."[12] All contemporary newspaper reports confirm this sequence of events, although the precise specifics of what happened were, naturally enough, subject to selective interpretation.

Russkii Invalid, for example, reported that when the priest appeared, "the condemned man kneeled and remained out of sight for a minute. The silence was undisturbed, but horrible. After the priest's parting words, they placed the shroud over the criminal, and within a few minutes he was no more."[13] *Golos* concurred, but included additional details: while the priest said a prayer and parting words, Karakozov, his head hanging, was on his knees, but then, "stood up, piously crossed himself, brought his lips to the cross, and, receiving the priest's blessing, kissed his hand."[14] A summary printed in a different local paper, *Petersburgskii Listok*, also agreed, but explicitly interpreted Karakozov's kneeling posture as prayer and his kissing the cross as expressive of reconciliation with God: "The criminal, when the priest approached him, zealously prayed and, evidently, with a feeling of complete repentance, brought his lips to the cross."[15] Yet another report understood Karakozov's being on his knees as confession: "When the priest approached, Karakozov, falling to his knees with folded hands, began to confess." Additionally, this last article included the following detail, which it placed after Karakozov's kissing of the cross: "The priest crossed him once more, then removed himself. Then Karakozov, held by the executioners, began to bow to the people. They brought him to the gallows."[16]

Concerning the crowd, one article reported that the people removed their hats after the verdict had been read and crossed themselves when the executioners placed the rope around Karakozov's neck.[17] In another paper it was observed that, after the execution, "some women and some pious old men, taking off their caps, crossed themselves, and we heard the voice of a passing woman, 'in the next world, Lord, forgive him his grave sin.'"[18]

No account besides Repin's, in sum, describes the transformative bow exchanged between crowd and criminal; the closest approximation is the above-cited report that, on his way from the priest to the noose, Karakozov "began to bow to the people." Lining up all that has been culled from these varied recitals, it appears that when Repin awoke his memory, some of the event's details were crushed under the weight of hindsight. Priest, Orthodox ceremonials, and Karakozov's reconciliation with the cross were evidently obliterated during Repin's mnemonic reconstruction— and any religious atmospheric residue transferred to the monument erected in their stead, namely the people.

It is conjecture, of course, but quite possible that when Repin remembered the execution, he did so in accordance with a revolutionary behavioral code he had himself decided in his paintings, i.e. that his own works mediated the past to him. In Repin's art, a revolutionary does not quite quit the world with a priest's blessing.

Later revolutionaries—most notably the tsaricides hanged for the 1881 assassination of Alexander II and, without significant exceptions, members of the terrorist wing of the early-twentieth-century Party of Socialist-Revolutionaries—all exited life defiantly, stoically, and alone. But when Karakozov gazed down from the scaffold into a crowd of several tens of thousands on the morning of September 3, the proper way to die for a revolutionary had not yet been codified: the Decembrists (1825) were not executed in public, the Petrashevtsy (1849) were pardoned at the last moment. Karakozov stood as the modern era's first public example of a revolutionary death.

The evidence from newspapers (that a priest presided over Karakozov's passage into death, and in the most Orthodox fashion at that), however, creates the impression that there was nothing paradigmatically revolutionary about the death of this first modern tsaricide. Rather, from a revolutionary angle, it is as if something defeated, failed, and even unethical attaches itself to Karakozov's buckling body, as if his political resolve crumpled under the sheer weight of religion, as if with this kiss, he becomes a Judas. Seen through a whole spectrum of media filters, the image of Karakozov's last stance even looks consistent enough to serve as proof of the past: Karakozov kneeled and so on, therefore he repented his crime, was reconciled with God, state, and tsar, and, by implication, betrayed the revolutionary cause.

But if Repin's image was doubly exposed, this media representation is too quick. We will have to look elsewhere yet. The truth is that at this moment in Russian history, the relation between religion and revolutionary politics had not been definitively decided at all. Rather than already having been divided into enemy camps, the two were still engaged, however tendentiously, in some form of a dialogue—something nowhere better seen than in the struggles of—and over—Karakozov's soul.

Karakozov's Faith

Born into an Orthodox family, Karakozov was an atheist by conviction. According to Nikolai Peterson, who was closer to him than were most others, Karakozov was open about his antireligious sentiments and "believed according to Renan,*" i.e. he did not believe.[19] During the trial, Karakozov also spoke plainly about his atheism, and tied it directly to the psychological condition that fomented his crime: "Had I been more religious, my condition would have led me onto a different path, in any case, not to suicide. But I was sick, nervous, and irreligious—so of course it was completely natural that the idea of suicide came to me."[20]

That matters may have been more ambiguous, however, is suggested by the following details. According to one acquaintance, for example (and as the reader will recall), when Karakozov was hospitalized in Moscow University Clinic, he sent his friends a letter requesting opium and containing the line: "If God doesn't help"—if God does not either cure or kill him—"the devil will."[21] Second, between being released from the clinic and leaving for Saint Petersburg, there was that trek to Trinity-Sergius Lavra Monastery: "Yes, exactly, when my condition was heavy, I went to the monastery of the Trinity."[22] (On the other hand, the monastery seems not to have been his final destination: "When my illness developed, I had had enough of life itself, and I didn't just want to go to Trinity, but even further, wherever.")[23] Lastly, on April 15, the Investigative Commission asked Karakozov to explain the meaning of a scrap of paper found in his abandoned hotel room and bearing the following markings in Karakozov's handwriting:

+ + +
Great is the Christian God.[24]

It had "no symbolic meaning," answered Karakozov, and was written "absolutely mechanically," but then added: "or maybe under the influence of the depressing ideas about my situation at the time."[25] Obviously, and even precisely because it was written "absolutely mechanically," the note does have symbolic meaning, ambiguous though it may be. In any case, all three details suggest that if Karakozov had any religious feelings

around the time of the assassination, they were probably un- or precon-
scious, and definitely in direct conflict with his stated convictions.

By mid-June, however, it was reported to Alexander II that religious
sentiments seemed to have stirred in Karakozov: "In his cell, he prays to
God on his knees for several hours."[26] Karakozov's prayers evidently became a known fact in official circles: "They say you've been praying," a
stern Count Panin addressed Karakozov during the trial, "which must
mean that you're a believer."[27] In a retrospective article, D. V. Stasov,
counsel to Ishutin, actually recalled seeing Karakozov pray: just before the
verdicts were read on August 31, Stasov noticed Karakozov kneeling in
the middle of the church that stood on the prison grounds: "He was completely alone and prayed with such zeal, he was so engrossed in his prayer,
that is, he was in a state of inspiration such as I have never encountered
in my whole life."[28] Finally, Karakozov's September 1 plea for clemency
from Alexander II reads: "I ask Your forgiveness as a Christian of a Christian and as a human being of a human being."[29] All of this certainly suggests that Karakozov experienced a conversion during his incarceration.
And yet there was one person who may have doubted the conversion's
sincerity: Karakozov's own priest.

The Priest Polisadov

On April 4, immediately following Karakozov's detention, Count Dmitry
A. Tolstoy, procurator of the Holy Synod, and soon to be appointed minister of education as part of the political reaction that followed the failed
assassination, noted that he had been asked to recommend "a priest for
the admonition of today's criminal."[30] For the next two days, the minutes
of the Investigative Commission included entries stating that "so that [the
criminal] would tell the truth . . . a priest admonished him for several
hours."[31] The name of this priest was Vasily Petrovich Polisadov* (1815–
78).[32]

Having completed his studies at the Moscow Ecclesiastical Academy,
the young Polisadov briefly taught at a seminary in Saint Petersburg before being dispatched abroad in 1847. During a decade spent primarily
in Geneva, Paris, and Berlin, Polisadov held clerical positions in various
Orthodox churches and, naturally enough, acquainted himself with the
cultural-intellectual climate of postrevolutionary Europe. The revolutionary violence of 1848 negatively impressed Polisadov, and his political
conservatism thereafter appears to have received further fortification
from his friendly ties with a number of German professors of a Right
Hegelian bent.[33] In 1858, he traded in his post as archpriest of the
Orthodox church at the imperial embassy in Berlin for a prestigious

appointment as professor of theology, logic, and psychology at Saint Petersburg University.[34] Things were going well for Polisadov: at roughly the same time, he was named archpriest of the Peter-Paul Cathedral, located on the grounds of the Peter-Paul Fortress. Here, his duties obligated him to preach to the convicts (including politicals), administer all religious rites, take confession, and, whenever necessary, admonish the recalcitrant, taciturn, and unrepentant.[35] It was in this last capacity, that is, to solicit a confession, that Polisadov was summoned to the headquarters of the Third Section following Karakozov's arrest.

Given the old legal status of confession as "the best evidence in the world" and the fact that it entailed automatic conviction, religious exhortation had been a central feature of pre-reform judicial procedure. Technically, the old procedure became illegal after the judicial reforms of 1864, but the government continued to take advantage of archaic practices. One of these was the religious admonition of those too obstinate to confess their crimes upon arrest. In Karakozov's case, however, the rather usual several hours of rebuke marked only the beginning of a complicated dialogical collision between the representatives of regal, religious, and revolutionary politics.

Overall, the paper trail detailing this dialogue is sparse, patchy, and full of gaps. Though a number of very remarkable sources survive, the vestiges primarily consist of bureaucratic memoranda. Polisadov's exhortations of Karakozov, for example, have not been preserved; he preferred to deliver much of his oratory extemporaneously.[36] Nevertheless, from a patchwork of sources, it is possible to create a sense of the dialogue that developed between the priest and the tsaricide. This dialogue, which was no doubt the most intimate of the last period of Karakozov's life, is the closest thing to a cipher for comprehending Karakozov's death—and especially so since Polisadov actively sought to shape the image of this death. So as to be able to decode this cipher, it will be useful to first briefly consider a few sources that will deepen our understanding of Polisadov.

Polisadov's Habits

Rather than restricting himself to the pulpit or altar, and his penchant for improvisation notwithstanding, Polisadov published a number of articles in religious journals that provide a composite look at his religious activities, views, and style, and help establish a picture against which to evaluate his relations with Karakozov. For example, "The Death of the Criminal Gudzevich," an article Polisadov wrote about his experiences with a notorious murderer, not only reveals his admonitory techniques— among them allusion ("Where is Abel your brother?"), shame ("God sees your heart's innermost thoughts; he knows the truth and will disclose it in front of everyone"), and the promises of 1 John 1:9 ("If we confess our sins, he is faithful and just, and will forgive our sins and cleanse us from all unrighteousness")—but also provides a comparative framework for Polisadov's approach to deciding if and when to reconcile sinners with God.[37]

Furthermore, because Polisadov repeatedly overstepped the boundaries proper to his designated station in life, he was on a number of occasions forced to write letters explaining his conduct to his superiors, and these hasty apologias, composed as they were under exceptional circumstances, contain a number of rhetorical tics that are extremely revealing of his beliefs, method, and character.

In 1859, for example, a rumor that Polisadov had confused his students with obscenities ("les expressions scabreuses") drove him to justify himself to the authorities. Admitting his slips of the tongue, he insisted they had been taken out of context: to prove the link between polytheism and immorality, Professor Polisadov explained, "I had to quote some passages from ancient writers."[38] The obscenities, it turns out, were Ovid's: the poet had somewhere asserted that it would be better if women remained outside the temple of Jupiter, given how many the god had already impregnated. Clearly, thus Polisadov's scholarly argument, little morality could be expected from a society whose deities were so sleazy that they seduced their own supplicants. At the letter's end, Polisadov added a last line of defense: "that phrase was said in Latin, and I did not translate it into Russian so as to hide its vile meaning."[39]

Polisadov's 1859 apologia is relevant in three respects. First, it reveals an instance where what the priest presumed to be self-evident logic was in fact neither transparent, nor acceptable. Second, it evidences that Polisadov was not in the habit of keeping silent about ideas he opposed; he overtly confronted them. Finally, it shows Polisadov purposefully using language as a protective curtain, a means of containment, and a screen with which to distinguish one community from another.

In 1863, Polisadov was called to justify himself once more because he had dared to discuss Chernyshevsky in a theology lecture at Saint Petersburg University. This second apologia actually creates the impression that it had been an altogether very unusual semester: Polisadov admits having delivered his lectures "with heat and some oratory" (in response to all too frequent complaints that "theology was being taught in a cold way") and—most unconventionally—having taught his entire course on religion via the history of philosophy.[40] His faux pas occurred during the last week of the semester, immediately following his—improvised, of course—lecture series on Hegel's *Religionsphilosophie*.[41]

The day of the incident, Polisadov was forced to acknowledge, he had lectured on the epoch's most infamous intellectual tradition. He had covered the Left Hegelians ("Feuerbach, Bruno Bauer, Strauss, Proudhon, Max Stirner"); expounded the history of scientific materialism; and discussed the enormously popular materialists Vogt, Moleschott, and Büchner. Going overtime, Polisadov's lecture had stretched itself out towards Russian materialism, whose proponents, however, unlike their European counterparts, he had left nameless. It was at this point that "some rude tongue" had yelled out Chernyshevsky's name and propelled Polisadov into a raging fit. Whatever its contents, this diatribe was the immediate cause of the second apologia. "But if professors of Berlin University do not find it malapropos to treat Bruno Bauer, Büchner, Karl Vogt, and others," Polisadov defended his explicit attack on the jailed radical, "then why do I not have the right to point to Chernyshevsky? Why do I, a professor-priest, not have the right to convince the youth to turn away from subversive ideas spread by underground literature?"[42] Besides, he argued, this event had taken place beyond the boundaries of regular academic time and in the midst of what he called "a sincere talk" (*iskrennaia beseda*) with his students.

To Polisadov's classical education, improvisation, and tricks of language, the second apologia allows us to add the following observations. The first is simply to note that he distinguishes between formal and informal times, that he refers to dialogue that seeks to convince as "sincere talk," and that such dialogue occurs during informal times. Second, Polisadov was not only familiar with canonical philosophy, but also well versed in the materialist knowledge of his ideological enemies. Both apologias reveal his conviction, in fact, that in order to disarm enemy ideology, it must first be openly engaged and then turned against itself. Third, Polisadov's letters convey a sense that he was a proud man: why is this well-traveled, learned professor-priest not guaranteed the same degree of trust as are his respected German colleagues? In sum, the second apologia thus confirms as patterns of behavior (1) Polisadov's assumption of dialogical rights that were not his to assume; (2) his unorthodox approach to rhetoric; and (3) a peculiar bearing that flashed up when he was under what he perceived as a threat.

Relations

Around the third week of April, a small flurry of memoranda passed back and forth among the uppermost echelons of Russian officialdom. Tracking Polisadov's visitation rights with Karakozov, this paper trail evidences a second, distinct phase in the relations between priest and tsaricide following the period of admonition at the Third Section. For the record, the names and positions of this paperwork's most relevant personages are: Aleksei Fedorovich Sorokin (governor of the Peter-Paul Fortress); Nikolai Vladimirovich Mezentsev (chief of staff of the gendarmerie and leading official of the Third Section); Petr Andreevich Shuvalov (commander of the gendarmerie and head of the Third Section); and, a bit further in the background, Murav'ev and Alexander II.

On April 19, once Murav'ev had ordered Karakozov's transfer to the Peter-Paul Fortress, Mezentsev formally requested of Sorokin, its governor, that he take the strictest care in locking up the prisoner in one of the cells of the fortress and instruct the guards to allow the priest Polisadov plus member of the Investigative Commission Colonel Losev admission to Karakozov "at all times."[43] Whether the idea that Polisadov and Karakozov would continue to meet originated with Murav'ev, Mezentsev, or even the priest himself is impossible to prove. It appears, however, that Sorokin hesitated to fulfill the unusual request and first addressed himself to someone of higher rank—probably Mezentsev's direct superior, Count Shuvalov—for official consent. He received the highest possible permission: on April 20, Shuvalov first humbly addressed himself to Alexander II and then, having obtained the requisite imperial scribble, sent word to Sorokin.[44]

Thus duly informed, Sorokin notified the tsar that Karakozov had been secured and only then responded to Mezentsev's initial request.[45] Though the cells of the Peter-Paul Fortress were separated by thick enough walls, he wrote to Mezentsev, they were already stuffed with prisoners arrested in connection with April 4; Karakozov would be best kept segregated and in the complete isolation provided by the Alekseevsky Ravelin. Here, Polisadov and Losev would be freely admitted.[46]

Such access to a prisoner in what was known as the "secret house" of the Alekseevsky Ravelin was unprecedented in the history of this most dreaded of tsarist prisons. Sorokin's April 24 follow-up report to Shuvalov, moreover, shows that not just the fact, but also the format and content of the meetings between priest and tsaricide were extraordinary. Sorokin reports that despite a strict proscription against unchaperoned admission, given that Polisadov and Losev had been authorized to visit Karakozov in order to obtain from him "an explanation of the crime," he had given orders that they be permitted to meet with Karakozov privately (*na edine*).[47]

In fact since the time of Peter the Great, priests were required by law, on penalty of losing their robes, to inform the authorities of any details related to crimes revealed during confession. When Sorokin speaks of "an explanation of the crime," therefore, he complies with legal protocol. But while Mezentsev's original memo had indeed requested that Sorokin allow Polisadov and Losev to gain access to Karakozov "at any time," it neither explicitly mentioned "an explanation of the crime," nor suggested that Polisadov and Losev meet with Karakozov privately.[48] These important addenda are only accounted for if we turn to Polisadov's April 23 report of his first visit.

Polisadov opens with an informative account of his activities with Karakozov:

> The first time [I visited him] for a simple conversation (*dlia prostogo sobesedovaniia*), and the second, for a service . . . after which, in accordance with the ceremony, a speech was given . . . with the goal of arousing in him faith in God . . . who is always prepared to forgive the sincerely repenting sinner . . .
>
> As far as the future is concerned, I intend to visit the criminal three times a week—and if You will permit it, then even more frequently—mornings from 9–10 and evenings around 6–7. It will be useful to report to Your Excellency that each visit will begin with a private service (liturgies in the mornings; vespers in the evenings) and finish with a sermon, different each time, but all on the theme that the Lord Christ extends his merciful embrace to each sincerely repentant sinner and on the terms of a sincere repentance. At the time of these activities I will be in vestments, and the criminal needs to be on his feet.[49]

All the talk occurs in accordance with official church regulations: ceremonies, rituals, speeches, sermons, Polisadov in sacerdotal robes, and Karakozov, hour upon hour, on his feet, being talked at.

In the next paragraph, however, Polisadov writes, "After that, I will talk with (*besedovat's*) the criminal specifically about his great crime, inducing him to an open explanation (*otkrovennoe ob'iasnenie*)." He adds, "If he reveals to me something suitable for the judicial explanation (*sudebnoe raz'iasnenie*) of his crime, I will ask and persuade him to inform whomever it may concern about everything." First, we note, Polisadov strips the dialogue of certain formalities: "After that," i.e. after the activities requiring that Polisadov be in sacerdotal robes and Karakozov on his feet, implies that, during what follows, those regulations no longer apply. Second, the use of the verb *besedovat's* eases the formality of the situation, as it means "to talk/converse with"; it is, in fact, the first time Karakozov is being talked *with* ("s" in "besedovat's," means "with"). Additionally, Polisadov seems to differentiate between an "open explanation" (*otkrovennoe ob'iasnenie*) and a more formal "judicial explanation" (*sudebnoe raz'iasnenie*). This suggests that the relevance of these talks stretches beyond whatever details reveal themselves as suitable for the court, and that even while he cooperates with the government, Polisadov sees this politico-judicial dimension as a narrower aspect of his much broader religious duties.[50]

Polisadov then distances himself even further from his bureaucratic superiors:

But in order not to appear to him like a person who is, however spiritual, too official or even an investigative police officer, I wish, in my personal conversations with him (*v chastnykh moikh s nim sobesedovaniiakh*), to enter into discussion (*rassushdenie:* reasoning, debate, argument, discourse) of science, literature, art, their various tendencies, and finally [of] when science and literature act beneficially and when destructively on the young generation and society. Also I would hope to permit myself to discuss (*rassushdat'*) the social condition of society. All these discussions (*rassushdeniia*) (that is, about science, literature, art, society), conducted in a strict Christian and conservative direction, will have the goal of changing the mind of the criminal, of changing the ruinous theories from which sprang, in my opinion, his crime, and which he, of course, has not yet repudiated.[51]

Polisadov is proposing to engage Karakozov in dialogue. Yes, "in a strict Christian and conservative direction," but mentioning this only suggests there are other, competing perspectives. After the sermons, what will Polisadov and Karakozov be discussing? Science, literature, art, society, and theory. It is noteworthy that on April 23, after nearly three weeks of torturous interrogations, Karakozov, whom Western historiography has branded a mentally unstable half-wit, had "not yet repudiated" the ruinous theories. But if Polisadov is asking for permission to hold a dialogue, he must think there exists a possibility that dialogue be fruitful. Lastly, it should be briefly noted that Polisadov's goal stretches beyond the elucidation of the crime into nothing less than changing Karakozov's mind and theories through dialogue, and doing so in the course of a time marked as informal—conduct that Polisadov's apologias revealed as the modus operandi proper to a direct engagement of enemy ideology. For Polisadov, evidently, the way to Karakozov's soul is via his mind.

Polisadov concludes his letter with the suggestion that, "In order to induce the criminal to a sincere explanation (*iskrennoe ob'iasnenie*) with me, it would be useful if the guard and his assistants let us talk privately (*besedovat' na edine*)." Thus, we find the request for the private meetings between the priest and the tsaricide that reappears a day later, approved, in Sorokin's April 24 note to Shuvalov.[52] Polisadov's idea of the content and purpose of these visits, however, clearly exceeded that of the officials.

On May 2, 1866, Polisadov wrote a second—and, as it turned out, last—report, which was dispatched to Shuvalov along with an accompanying note from Sorokin.[53] Since April 23, the priest reported, he had met with Karakozov six times for one and a half to two hours of services, sermons, and private talks. Polisadov could not say how successful he had been, but what he could say was that Karakozov had been so thoroughly admonished that "all his religious, moral, and intellectual needs . . . must have received complete satisfaction." Perhaps it had even been excessive. At the end of this May 2 letter, Polisadov suggests halting his visits to Karako-zov for a period of eight to ten days:

> Presently being afraid of the surfeit of spiritual-intellectual food for the per-son, generally weak in faith and doctrine, given to my spiritual care, I would consider it useful to give him time, so to say, to digest everything he has been told, so that he, in the words of the prophet, will become aware of the smoothness of listening to the words of God, prayers, and discussions sober-ing for the mind.[54]

However, this interruption, after which Polisadov intended to take up his care of Karakozov's soul again "with complete zeal and dedication," turned out to be the end of all private discussions as Polisadov had de-scribed them in his April 23 report. The meetings were either adminis-tratively curtailed, or suspended because during the months of May and June, both Karakozov and Polisadov suffered health problems. (Karako-zov, as the reader will recall, was eventually even medically excused from questioning for a brief period, and Polisadov was away for weeks while taking the waters.)[55] For what remained of Karakozov's life, the priest and the tsaricide would continue to meet in church and sometimes in the pri-vacy of the tsaricide's cell, but never again informally.

Faux Pas

Fast-forward now to September 4, the day after Karakozov's execution, when Polisadov hurriedly took up his pen and wrote the following letter to Count Shuvalov:

> Your Highness, Worshipful Lord, Count Petr Andreevich!
> Yesterday, when, having performed the last pastoral duty for the criminal Karakozov, I moved away toward a group of people standing on a special podium, one of the military gentlemen asked me, "Did the criminal repent sincerely?" to which I laconically replied, "That is the confessor's secret."
> That reply was given by me because I really did not recognize You (Your appearance is much changed, High Count), and because a clearer and more satisfactory answer would also be heard by someone in the crowded group and be interpreted in a manner unfavorable for my pastoral modesty.
> Soon afterward I was told that Your Highness had posed that question.
> Knowing what great assistance you have shown me in the pastoral guid-ance of Karakozov, I hasten to satisfy Your Highness's wish, expressed in Your question: did he repent sincerely? Not in the least afraid of violating the Divine seal of Confession, I can announce—to Your Highness or any-one else who asks me about Karakozov's last days, not out of sheer curios-

ity, but out of a Christian concern for his soul and eternal fate—that the criminal died with salvific Christian dispositions, beliefs, and feelings. And that upon hearing his detailed, most seriously conducted confession there slumbered in my soul a weight that had been pressuring me especially in recent times on account of a thought that consistently pursued me: Will the distinctive will of this grave criminal entirely give itself up to my guidance and will he fulfill the terms of a Christian confession? Of course, in the words of the Apostle Paul: What man knows the things of a man, save the spirit of man which is in him? (1 Corinthians 2:11) and in the words of the Prophet, only God feels the heart and the inward parts of people. But all the same, Karakozov's overall conduct over the last two days allows me to preserve the persuasion that his confession was not vain (*nesuetnyi*), so that I, relieved in my conscience, thanked the Lord Jesus for saving the lost sheep, and dared [or decided, *reshilsia*] to teach Karakozov the Holy Secret of Christ, toward eternal life.

The comforting result of my efforts to save Karakozov's soul I owe to Your Highness, and to Your predecessor Prince Andreevich [*sic* Prince V. A. Dolgorukov*], who gave me the right to go into the cell of the criminal and, what had never before been permitted, to talk with him privately. That was in April. Consequently, since mid-June, of course with Your permission, they took Karakozov to the Kommendantsky Church for the divine service; even though I did not have the possibility to properly converse (*besedovat'*) with the criminal about the ulcers of his soul, I had the possibility to preach the New Testament with respect to his condition. All that gave me the possibility to turn Karakozov toward better, salvific feelings. Giving Your Highness the humblest gratitude for your timely and kind assistance in my difficult service for the benefit of the soul of the great but repentant sinner, I dare to hope that Your Excellency will not abandon me and deny me assistance with respect to other political convicts kept in the Alekseevsky Ravelin and in prison. As for me, I am wholeheartedly ready to serve the good and salvation of their souls.

All-humble, diligent, and devout,

Vasily Polisadov, Archpriest of Peter-Paul Cathedral.[56]

There is more to this simple, albeit tense, apology than meets the eye. What follows will suggest a reading of Polisadov's short passage from the scaffold to the podium as a metaphor for his hazardous dwelling simultaneously in two conflicting realms—namely the world of spirit and the world of the flesh, God and Man, religion and politics—and explains how this condition directly affected the priest's relationship with the tsaricide.

Imagine Polisadov solemnly descending the scaffold and still wrapped up in the ceremony of the occasion when "one of the military gentlemen" pierces the silence with a strange, even insolent question: given that Polisadov has just administered rites that are predicated on repentance, the blunt question challenges Polisadov's honor and honesty. The archpriest has his protocol, too, and within the spheres of religion and etiquette, his curt retort is quite correct. But he forgets where he is: after the ceremony, after his descent from the platform, after his movement toward the crowd, Polisadov walks in the world, and among men of the world. Misfortune dictated that the man he arrogantly dismissed happened to be not only his superior, but also the empire's most powerful official.

The actions that follow are easily understood: Shuvalov's identity is revealed to Polisadov, who then hastens to apologize, lest the privileges he has gained over the last few months be taken from him again. The content of the letter thus reads as follows: "After all you've done for me, yes, I will tell you; yes, he died a Christian; I was worried for a while (after all, who but God really knows what goes on inside a person's mind?), but the criminal's behavior indicated that he was sincere, so I administered him the last sacraments." And thus emerged what Polisadov intended to communicate to Shuvalov: a portrait of a humble priest who may have momentarily forgotten himself, but essentially knows his place in a strict hierarchy. There is no doubt about the respective placement of Shuvalov and Polisadov: Your Highness, all you've done for me, what had never been allowed before, please do not deny me your assistance in the future, etc. Read with this slant, the text from 1 Corinthians further deflates any impression of priestly pride. In contrast to the previous day's arrogance ("That is the confessor's secret"), Polisadov now presents an image of humility ("What man knows the things of a man, save the spirit of man which is in him? . . . only God feels the heart and the inward parts of people"). This way, Polisadov not only hesitates to express certainty on the state of Karakozov's soul, but also relegates responsibility for its eventual salvation to the count. In the end, it was Shuvalov who made salvation possible, while Polisadov merely performed a service that was expected of him as a servant of the state, church, and God.

But a very different Polisadov stares us in the face when we check his reference to Paul's first letter to the Corinthians, Chapter 2:

1. When I came to you, brethren, I did not come proclaiming to you the testimony of God in lofty words or wisdom . . .

6. Yet among the mature we do impart wisdom, although it is not a wisdom of this age or of the rulers of this age, who are doomed to pass away . . .

9. *What no eye has seen, nor ear heard*
nor the heart of man conceived,
what God has prepared for those who love him,

10. God has revealed to us through the Spirit. For the Spirit searches everything, even the depths of God.

11. For what person knows a man's thoughts except the spirit of the man which is in him? So also no one comprehends the thoughts of God except the Spirit of God . . .

14. The unspiritual man does not receive the gifts of the Spirit of God, for they are folly to him, and he is not able to understand them because they are spiritually discerned.

15. The spiritual man judges all things, but is himself to be judged by no one.[57]

Whether Polisadov quoted from 1 Corinthians coincidentally or cunningly, this chapter not only contains his defense, but also elucidates the archpriest's understanding of the world, the W/word, and its purpose—again, essential for assessing his relationship with Karakozov.

Wherein consisted Polisadov's verbal transgression? Though in the world of the Church, "the confessor's secret" is but a truism, it offends in the world of men. Given Russian law and the fact that Polisadov was dealing with a state criminal, factually the phrase could even approach a criminal offense. But more broadly, Paul's first letter to the Corinthians suggests that, speaking in the world, a man of God is practically guaranteed to offend: "I did not come proclaiming to you the testimony of God in lofty words or wisdom . . . my speech and my message were not in plausible words of wisdom." Reading Polisadov with 1 Corinthians, it becomes apparent that the priest's reality is split in two, and the division indicated by a linguistic barrier. The truth of spiritual statements is *eo ipso* unintelligible in the world, for the wisdom of God is folly to the unspiritual man and misunderstood by the rulers of this age—including Shuvalov.

And yet Shuvalov, though "doomed to pass away," may nevertheless be judging Polisadov—in an explicit inversion of the Pauline dictum that "The spiritual man judges all things, but is himself to be judged by no one." A world where a spiritual man must answer not only to God, but also "to military gentlemen" is an inverted world, and a world that places the spiritual man in a very awkward position vis-à-vis God. Polisadov seems to have suffered acutely from this inversion: Sorokin's archive includes several letters expressing Polisadov's severe distress at seeing his religious authority challenged by state power. Once, for example, upon being told that Sorokin had ordered the rearrangement of certain relics in the Peter-Paul Fortress, Polisadov was so distraught that he became ill: "I had to move away from the holy altar and, having refreshed my face and head with cold water, to sink down in a chair for several minutes"; another time, Polisadov formally requested of Sorokin, who had twice publicly scolded him, that he spare him from further "humiliation."[58] Of course, considering Polisadov's seasoning of his apology with a little "Your Excellency" here, a little "Your Highness" there, his implicit references to a Pauline distaste of "lofty words or wisdom" might still provoke a frown, also because surely one was not appointed archpriest of the Peter-Paul Fortress without possession of the requisite talents in the socio-political realm. Nonetheless, Polisadov constantly and uncomfortably negotiated between his commitments to God and the world, and the letter to Shuvalov evidences the peril and unease of the priest's service to two masters—a fact that directly challenged his work with Karakozov.

Why, in a letter concerning the "state" of the tsaricide's soul, does the priest's own psychological state begin to obscure everything else? Why does Polisadov presume that details about the condition of his own soul ("in my soul slumbered a weight") amplify the sincerity of Karakozov's confession? Why confess the turmoil of his own psychology ("a thought that consistently pursued me") to Shuvalov, a man he obviously does not know well? The tension with which the letter is wrought cannot only be explained by Polisadov's nervous compensation for his political faux pas; rather, the archpriest had been pursued by doubts of his own capacity, challenged by the conditions in which he was supposed to perform his "difficult service"—and by Karakozov himself. Beyond the apologetic text and insolent subtext of his dialogue with Shuvalov, Polisadov-servant-of-the-state also dialogues with Polisadov-servant-of-God, and seeks to convince himself—and God—that, given the circumstances, he performed his service as best he could.

Consider once more the conditions of his service. Polisadov had been allowed to visit Karakozov, even—"what had never before been permitted"—to speak with him privately. He had not, however, been allowed "to properly converse with the criminal about the ulcers of his soul." Since "the ulcers of his soul" cannot but refer to the painful digestive results of the "ruinous theories," the letter suggests that Polisadov's April 23 request to enter into discussions about science, art, literature, and society had been denied—conceivably by Shuvalov himself. Polisadov had not been allowed, in other words, to engage the enemy directly. Instead, he had been restricted to admonishing him. But after nearly half a year of preaching the gospel, Polisadov's soul was still weighed down by the resistance he sensed in Karakozov's "distinctive will." Will he submit? Has he changed his mind? *Did* the criminal repent sincerely? Absent dialogue (or rather, dialectics), Polisadov hesitated, granted Paul the authoritative word on the riddle of the tsaricide's soul, and left dangling a revealing reference, or clue, to his own conscience.

His own—and that of the Church. Given that Polisadov was an official, albeit peculiarly progressive, representative of the Orthodox Church, ultimately his doubts about Karakozov are a measure of religion's attitude to revolutionary politics in general. If Polisadov was nervous, this was because Karakozov represented the moment when nihilism—which for the Church meant, first and foremost, atheism—violently attacked the Russian autocracy, which the Church was sworn to defend. For Polisadov, in fact, nihilism and the political violence that would become known as revolutionary terrorism were directly related: the "ruinous theories" were the cause of Karakozov's crime, and because these theories were everywhere, his was possibly the first of many such crimes. So a lot was at stake for the Church, for if Karakozov repented, this would mean the Church could still defend the State from modernity. Polisadov's doubt is thus essentially meaningful, no less so than his conviction that the only sure way to get Karakozov to repent was to get into the tsaricide's head via very modern means: both suggest that religion suspected that it was facing a new, as yet unknown enemy. It might be possible to defeat this enemy, but it would take some fairly unorthodox measures: talking to political criminals about science and art, lecturing to theology students about Chernyshevsky, and so on. In recognizing this, the Church was markedly more progressive than the State, which only knew to respond to the new by means of the old. Hereby, in the view of the Church, the State not only fueled the fire of the opposition, but also tied religion's hands in the midst of its battle with revolution.

Letters

Finally, another way in which Polisadov's reference to Paul is very illuminating is in terms of understanding his approach to the souls of his criminals. Because "[Karakozov's] confession was not vain [*nesuetnaia*; also empty, rushed, or fussy]," writes Polisadov, "I dared [or decided, *reshilsia*] to teach Karakozov the Holy Secret of Christ, toward eternal life."[59] His 1863 portrayal of the criminal Gudzevich is slightly more elaborate, its tone bolder, but the logic of the priest is the same here as it will be for Karakozov:

> [Gudzevich's] confession was conducted without any hurry (*bez vsiakoi pospeshnosti*). . . . Thanks to such repentance . . . I absolved (*razreshil*) him from all sins. . . . I dared [or decided, *reshilsia*] acquaint him with Jesus Christ's Secret, into eternal life.[60]

A temporal function—speed—indicates the sincerity of repentance; the psycho-spiritual distance from crime is measured by duration. Perhaps the link between haste and insincerity is self-evident. Nevertheless, it seems worthwhile to underline that a penitent confession is free of rush because it has nowhere it needs to get to and has no time to run out of; freedom means freedom from time, and repentance delivers a different time signature that allows for confession to unfold in its own time and in time with itself.

Whenever Polisadov reconciles a criminal with God and the world, the priest is thus called to make a temporal judgment that, at least to human eyes, determines the fate of the criminal's eternity. Polisadov bears this power (vested in him by Christ) to decide eternal life and death, yet interestingly enough Polisadov's writings reveal that each time he must so decide, this decision is a leap of faith, and that each time he must answer for so momentous a wager, he defers to Paul. In fact, whenever Polisadov must defend himself, provide proof, or take a leap of faith, he reaches specifically for the Pauline Epistles, and so the text from 1 Corinthians in his letter to Shuvalov is no mere chance citation.

Even with the limited number of sources related to Polisadov that have survived, there are no less than three examples of this rhetorical tic, two of which are specifically related to decisions of life and death. First, "It was not given to us by God to penetrate conscience," Polisadov sums up at the end of an essay that had required of him to publicly decide on the moral character of Gudzevich, "but if *in Jesus Christ all God's promises are "yes" and amen,* that is, true and immutable, then we must believe without a doubt that the criminal Gudzevich died a Christian death."[61] The passage sourcelessly emphasized in Polisadov's text is actually from Paul's second letter to the Corinthians 1:19–20, whose full text reads: "For the Son of God, Jesus Christ, whom we proclaimed among you, Silvanus and Timothy and I, was not 'Yes and No'; but in him it is always 'Yes.' For in him every one of God's promises is a 'Yes,'"—that is to say, it may be trusted that, in Christ, for once, things are as they appear to be. Second, in the above-mentioned 1863 apologia to a superior at the Saint Petersburg University, Polisadov also justifies himself via the apostle: "Forgive my insolence! I have great sorrow and unceasing anguish in my heart, I say along with the apostle Paul."[62] This text is from Romans 9 and is immediately preceded by: "I am speaking the truth in Christ—I am not lying; my conscience confirms it by the Holy Spirit." (Rom. 9:1–2) The last example, of course, is the September 4 letter to Shuvalov, in which Polisadov justifies his decision to absolve Karakozov by citing the authoritative wisdom of the apostle: "Of course, in the words of the Apostle Paul: What man knows the things of a man, save the spirit of man which is in him?" What these examples reveal is that these decisions, which in temporal terms are questions of life and death, are absolutely groundless: no more—but also no less—than leaps of faith, in fact. And this means, of course, that they are exceedingly difficult to narrate and/or justify.

Polisadov's "along with the apostle Paul" may be read, perhaps, as a replica of Paul's own unshakeable habit of using the expression "speaking in Christ" to couch in humble terms what might otherwise appear as his insolence and to prove, whenever he must, his sincerity. A verse from Romans, for example, reads: "Nevertheless on some points I have written to you rather boldly. . . . In Christ Jesus, then, I have reason to boast of my work for God" (Rom. 15:15–17). And in a verse from 2 Corinthians, Paul writes, "For we are not peddlers of God's word like so many; but in Christ we speak as persons of sincerity" (2 Cor. 2:17).

In light of Polisadov's strategic withdrawals behind the apostle, especially this last sentence from 2 Corinthians is very interesting; it is followed by the opening lines of chapter 3: "Are we beginning to commend ourselves again? Surely we do not need, as some do, letters of recommendation to you or from you, do we? You yourselves are our letter, written on our hearts, to be known and read by all" (2 Cor. 3:1–2). This indeed seems like language proper to the type of man who, to justify himself, refers not to law, but his conviction/Christ. But however sincere he may have been "along with the apostle," Polisadov was also often simply too proud—and perhaps not quite as daring in his faith as Paul. Evidently, besides being haunted by the possibility that Karakozov's "distinctive will" would not defer to his spiritual authority, Polisadov fretted that even if it did, this submission would not be written plain enough "to be known and read by all." It is perhaps only partly surprising that this priest felt he needed an *actual* "letter of recommendation" to prove the tsaricide's repentance, and so the archival holdings include the following, remarkable document from Karakozov:

> Thinking of the approaching hour of my death and that I shall soon stand before God's dreadful court, I, besides the secret confession before my spiritual Father, dared [or decided, *reshil'sia*], for the pacification of my conscience, to put forth in this written explanation my last feelings and humble requests: I die with gratitude to God for all his gifts . . .

Thus wrote not Karakozov, however, but Polisadov as Karakozov.[63] This "forgery," which the tsaricide was meant to sign (but did not), stands as a lasting testament to the signature doubt of the priest in the ways of his God.

Not forgetting to thank himself for his "zealous care" of the tsaricide, Polisadov has Karakozov apologizing to God, tsar, and country; pleading with the young generation not to follow his example; begging forgiveness of the Investigative Commission and Supreme Criminal Court for having "tortured them so much with my lies, insincerity, and all sorts of evasions"; and even waxing lyrical over tears that were apparently shed by the president of the court, Prince Gagarin, when he pronounced the verdict: "I would like to gather [these tears], like costly pearls, take them into the grave, and place them in front of the Lord God myself."[64] Finally, in a phrase that hurls out the question whether it is possible for a Christian to write it and remain a Christian, Polisadov has Karakozov say to the tsar: "I believe that your Angelic heart would have pardoned me, if the highest justice did not demand of You to reveal on me, a fiend, Your lawful truth," in other words, if murder was not necessary to prove the existence of temporal law.[65]

Probably, the last-cited line actually referred to the answer the tsaricide had heard from the tsar in response to a final plea for clemency. In response to, "I ask Your forgiveness as a Christian of a Christian and as a human being of a human being," Karakozov had been told that "as a

Christian, His Majesty forgives you, but as Emperor, he cannot."[66] Indeed Karakozov's death sentence was not just punishment commensurate to his crime. (Arguably, it was even incommensurate: Karakozov had not killed the tsar, after all.) Rather, tsar and court justified rejecting Karakozov's plea by underlining the need to prevent future assassination attempts "through the example of an execution" (*primerom kazni*).[67] Karakozov's death, that is, was to be exemplary. And the exceptional nature of this death was evidently well understood. Wrote one eyewitness whose letter was intercepted by the Third Section:

> Such things had not happened on Smolensk Square yet. Sometimes it happens that they cart someone to the gallows and tell him, listen, we're going to hang you, then they bring him up to the scaffold and even put a rope around his neck, but then, after some three minutes, they say, just kidding, we're not going to hang you; we're sending you into lifelong exile.[68]

In deciding to kill Karakozov, both the executive and the judiciary branches of the state authenticated his challenge as a real exception. Karakozov's execution was thus high politics: it exposed the figure of the revolutionary as enemy, as a type of being it was henceforth lawful to kill. Politically, perhaps, how Karakozov faced death therefore mattered rather less than the very fact of his death: since it represented a rule of which it was also an example, Karakozov's death was paradigmatic by definition.

The End, As It Was in the Beginning

On the scaffold, while an official was pronouncing the justice of a murder that a priest agreed was necessary to prove the law, Karakozov could not hold up his head: "the whole time it was heavily bent to the side," wrote someone for *Golos*.[69] Other eyewitnesses confirmed his moral weakness, but *Golos*, singularly, added the following description of Karakozov's last moments:

> When the priest left the scaffold, the verdict began to be carried out. The *armiak* the criminal had been wearing was taken from him. In that minute it was as if vitality stirred in him; he lifted his head and straightened his hair, though his face was pale and his lips twitched convulsively. They blindfolded him with a white shawl and dressed him in a long-sleeved, hooded, white shroud . . . [70]

"My death," he knew, "will be an example and inspiration."

CONCLUSION

The Point of April 4, 1866

This book has shown that the birth of terrorism was intimately related to modernity—economically, politically, socially, and culturally. Now, therefore, it should be possible to discern that this violence essentially expresses the spirit of things modern, a spirit that senses that the world is historical, that history is contingent, and that contingency provides the chance for change. Modernity denotes historicity, above all, and terrorism knows it—for terrorism is not only modern, but self-consciously so: it is violence perpetrated by those who think they can deliver the future from the past by intervening in the present, because in their time, every now promises the new.

Nothing New

But suppose someone says, "There is nothing modern about terrorism, and nothing to be gained from arguing that there is. Arguments about modernity just fall for the modern era's own hype about historical change, and then are blinded to precedents and permanence. Terrorism is in fact an old violence: there are countless early examples to counter the claim that it is new."

Generally, what animates this—quite common—conviction is the long history of conflict between the powerful and the powerless, and their respective resort to illicit violence to either maintain or alter the balance of power. On this reading, terrorism is a weapon wielded by whomever, and whenever it erupts—be it in times ancient, medieval, or modern—it is the reemergence of barbarism in the midst of civilization. Of course most historians would not defend their views with such essentialisms. Rather, if and when they hold that terrorism is nothing modern, it is because they see strategic precedents stretching back to the earliest of times.

Tyrannicide, for example, was politically and philosophically authorized among the ancients in the event of misrule and usurpation: its purpose was to reconstitute legitimate rule.[1] "Sic semper tyrannis!" ("Thus ever to tyrants!"), legendarily cried Brutus—the classic case—as he and his co-conspirators fell upon Caesar (thereby coining a catchphrase for regicides ever after). When it emerged in the nineteenth century, indeed, terrorism mostly meant assassinating various VIPs, and therefore it sometimes seems as if terrorists followed in the footsteps of traditional tyrannicides.[2] But there is an important difference between the premodern and the modern regicide: the former attacks the king, the latter, kingship. Or, as one scholar has put it, "The assassin attacks those who are corrupting a system, the terrorist attacks a system that has already corrupted everyone."[3] Terrorism, unlike tyrannicide, seeks radically to reinvent the world; it is revolutionary, and so it is modern.

Even more frequently cited as "proto-terrorists" than the tyrannicides, however, are the first century Zealots-*Sicarii* and the eleventh century Nizari Ismaili (aka *Hashshashin,* whence the term *assassin*): both used public, high-profile assassinations to induce fear and provoke change. This certainly seems similar to terrorism, but it is important to note that the Zealots and the Assassins were religious groups—Jewish and Muslim respectively—from antiquity and the Middle Ages, which is to say that they stood in a premodern, nonsecular relationship to the concept of history: theirs was not what Walter Benjamin called "empty, homogeneous time," nor did they have an "awareness that they are about to make the continuum of history explode."[4] They were not driven by a despair born of the threat of historical superfluousness, nor did they fear exclusion from the coming community being constructed elsewhere on earth. Hence also their violence was not individual voluntarism: it emerged from a closed caste and did not mean to inspire, via factual propaganda, a whole series of singular assassinations.

There are other examples—and a few more will be taken up below—but none that can properly prove that terrorism is old—or even just "older" than this book claims. To take the most obvious one, the Terror of the French Revolution (1793–94) is not a precursor to terrorism, either. The Terror and terrorism do share some important and specifically modern characteristics—revolutionary consciousness, a secular concept of history, violence perpetrated under the sign of the spectacle—and of course, confusingly, terminology. But this should not obscure their differences. The Terror, famously, was legal—September 5, 1793, the Jacobins made "terror the order of the day"—and, together with virtue, officially functioned as the principle of popular government in revolution (Robespierre): it executed—and accelerated—change already in motion.[5] Terrorism, by contrast, was illegitimate, illegal, and irregular violence that, temporally speaking, meant to short-circuit the historical current and *ignite* historical change. In more ways than one, then, the Terror and terrorism belong to different times.

Terrorism, in sum, neither existed in an unchanging form since time immemorial, nor developed over time into its present form. It is a violence that emerged in modernity, first of all, and to understand its essence it must be differentiated from what are posited as its precedents. Unless there is a demonstrable connection between past and present—that is, unless there exists a reception history—"prototypes" only establish a false sense of continuity and, more harmfully, cover over those rare ruptures whence emerges the new.

Inertia of (Narrative) Form

A qualitative difference sets April 4, 1866, apart even from historically proximate violence. Unlike the April 14, 1865 assassination of United States President Lincoln, for example, April 4, 1866 was not staged as a traditional tyrannicide; if Karakozov did not sum up his violence as did John Wilkes Booth with a theatrical "Sic semper tyrannis!" this was because he hardly aimed to avenge a *particular* abuse of power by the Russian autocrat. Nor did April 4, 1866, structurally parallel the April 30, 1866 attempt on the life of the belligerent Bismarck, by means of which the republican nationalist Ferdinand Cohen Blind tried to prevent the Austro-Prussian War. April 4, 1866, was no corrective tinkering with an otherwise agreeable or partially still viable political order: Karakozov meant not to negotiate with the autocracy, but to eliminate it altogether.

That the radical nature of Karakozov's act has often gone unnoticed is shown by the obstinacy with which a particular account of his crime has persisted in the historical literature: "You cheated the people," or some such phrase, a just-detained Karakozov reportedly told Alexander II. Referring to despotic misrule—specifically, the tsar's betrayal of the promise contained in the 1861 abolition of serfdom—this is a phrase proper to a tyrant-killer, and because of this phrase the logic of vengeance has always structured narratives of Karakozov's attempt.[6]

The Soviet historian A. A. Shilov, to cite only the account that was the basis for most of the later histories, has the assassin first volunteer the phrase, "Your Highness, you offended the peasants!" as if Karakozov had somehow meant to chivalrously defend the people's wounded honor via a gentlemanly duel. He then adds that, "according to other witnesses the conversation was as follows . . . :

"Why did you shoot at me?"
"Because you swindled the people—you promised them land, but did not give them any."[7]

Shilov did not footnote this dialogue, but his source was probably either Khudiakov's *Notes of a Karakozovist*, or the testimony given by a peasant named Nikifor Fedotov. Khudiakov presents the following scene:

"Fools! I did this for you!" he said [to the crowd], "And you don't understand."
"Are you Polish?" the emperor asked him.
"No, pure Russian," Karakozov answered calmly.
"Why did you shoot at me?"
"Because you promised the people land, but did not give them any."[8]

But unless Khudiakov was an eyewitness (which would make him a co-conspirator, and this, as we have seen, is not at all certain), these phrases do not originate with him. "Fools! I did this for you!" for example, is probably a rewriting of the rumors reported in *Moskovskie Vedomosti* on April 7, 1866, that Karakozov, when the crowd moved to detain him, cried, "Guys, but I wanted to do this for you."[9] Khudiakov could have intercepted these same rumors or even read the paper; he was arrested the afternoon of April 7. But no witness, in any case, ever reported hearing either this outcry, or this exchange.

The eyewitness Fedotov, however, did tell investigative officers that he had overheard the following:

ALEXANDER II: "What do you want?"
KARAKOZOV: "What kind of freedom did you make?" (*Vy kakuiu voliu sdelali?*)[10]

Nevertheless, it is probably apocryphal, this tyrannicidal motive, if only because nowhere else did Karakozov explain his crime by reference to Alexander II's personal responsibility for the failed 1861 abolition of serfdom, and certainly not in this kind of language ("Vy kakuiu voliu sdelali?" is awkward not only in translation). Rather, this dialogue reveals what was at that time an imaginable crime for the eyewitness Fedotov, whose status as a peasant is all the more relevant in this context.

The trial records of the Karakozov case, in any event, present a very different account of what happened. According to the defense speech delivered by Karakozov's lawyer, when Alexander II asked his assassin what he wanted, the latter's answer consisted of a single word:

"Nothing."[11]

In court, no one contested this story, which was based on the eyewitness accounts of Karakozov's arresting officers, Stepan Zabolotin and Lukian Slesarchuk.[12]

Only one historian, Adam Ulam, has presented this version in narrating the Karakozov case:

> What was the point of this whole plot, which—probably even more than its successful repetition on March 1, 1881—changed the course of Russia's history? What did the people who inspired Karakozov really intend to accomplish? To repeat: despite all the legend to the contrary, the would-be assassin's only words when seized and asked by the emperor what he wanted were "Nothing, nothing."[13]

In Ulam's account, Karakozov's response only showed how senseless was April 4, 1866. A different reading of this "nothing," however, is much more to the point.

Nihil

There exists good evidence to prove that Alexander II *personally* meant nothing to Karakozov *politically*. Member of the Investigative Commission Cherevin, for example, remembered Karakozov saying: "I cannot but feel sorry that I made an attempt on the life of a ruler like Alexander II, but it was not at him that I shot; I took action against the emperor in him—and this I do not regret."[14] Karakozov's "split" assessment of Alexander II receives confirmation from a piece of testimony written during his incarceration: in a letter to the tsar, Karakozov wrote that the Great Reforms showed that "as a person you have a good heart, but as a monarch neither the power, nor the capacity to eradicate the poverty of the working class, which has been, is, and will be so long as . . ."[15] For Karakozov, the individual that is Alexander II is politically irrelevant, and to the extent Alexander II is tsar, there is nothing individual about him: Tsar Alexander II is as replaceable as he is obsolete, and must as such be eliminated.

The radicalism of Karakozov's political action can be brought into sharp relief by comparing April 4, 1866, with what the historiography frames as the first real act of terrorism: Vera Zasulich's 1878 shooting of the governor of Saint Petersburg, Fyodor Fyodorovich Trepov.[16] Zasulich's violence combined vengeance ("For Bogoliubov," she announced when asked why she had shot Trepov, that is for Trepov's illegal flogging of the student Arkhip Bogoliubov) and the desire to shock ("I could not find any other means to direct attention to this event"); her attack was directed against the tyrannical abuse of power.[17] As with Lincoln and Bismarck, Trepov himself was targeted: *he* was to be eliminated, not the office he occupied. Further, Zasulich's arguably modern resort to shock was grounded in a traditional view of honor besmirched: "I was determined to show that a human being may not be insulted in that way with impunity."[18] (Zasulich's lawyer, indeed, compared his client's violence to the *crimes passionnelles* committed against scores of dishonorable men by scores of jilted women over the course of the century.) Precisely here, on this point of honor, one notices a parallel with the many narratives of Karakozov's "offended peasants"—and a striking contrast with his "nothing." And while Zasulich quite literally approached Trepov as a petitioner (she brought her grievance during Trepov's official receiving hours), Karakozov's answer shows that Alexander II will no longer be petitioned for anything. "Nothing," therefore, is not ridiculous, but radical: it declares obsolete the power of the tsar to act at all.

Vision of Terror

Well known is the argument against terrorism captured by the quip Georgy Plekhanov made upon hearing of the March 1, 1881, assassination of Alexander II: another numeral, he noted, could now be added to "Alexander." That is, Alexander II would become Alexander III. In other words, terrorism does not "work," because it achieves no more than the replacement of a cog in the giant machinery of state; to dismantle the system, one must either place explosives at its base or short-circuit its connections, not cut off its figureheads.

But it is not the case that terrorists—at least Karakozov—did not know that the place occupied by the sovereign is structurally empty, always only filled with whomever. In fact, if anything, terrorism knew it first, for this is precisely what is at stake in Karakozov's proclamation when he writes: "Let the Russian people recognize their main, mightiest enemy, be he Alexander II, Alexander III, and so forth, that's all the same."[19] The idea is that after seeing autocrat upon autocrat assassinated and replaced by yet another autocrat (the nightmarish multiplication of Baudelaire's "The Seven Old Men" comes to mind), the people finally also sees the autocracy as a mythical monster, a monster rooted in myth, a myth rooted in power. And that was the point of April 4, 1866: nothing—a vision of power's void.

DRAMATIS PERSONAE

After Dmitry Vladimirovich Karakozov (Mitia, Dmitry Vladimirov, Aleksei Petrov, Petr Ivanov, Nikitushka Lomov, "Charles XII," the White Bear), the most important people in the text are:

ALEXANDER II (ALEXANDER NIKOLAEVICH ROMANOV): Tsar of Russia 1855–81.

AZEF, EVNO FISHELEVICH: provocateur, leader of the Party of Socialist-Revolutionaries terrorist organization, the Combat Division (BO, *Boevaia Organizatsiia*).

BAKUNIN, MIKHAIL ALEXANDROVICH: anarchist, revolutionary, close with Herzen and Ogarev.

BOTKIN, SERGEI PETROVICH: physician-therapist, founder of Russian neurology, Karakozov's doctor.

CHEREVIN, LIEUTENANT COLONEL PETR ALEKSANDROVICH: member of the Investigative Commission.

CHERNYSHEVSKY, NIKOLAI GAVRILOVICH: radical critic, author of *What Is to Be Done?*

DANILOV, ALEKSEI MIKHAILOVICH: Moscow university student who committed a double homicide in 1866 and was compared to *Crime and Punishment*'s Raskolnikov.

DECEMBRISTS: aristocratic-constitutionalist officers who attempted a coup d'état in December 1825.

DOLGORUKOV, PRINCE VASILY ANDREEVICH: head of the Third Section 1856–66.

DRENTEL'N, ALEXANDER ROMANOVICH: head of the Third Section 1878–80.

ELISEEV, GRIGORY ZAKHAROVICH: publicist, contributor to *Sovremennik*

ERMOLOV, PETR DMITRIEVICH: alleged member of "Hell" and "The Organization," defendant at the first trial.

ESIPOVICH, IAKOV GRIGOR'EVICH: secretary of the Supreme Criminal Court in 1866.

EVROPEUS, ALEXANDER IVANOVICH: former Petrashevets, contributor to *Sovremennik*, acquaintance of Kobylin's, arrested in connection with April 4, 1866.

FIESCHI, GIUSEPPE MARIA: French conspirator executed for his 1835 attempt on Louis-Philippe.

GAGARIN, PRINCE PAVEL PAVLOVICH: chairman of the Supreme Criminal Court in 1866.

GERASIMOV, ALEXANDER VASIL'EVICH: chief of the Saint Petersburg security police, 1905–9.

GLINKA, MIKHAIL IVANOVICH: composer of *A Life for the Tsar.*

HERZEN, ALEXANDER IVANOVICH: revolutionary (icon), man of letters, publisher of the exile journal, *Kolokol (The Bell)*.

HÖDEL, E. H. M.: German anarchist who attempted to assassinate Kaiser Wilhelm I on May 11, 1878.

ISHUTIN, NIKOLAI ANDREEVICH: Karakozov's cousin, alleged "founder" of "The Organization" and "Hell," defendant at the first trial.

IURASOV, DMITRY ALEEKSEEVICH: alleged member of "Hell" and "The Organization," defendant at the first trial.

IVANOVSKAIA, PRASKOV'IA SEMENOVA: member of the Party of Socialist-Revolutionaries terrorist organization, the Combat Division (BO, *Boevaia Organizatsiia*).

KATKOV, MIKHAIL NIKIFOROVICH: publisher of *Moskovskie Vedomosti* (*Moscow News*) and the literary journal *Russkii Vestnik* (*The Russian Herald*), conservative ideologue.

KHUDIAKOV, IVAN ANDREEVICH: writer, revolutionary, alleged conspirator, defendant at the first trial.

KOBYLIN, ALEXANDER ALEXANDROVICH: Karakozov's doctor, alleged conspirator, defendant at the first trial.

KOMISAROV-KOSTROMSKOI, OSIP IVANOVICH: "the new Susanin," Alexander II's alleged savior.

KONSTANTIN (KONSTANTIN NIKOLAEVICH ROMANOV): Grand Duke, Alexander II's brother.

KOREVO, IGNATY IGNAT'EVICH: acquaintance of Ishutin, Ishutin, Shaganov, and Stranden, important source of information about "Hell."

LANSKOI, MAJOR GENERAL PETR PETROVICH: head of the Investigative Commission, April 4–7, 1866.

LEVITSKY, SERGEI L'VOVICH: photographer.

MAIKOV, APOLLON NIKOLAEV: poet, friend of Dostoevsky's.

MEZENTSEV, NIKOLAI VLADIMIROVICH: chief of staff of the Gendarmerie and official of the Third Section 1864–76, head of the Third Section from 1876 until 1878, when he was assassinated by Sergei Mikhailovich Stepniak-Kravchinsky.

MIKHAILOV, MIKHAIL LARIONOVICH: radical poet, exiled for distribution of N. Shelgunov's proclamation, "To the Young Generation" (1861).

MIRSKY, LEON FILIPPOVICH: revolutionary exiled for his 1879 attempt on A. R. Drentel'n.

MOTKOV, OSIP ANTONOVICH: alleged member of "Hell" and "The Organization," defendant at the first trial.

MURAV'EV, MIKHAIL NIKOLAEVICH ("THE HANGMAN"): head of the Investigative Commission into April 4, 1866.

NECHAEV, SERGEI GENNADIEVICH: revolutionary, founder of *Narodnaia Rasprava.*

NIKOLAEV, PETR FEDOROVICH: alleged member of "The Organization," defendant at the first trial.

NIKOLSKY, ALEXANDER MARKELOVICH: defendant at the second trial, close with Khudiakov and Nozhin.

NOBILING, K. E.: German radical who attempted to assassinate Kaiser Wilhelm I on June 2, 1878.

NOZHIN, NIKOLAI DMITRIEVICH: biologist, radical, close with Khudiakov and Nikolsky.

OGAREV, NIKOLAI PLATONOVICH: poet, radical, close with Herzen and Bakunin.

OGRYZKO, IOSAFAT: leader of one of Saint Peterburg's Polish conspiratorial organizations during the late 1850s and early 1860s.

ORSINI, FELICE: Italian revolutionary executed for his 1858 attempt on Napoleon III.

OSTRIAKOV, ALEKSEI PETROVICH: Karakozov's defense lawyer.

PETRASHEVTSY: a group of radicals (including Dostoevsky) arrested in 1848 on charges of conspiracy.

PISAREV, DMITRY IVANOVICH: radical critic.

POLISADOV, VASILY PETROVICH: Karakozov's confessor, archpriest of the Peter-Paul Cathedral, professor of theology at Saint Petersburg University.

PUGACHEV, EMEL'IAN IVANOVICH: leader of a Cossack rebellion 1773–74.

PUTIATA, LIEUTENANT COLONEL ALEXANDER DMITRIEVICH: treasurer of the first *Zemlia i Volia* (Land and Freedom) organization, acquaintance of Kobylin's, arrested in connection with April 4, 1866.

RAZIN, STEPAN "STENKA": leader of a Cossack rebellion 1670–71.

RENAN, E.: author of *Life of Jesus* (1863).

REPIN, ILYA EFIMOVICH: painter, memoirist.

SAVINKOV, BORIS VIKTOROVICH: Socialist-Revolutionary terrorist and author of *Pale Horse,* etc.

SEREBRIANYI, IAKOV MARKOVICH: Kobylin's defense lawyer.

SERNO-SOLOV'EVICH, NIKOLAI ALEXANDROVICH: radical critic, close with Chernyshevsky, founder of the early 1860s revolutionary organization *Zemlia i Volia* (Land and Freedom).

SHAGANOV, VIACHESLAV NIKOLAEVICH: alleged member of "Hell" and "The Organization," defendant at the first trial.

SHUVALOV, COUNT PETR ANDREEVICH: head of the Third Section 1866–74.

SOROKIN, ALEKSEI FEDOROVICH: governor of the Peter-Paul Fortress.

STASOV, DMITRY VASIL'EVICH: Ishutin's defense lawyer.

STRANDEN, NIKOLAI PAVLOVICH: alleged member of "Hell" and "The Organization," defendant at the first trial.

TIKHOMIROV, LEV ALEXANDROVICH: member of *Narodnaia Volia* and, later, a revolutionary apostate.

TRAPP, JULIUS KARLOVICH: "the father of Russian pharmacology," professor at the Medical-Surgical Academy.

TREPOV, FEDOR FEDOROVICH: chief of police in Saint Petersburg 1866–73, governor of Saint Petersburg 1873–78, shot by Vera Zasulich in 1878.

VALUEV, PETR ALEXANDROVICH: minister of interior 1861–68.

ZAGIBALOV, MAXIMILIAN NIKOLAEVICH: alleged member of "Hell" and "The Organization," defendant at the first trial.

ZAICHNEVSKY, PETR GRIGOR'EVICH: author of "Young Russia" (1862).

ZAMIATNIN, DMITRY NIKOLAEVICH: minister of justice, prosecutor of the Karakozov case.

ZHELIABOV, ANDREI IVANOVICH: revolutionary, one of the principal members of
Narodnaia Volia.

Individuals Involved in the Investigation and Trials

Not all of those listed below appear in the main text (for example, some of the judges of the Supreme Criminal Court), and some only rarely (for example, some of the defendants at the second trial). They are listed here for the record.

Members of "Hell" According to the Indictments
Petr Ermolov
Nikolai Ishutin
Dmitry Iurasov
Dmitry Karakozov
Osip Motkov
Viacheslav Shaganov
Nikolai Stranden
Maximilian Zagibalov

Members of "The Organization" According to the Indictments
Feofan Borisov
Petr Ermolov
Nikolai Ishutin
Dmitry Iurasov
Alexander Ivanov
Dmitry Ivanov
Dmitry Karakozov
Konstantin Kichin

Fedor Lapkin
Alexander Malikov
Orest Malinin
Osip Motkov
Petr Nikolaev
Apollon Polumordvinov
Aleksei Sergievskii
Viacheslav Shaganov
Vasilii Sobolev
Nikolai Stranden
Dmitry Voskresensky
Maximilian Zagibalov

The Accused at the First Trial (August 28–31, 1866)
Petr Ermolov
Nikolai Ishutin
Dmitry Iurasov
Dmitry Karakozov
Ivan Khudiakov
Aleksander Kobylin
Osip Motkov
Petr Nikolaev
Viacheslav Shaganov
Nikolai Stranden
Maximilian Zagibalov

The Accused at the Second Trial (September 7–12, 1866)
Aleksei Bibikov
Feofan Borisov
Varlaam Cherkezov
Viktor Fedoseev
Alexander Ivanov
Dmitry Ivanov
Konstantin Kichin
Nikolai Kutyev
Adolf Langhaus
Fedor Lapkin
Pavel Maevsky
Alexander Malikov
Orest Malinin
Maximilian Marks
Fedor Nikiforov
Alexander Nikolsky

Leonid Obolensky
Nikolai Peterson
Apollon Polumordvinov
Aleksei Sergievsky
Boleslav Shostakovich
Vasily Sobolev
Boleslav Trusov
Dmitry Voskresensky

Investigative Commission under Major General P. P. Lanskoi
Privy Councillor Count Vrangel
Major General Ogarev
Major General Mezentsev
Major General Sleptsov
Lieutenant General Annenkov

Reconstituted Investigative Commission under Count M. N. Murav'ev
Chief of Gendarmerie Prince Dolgorukov
Head of the Third Section Major General Mezentstev
Chief of Police Major General Annenkov
Major General Trepov
Adjutant General Schwarz
Colonel Losev
Lieutenant Colonel Cherevin
Captain of the Guards Nikiforaki

Supreme Criminal Court
Prince P. P. Gagarin: president
D. N. Zamiatnin: prosecutor, minister of justice
Prince P. G. Ol'denburgsky: member
Privy Councilor V. N. Panin: member
Privy Councilor A. D. Bushnitsky: member
Privy Councilor M. M. Korniolin-Pinsky: member
Admiral N. F. Metlin: member
Ia. G. Esipovich: secretary
V. A. Sobolevsky: stenographer

The Karakozov Case, 1866–Present: Sources and Historiography

Sources

In the aftermath of April 4, 1866, and for a long time following, the only sources of information about the Karakozov case were newspaper and journal articles consisting of official announcements, reportage, and a few opinion pieces. Unless these happened to be published abroad, primarily in Herzen's *Kolokol*, they were subject to censorship.

A few prerevolutionary scholars, both Russian and foreign, touched on the Karakozov case here and there, but obviously their labors were enormously restricted by the poverty of the source base.[1] The same limitation is evident in the earliest anthologies related to the revolutionary movement: nothing but a few early reports from two official newspapers, *Severnaia Pochta* and *Senatskie Vedomosti* (*The Senate News*), were reprinted in *Za Sto Let (1800–1896)* (*A Century of Political Life in Russia;* 1897) and *Gosudarstvennyia prestupleniia v Rossii v XIX veke* (*State Crimes in Russia in the Nineteenth Century;* 1903).[2]

Some new sources surfaced after the revolutionary upheavals of 1905–7. These consisted of some archival materials and a few autobiographical accounts by some of the case's principal defendants, Petr Fedorovich Nikolaev and Viacheslav Nikolaevich Shaganov; Ishutin's defense lawyer, Dmitry Vasil'evich Stasov; the secretary of the Supreme Criminal Court, Iakov Grigor'evich Esipovich; and a friend of Dostoevsky's and contemporary of April 4, Petr Veinberg.[3] Like most new materials related to the revolutionary movement that were published at this time, many of these appeared in Vladimir L'vovich Burtsev's journal, *Byloe* (*The Past*). In turn, these publications facilitated the composition of, first, some broad works on the period Lenin later defined as the "*raznochinsky,* bourgeois-democratic, populist" phase of the revolutionary movement; and, second, a few critical essays specifically on the Karakozov case: V. E. Cheshikhina-Vetrinskii's "N. G. Chernyshevskii i karakozovtsy" ("N. G. Chernyshevsky and the Karakozovists"), which includes a letter penned by "Organization" member Nikolaev, and V. Evgen'ev-Maksimov's "Delo Karakozova i redaktsiia *Sovremennika*" ("The Karakozov Case and the Editorship of *The Contemporary*").[4]

Only 1917, however, gave scholars real access to the tsarist archives. For the early Soviet period, the remarkable research done on the Karakozov case by Shilov and especially Klevensky must be singled out. Among other things, Shilov wrote an article in 1918 that made public Karakozov's proclamation, "Druz'iam-rabochim" ("To My Worker Friends"), which had been buried in the archives since the day of the failed attempt. Shilov followed this with a short popular book based on his archival work, *D. V. Karakozov i pokushenie 4 aprelia 1866 g.* (*D. V. Karakozov and the Attempted Assassination of April 4, 1866;* 1920).[5] Klevensky wrote two books, *Ishutinskii kruzhok i pokushenie Karakozova* (*The Ishutin Circle and Karakozov's Attempted Assassination;* 1928) and *I. A. Khudiakov, revoliutsioner i uchenyi* (*I. A. Khudiakov, Revolutionary and Scholar;* 1929).[6] Under Klevensky's auspices, moreover, the journals *Krasnyi Arkhiv* (*Red Archive*) and *Katorga i ssylka* (*Penal Servitude and Exile*) printed a series of primary sources produced by the Investigative Commission into the Karakozov case and, most valuably, the stenographed protocols of the Karakozov trials were transcribed and published in 1928–30 as *Pokushenie Karakozova: Stenograficheskii otchet po delu D. Karakozova, I. Khudiakova, N. Ishutina i dr* (*Karakozov's Attempted Assassination: Stenographic Report of the Case of D. Karakozov, I. Khudiakov, N. Ishutin, and others*).[7] Klevensky's introduction and endnotes to *Pokushenie Karakozova,* in fact, are probably one of the best places from which to approach the case.

The great majority of sources pertaining to the Karakozov case, nevertheless, remains unpublished, and is located at the State Archive of the Russian Federation. Other holdings are located at the Russian State Historical Archive and in the manuscript divisions of the State National Library and at the State Public Library.

As for the quantity of the archival holdings, suffice it to say that the records held in the collection of the Investigative Commission alone exceed five thousand items. The contents of the combined records related to the Karakozov case held at GARF include all written testimonies, all official documentation produced by the investigation, all court-related materials, as well as all sorts of records on related investigations (no matter

how seemingly insignificant), surveillance reports, intercepted letters, reported rumors, public responses (telegrams, letters, poems, church services, and songs), death threats, statistics, photographs, and so on and
so forth. These, moreover, come from all across the Russian empire and
in some cases stretch forward in time as far as the late 1870s. The number of sources, in sum, is enormous, and this book hardly pretends to
exhaust them. It is worth emphasizing that the archival holdings—not
just for the Karakozov case, but also for the whole of the revolutionary
movement—are well-worth (re)visiting, and this applies to the (often-
times published) materials related to nineteenth-century political trials,
as well. Outside of Russia, these incredibly rich sources have barely even
been touched.

Historiography

The central question to puzzle and polarize contemporaries and commentators of the Karakozov case alike has always been the same: was this
the act of a lone lunatic or a calculated conspiracy? In 1866, the loudest
cries of "conspiracy!" came from the conservative, complex, and proud
Mikhail Katkov, publisher and chief editor of *Moskovskie Vedomosti* and
Russkii Vestnik, a literary journal whose pages were graced by the likes of
Turgenev, Tolstoy, and Dostoevsky. Meanwhile, Alexander Herzen—at
this time still widely thought to be the liberation movement's *éminence
grise*, though his star over revolutionary skies had already much faded—
eloquently swore all over the pages of *Kolokol* that Karakozov was no more
than a pitiful fanatic. Very broadly speaking, and exceptions granted, Soviet historians adopted Katkov's convictions (minus the value judgments)
while Westerners were more inclined to toe Herzen's line.[8] More recently,
Russian historians have reemphasized the crazy/crass core of Karakozov's
logic: F. M. Lur'e insists that "investigators and judges, doubtlessly, saw
that Karakozov was insane," and Budnitsky, more evenly, characterizes
Karakozov as "not entirely responsible."[9]

In the non-Russian historiography, Karakozov's attempted assassination is frequently mentioned, but rarely studied. The most complete treat-
ments can be found in Franco Venturi's classic *The Roots of Revolution*
(1952), Philip Pomper, *The Russian Revolutionary Intelligentsia* (1970),
Adam Ulam, *In the Name of the People* (1977), and Abbot Gleason, *Young
Russia* (1980), each of which contains a chapter or so devoted to April
4.[10] For the bottom line on the Karakozov case, however, one may turn
to Nicholas V. Riasanovsky's still standard textbook, *A History of Russia:*
"The decisive change away from reform came, in the opinion of many historians, in 1866, following an attempt by an emotionally unstable student,

Dmitrii Karakozov, to assassinate the emperor."[11] Rational age, irrational radical, progress ends, reaction starts.

Soviet scholarship was rather more seriously engaged in determining the exact nature of the Karakozov case and, thus, its proper place in the revolutionary past. Again, the debate may be seen to center on whether "The Organization" was a propagandist group and Karakozov's shooting an aberration or, alternatively, a proto-terrorist group that naturally, albeit perhaps prematurely, produced a Karakozov.[12] It is worth noting that Soviet scholars knew well enough that any interpretation of the political nature of nineteenth-century revolutionary phenomena was itself political and bore legible meaning for the legitimacy of the regime. During the 1960s, for example, they explicitly interpreted the historiography written in the early twentieth-century with an eye towards the struggles that were then going on between Social-Democrats, Socialist-Revolutionaries, and the Constitutional Democrats.[13]

Following the first wave of works on the Karakozov case, there was a relative dearth of publications until the early 1960s, when there appeared a few essays related to Khudiakov and finally two important monographs by R. V. Filippov, *Revoliutsionnaia narodnicheskaia organizatsiia N. A. Ishutina–I. A. Khudiakova (1863–1866)* (*The Revolutionary Populist Organization of N. A. Ishutin and I. A. Khudiakov*), and E. S. Vilenskaia, *Revoliutsionnoe podpol'e v Rossii (60-e gody XIX v.)* (*The Revolutionary Underground in Russia during the 1860s*).[14] Both these authors are deeply grounded in archival research using the same sources, but arrive at contradictory conclusions. The source of their scholarly strife is, once again, the exact political nature of the young revolutionaries: whereas Filippov characterizes them as proto-populist, Vilenskaia stresses their conspiratorial activities.

The development of this historiography may be characterized as the rather usual social-scientific zigzag: an emphasis in one direction produces blowback from the other side. So, Filippov reacted against an overemphasis on "The Organization's" conspiratorial nature; Vilenskaia, reacting against Filippov, wove conspiracy and terror back in; historians during the 1970s and 1980s reread the terrorist strand as an aberration and Karakozov as a solitary fanatic; and post-perestroika historians have begun to reread April 4 under a proto-terrorist heading again. Recently, for example, an article by E. I. Shcherbakova embedded Karakozov's act in his immediate psycho-social environment.[15]

What was April 4? Why this question is difficult to answer is easily explained. Among the hundreds of testimonies written by those arrested after Karakozov's attempt, scholars can find references not only to school projects, mutual aid societies, cooperative ventures, work associations, socialist factories, populist publications, and provincial propaganda, but also to conspiracy, weapons, drugs, robberies, holdups, jail breaks, mail bombs, sabotage, intra-organizational murder, political assassination, and tsaricide. The problem with these testimonies is that they were all produced under extreme duress, and that at one time or another their authors, to put it bluntly, were all lying: "In my whole life I have never seen such an enormous written mass of lies of all sorts," retrospectively wrote one of the case's main defendants, Ivan Khudiakov.[16] Only after long, slow sittings does the researcher get a rather unscientific "sense" of the truth of these sources. But it is equally true that whenever these materials are pushed too far in a given direction, they begin to resist—and pushing back, they end up protruding. And what does this mean but that the Karakozov case actually bears within itself a most important scientific principle? It is because its sources provoke falsifiability that this book could not only turn toward the production of knowledge about April 4, but also give this knowledge a critical reading.

Abbreviations

CP	Fyodor Dostoevsky, *Crime and Punishment,* trans. Richard Pevear and Larissa Volokhonsky
CP (Coulson)	Fyodor Dostoevsky, *Crime and Punishment:* The Coulson Translation
G	*Golos*
GARF	Gosudarstvennyi Arkhiv Rossiskoi Federatsii (State Archive of the Russian Federation, Moscow)
I	*Iskra*
IG	*Illiustrirovannaia Gazeta*
MV	*Moskovskie Vedomosti*
PL	*Peterburgskii Listok*
PSS	F. M. Dostoevskii, *Polnoe sobranie sochinenii v tridtsati tomakh*
PSZ	*Polnoe sobranie zakonov Rossisskoi Imperii*
RGIA	Rossiskii Gosudarstvennyi Istoricheskii Arkhiv (State Russian Historical Archive, Saint Petersburg)
RNB OR	Rossiskaia National'naia Biblioteka, Otdel Rukopisei (National Library of Russia, Manuscript Division, Saint Petersburg)
RV	*Russkii Vestnik*
SA	*Sekretnyi arkhiv* (Secret archive—archive)
SP	*Severnaia Pochta*

NOTES

Introduction

1. Fyodor Dostoevsky, *The Brothers Karamazov*, trans. Richard Pevear and Larissa Volokhonsky (New York: Farrar, Straus and Giroux, 1990), 3; *PSS* 14:5.

2. Ibid.

3. Joseph Frank, *Dostoevsky: The Mantle of the Prophet, 1871–1881* (Princeton: Princeton University Press, 2002), 727. Frank cites from Grand Duke Alexander Mikhailovich, *Velikii kniaz' Aleksandr Mikhailovich, 1866–1933: Kniga vospominanii* (Moscow: Zakharov-AST, 1991), 42. Or see D. I. Iakubovich, *Letopis' zhizni i tvorchestva F. M. Dostoevskogo*, 3 vols. (Saint Petersburg: Akademicheskii proekt, 1993–95), 3:536.

4. Walter Laqueur, *The Age of Terrorism* (Boston: Little, Brown, 1987), 9.

5. "Programma Ispolnitel'nogo Komiteta," *Narodnaia Volia; Sotsial'no-revoliutsionnoe obozrenie* 2, no. 3 (1 January 1880). Reprinted in *Literatura Partii Narodnoi Voli*, ed. B. Bazilevskii (Paris: Société nouvelle de librairie et d'édition, 1905), 165.

6. *Dnevnik A. S. Suvorina*, ed. M. G. Krichevskii (Moscow: Izdatel'stvo L. D. Frenkel', 1923), 16.

7. Philip Pomper, *The Russian Revolutionary Intelligentsia* (Wheeling, Ill.: Harlan Davidson, 1993), 86; Nicholas V. Riasanovsky, *A History of Russia* (Oxford: Oxford University Press, 1993), 380; Feliks M. Lur'e, *Nechaev: Sozidatel' razrusheniia* (Moscow: Molodaia Gvardiia, 2001), 96; Oleg V. Budnitskii, *Terrorizm v rossiiskom osvoboditel'nom dvizhenii: Ideologiia, etika, psikhologiia (vtoraia polovina XIX—nachalo XX v.)* (Moscow: Rosspen, 2000), 339; Walter G. Moss, *Russia in the Age of Alexander II, Tolstoy, and Dostoevsky* (London: Anthem Press, 2002), 90.

8. Petr I. Veinberg, "4-e aprelia 1866 g.: Iz moikh vospominanii," *Byloe*, no. 4 (1906): 299–300.

Chapter 1. From the Files of the Karakozov Case

Epigraph: Alexander Herzen, "Viselitsa i Murav'ev," *Sobranie sochinenii v tridtsati tomakh*, vol. 19 (Moscow: Izdatel'stvo Academii Nauk SSSR, 1960), 138. An American diplomatic mission sailed from Saint Petersburg on September 3, 1866, the day Karakozov was hanged. *The Kamarinsky* is a Russian folk tune; a journalist had reported in *Golos* that the two tunes, *Yankee Doodle* and *The Kamarinsky*, could be heard simultaneously when the Americans made a visit to Pavlovska. See notes to "Viselitsa i Murav'ev," ibid., 415–416. Herzen's citation of "The Kamarinsky Peasant" likely refers to Osip Ivanovich Komisarov, the peasant ennobled for ostensibly saving Alexander II from Karakozov's bullet.

1. *G*, no. 243, September 3, 1866.

2. Ibid.

3. *CP* (Coulson), 287; *PSS* 6:261.

4. Cited in Samuel Kucherov, *Courts, Lawyers, and Trials under the Last Three Tsars* (New York: Praeger, 1953), 7.

5. John P. LeDonne, "Criminal Investigations before the Great Reforms," *Russian History*, no. 1 (1974): 108.

6. Written testimony of Khudiakov, April 13, 1866. GARF f. 272, op. 1, d. 11, l. 154.

7. Ia. G. Esipovich, "Zapiski Senatora Esipovicha," *Russkaia Starina*, nos. 1–3 (1909): 136.

8. Vysochaishii reskript, May 13, 1866, No. 43298. *PSZ*, 41:547–549.

9. "Reskript 13 maia 1866 g.," *SP*, no. 102, May 14, 1866.

10. Penciled note in Alexander II's hand on Murav'ev's June 9, 1866 report (see below) specifying its consideration by the Council "to stop, if possible, the evil from disrupting our young generation." GARF f. 272, op. 1, d. 5, l. 2.

11. See V. Evgen'ev-Maksimov, "Delo Karakozova i redaktsiia Sovremennika," *Zavety*, no. 6 (1914): 95–96.

12. See Jonathan Daly, "Origins of a Modern Security Police," chap. 1 of *Autocracy Under Siege: Security Police and Opposition in Russia, 1866–1905* (DeKalb: Northern Illinois University Press, 1998), esp. 17–20.

13. For the original, see N. A. Vorms, "Belyi Terror," *Kolokol*, nos. 231–232, January 1, 1867, 1891.

14. Cited in A. Volodin, "Raskol'nikov i Karakozov: K tvorchestkoi istorii D. Pisareva 'Bor'ba za zhizn,'" *Novyi Mir*, no. 11 (1969), 216.

15. Extract from a letter from A. Rudkov in Kiev to Dmitry Konstantinovich Girs in Petersburg dated August 11, 1866. GARF f. 109, SA, op. 1, d. 1817, l. 2.

16. W., "Karakozov, tsar, i publika," *Kolokol*, no. 224 (August 15, 1866), 1329–1334.

17. Cited in Daly, *Autocracy under Siege*, 16.

18. His reference was to the two Murav'evs executed for their part in the Decembrist uprising. The Murav'evs were one of imperial Russia's most notable families. The prosecutor at the trial of the 1881 tsaricides, for example, was also a Murav'ev.

19. GARF f. 109, op. 3, d. 3242, l. 5.

20. P. A. Cherevin, *Zapiski P. A. Cherevina (Novye materialy po delu Karakozova)* (Kostroma: Izdanie "Kostromskogo Nauchnogo Obshchestva po izucheniiu mestnogo kraia," 1918), 11.

21. Ibid., 12.

22. First Report of Investigative Commission under Lanskoi. GARF f. 95, op. 1, d. 439, ll. 1–2ob.

23. Cherevin, *Zapiski P. A. Cherevina*, 5–6.

24. Cf. Karakozov's written testimonies for April 4–6 with that for April 10. GARF f. 272, op. 1, d. 10, ll. 19–51ob, and f. 95, op. 1, d. 163 T. I, ll. 71–83.

25. See testimony of Ishutin, GARF f. 272, op. 1, d. 5, ll. 383–384; trial testimony of Lapkin, *Pokushenie Karakozova: Stenograficheskii otchet po delu D. Karakozova, I. Khudiakova, N. Ishutina i dr.*, ed. M. M. Klevenskii and K. G. Kotel'nikov, 2 vols, Seriia Politicheskie protsessy 60–80 gg., ed V. V. Maksakov and V. I. Nevskii, 2 vols. (Moscow, 1928; Moscow and Leningrad, 1930), 2:48; and Ivan Khudiakov, *Zapiski Karakozovtsa* (Moscow: Molodaia gvardiia, 1930), 129. Written in 1867 and originally published as *Opyt avtobiografii* (Geneva: Vol'naia russkaia tipografiia, 1882).

26. GARF f. 95, op. 1, d. 439.

27. See Alexander II's note on Murav'ev's report. GARF f. 95, op. 1, d. 439, l. 27. Murav'ev's recommendation appears in a June 9 note to Alexander II, GARF f. 109, SA, op. 1, d. 283, l. 2.

28. GARF f. 95, op. 1, d. 439, ll. 27ob–28.

29. Ibid., ll. 28ob–29.

30. Ibid., l. 29ob.

31. Ibid., ll. 29–29ob.

32. "Orsini bombs" were bombs of the type hurled at the carriage of Napoleon III in 1858 by the Italian nationalist revolutionary Felice Orsini.

33. Murav'ev's June 9, 1866, report to Alexander II. GARF f. 95, op. 1, d. 439, l. 31ob.

34. Ibid., l. 32.

35. Ibid., l. 32ob.

36. Ibid., l. 31.

37. Ibid., l. 35.

38. Ibid., l. 35ob.

39. Ibid., l. 36.

40. Ibid., l. 36ob.

41. Ibid.

42. Ibid.

43. *PL*, no. 114, August 4, 1866. Reprint from *SP*, no. 189, August 3, 1866.

44. Esipovich, "Zapiski Senatora Esipovicha," 133.

45. P. A. Valuev, *Dnevnik P. A. Valueva Ministra Vnutrennikh Del*, vol. 2: *1865–1876* (Moscow: Izdatel'stvo Akademii Nauk SSSR, 1961), 144–145.

46. Katkov's commentaries on the *Severnaia Pochta* report appear in *MV*, nos. 163, 168, and 180, August 4, 11, and 26, 1866.

47. Esipovich, "Zapiski Senatora Esipovicha," 137–138.

48. "Ob uchrezhdenii Verkhovnogo Ugolovnago Suda dlia razsmotreniia sledstvennago dela o prestupnykh zamyslazkh protiv Verkhovnoi Vlasti i ustanovlennago zakonami obraza pravleniia i dlia postanovleniia okonchatel'nago po semu delu prigovora," June 28, 1866, no. 43442. *PSZ*, 2d ser., 41 (part 1), 743.

49. Esipovich, "Zapiski Senatora Esipovicha," 133.

50. Ibid., 270.

51. Ibid., 134.

52. See *Pokushenie Karakozova*, 1:xvi.

53. Note from Sorokin to Gagarin, July 16, 1866. GARF f. 272, op. 1, d. 5, l. 37.

54. See G. N. Bhat, "Trial by Jury in the Reign of Alexander II: A Study in the Legal Culture of Late Imperial Russia, 1864–1881" (Ph.D. diss., UC Berkeley, 1995), 43–55.

55. Khudiakov, *Zapiski Karakozovtsa*, 150.

56. Esipovich, "Zapiski Senatora Esipovicha," 129–130, 138.

57. *Pokushenie Karakozova*, 1:261.

58. Ibid., 281. Or see, for example, *PL*, no. 126, September 3, 1866.

59. *Pokushenie Karakozova*, 2:343–344.

60. Ibid., 345.

61. Ibid.

62. Ibid., 346.

63. Ibid., 346–349.

64. *Polnyi Svod Zakonov Ugolovnykh*. Ulozhenie o nakazaniiakh ugolovnykh i ispravitel'nykh, s vkliucheniem teksta vsekh statei Svoda zakonov, na kotoryia ukazany ssylki v ulozhenii o nakazaniiakh starago 1857 i novago 1866 g. izdaniia (Moscow, 1867), 84.

65. *Pokushenie Karakozova*, 2:352. Article 318, *Polnyi svod zakonov ugolovnykh*, 113–114.

66. *Pokushenie Karakozova*, 2:352–355.

67. Esipovich, "Zapiski Senatora Esipovicha," 562.

68. *Pokushenie Karakozova*, 2:357–258. Or see *SP*, no 112, October 5, 1866.

69. *Pokushenie Karakozova,* 2:358–359. For a report on the events of October 4, 1866, see also *SP,* no. 112, October 5, 1866.

70. "Pokushenie Karakozova 4 aprelia 1866," introd. A. A. Shilov, *Krasnyi Arkhiv* 4, no. 17 (1926): 131n7.

71. Notes to the emperor on the activities of the Investigative Commission, June 16, 1866. GARF f. 95, op. 1, d. 439, l. 12.

72. "Pokushenie Karakozova," 131 n. 7.

73. Notes to the emperor on the activities of the Investigative Commission, June 16, 1866. GARF f. 95, op. 1, d. 439 T. III, ll. 82–83.

74. "Pokushenie Karakozova," 106–107.

75. Ibid., 107.

76. GARF f. 272, op. 1, d. 12, ll. 30–30ob.

77. Trial testimony of Ermolov, *Pokushenie Karakozova,* 1:73.

78. Trial testimony of Shaganov, ibid., 26.

79. Trial testimony of Stranden, ibid., 27–28.

80. Trial testimony of Ishutin, ibid., 28–29.

81. Trial testimony of Motkov, ibid., 23.

82. Trial testimony of Ishutin, ibid., 167.

83. Trial testimony of Stranden, ibid., 137.

84. Ibid., 118–120. Cf. trial testimony of Iurasov, ibid., 85.

85. Trial testimony of Polumordvinov, ibid., 114.

86. Trial testimony of Dmitrii Ivanov, ibid., 2:337.

87. Trial testimony of Nikolaev, ibid., 1:198.

88. Trial testimony of Khudiakov, ibid., 40–41.

89. Trial testimony of Malinin, ibid., 2:9–10.

90. Trial testimony of Motkov, ibid., 64.

91. Trial testimony of Sobolev, ibid., 71.

92. Trial testimony of Voskresensky, ibid., 92.

93. Articles 318–324 (*O tainykh obshchestvakh i zapreshchennykh skhodbyshchakh*) of the penal code for 1857–66 appear in *Polnyi svod zakonov ugolovnykh,* 113–115. For the revision, see "O protivozakonnykh soobshchestvakh," March 27, 1867, No. 44402, in *PSZ,* 2d ser., 42 (part 1): 329–331.

94. Ibid., 330.

Chapter 2. The Real Rakhmetov

Epigraph: Nikolai G. Chernyshevsky, *What Is to Be Done?* (Ithaca: Cornell University Press, 1989), 300; N. G. Chernyshevskii, *Chto delat'?* ed. T. I. Ornatskaia and S. A. Reiser (Leningrad: Nauka, 1975).

1. K. S. Malevich, "I/49: The World as Non-Objectivity," in *The World as Non-Objectivity: Unpublished Writings 1922–25,* vol. 3, ed. Troels Andersen (Copenhagen: Borgen, 1976), 311.

2. Scholarship has remained undivided in its agreement with Lenin, who lauded Chernyshevsky for having taught young revolutionaries "what was to be done." See Michael R. Katz and William G. Wagner, introduction to Chernyshevsky, *What Is to Be Done?,* 21; Joseph Frank, "N. G. Chernyshevsky: A Russian Utopia," *Southern Review* 3, no. 1 (1967): 83; Katerina Clark, *The Soviet Novel: History as Ritual* (Chicago: University of Chicago Press, 1981), 51; and Avrahm Yarmolinsky, *Road to Revolution: A Century of Russian Radicalism* (New York: Collier Books, 1962), 120.

3. Verdict of the Supreme Criminal Court, *Pokushenie Karakozova,* 2:345–346. My emphasis.

4. See Franco Venturi, *Roots of Revolution: A History of the Populist and Socialist Movements in Nineteenth-Century Russia,* trans. Francis Haskell (London: Phoenix Press, 2001), 331–335. Originally published in 1952 by Einaudi as *Il popolismo russo;* Frank, "N. G. Chernyshevsky," 83; Irina Paperno, *Chernyshevsky and the Age of Realism: A Study in the Semiotics of Behavior* (Stan-

ford: Stanford University Press, 1988), 29; and also Vladimir Nabokov, *The Gift*, trans. Michael Scammell (New York: Vintage Books, 1991), 283.

5. The speaker was Pavel Petrovich Maevsky. E. I. Shcherbakova, "Roman N. G. Chernyshevskogo *Chto delat'?* v vospriiatii radikol'noi molodezhi serediny 60-kh godov XIX v.," *Vestnik Moskovskogo Universiteta* 8 (Istoriia), no. 1 (1998): 68, citing GARF f. 272, op. 1, d. 16, l. 432.

6. Chernyshevsky, *What Is to Be Done?*, 292; Chernyshevskii, *Chto delat'?*, 214. As against Katz's "specimen," I have translated *ekzempliar* literally to make explicit that Rakhmetov's status is level with the likes of Socrates, Christ, Cato, as "exemplars," in Seneca's words, "according to whom we may regulate our characters." Seneca, *Epistles* (Cambridge, Mass.: Loeb Classical Library, 1996), 65.

7. P. F. Nikolaev, "N. G. Chernyshevskii i Karakozovtsy," *Russkaia Mysl'* 2 (1913): 104. Another alleged co-conspirator, Leonid Egorovich Obolensky, wrote about Karakozov, "I compared him to Rakhmetov from Chernyshevsky's novel." Cited in *Pokushenie Karakozova*, 1:316.

8. One of the few exceptions to this interpretive rule is Andrew M. Drozd's *Chernyshevskii's What Is to Be Done?: A Reevaluation* (Evanston: Northwestern University Press, 2001), but readers familiar with Drozd's text will notice a divergence between our readings of *What Is to Be Done?*

9. Correspondence between Mezentsev and Colonel Duving at police headquarters in Irkutsk, May 26 and 27, 1866. GARF f. 109, 1 eks., op. 1, d. 230 ch. 26, l. 270.

10. Paperno, *Chernyshevsky*, 20.

11. Report of Shuvalov to Alexander II from 1870. GARF f. 109, 1 eks., op. 1, d. 230 ch. 26, l. 313.

12. See A. D. Margolis, "N. G. Chernyshevskii v doroge na katorgu," in *Tiur'ma i ssylka v imperatorskoi rossii* (Moscow: Lanterna Vita, 1995), 95–106; N. A. Troitskii, "Vosem' popytok osvobozhdeniia N. G. Chernyshevskogo," *Voprosy istorii*, no. 7 (1978): 122–141.

13. *IG*, no. 14, April 14, 1866.

14. Karakozov's last letter, September 1, 1866. GARF f. 272, op. 1, d. 5, l. 577.

15. See for example, *MV*, nos. 70–72, April 5–7, 1866, and *PL*, no. 54, April 14, 1866.

16. See for example *G*, no. 102, April 14, 1866, or *MV*, no. 163, August 4, 1866.

17. Indictment of Karakozov, *Pokushenie Karakozova*, 1:6.

18. *MV*, no. 73, April 8, 1866.

19. *G*, no. 98, April 10, 1866.

20. *MV*, no. 88, April 26, 1866. My emphasis.

21. Ibid. The correspondent was Sergei A. Raikovsky. His original report reads, "what terrible consequences there might have been without Komisarov," and specifically names the culprits of the chicaneries as "muzhiki." For the unedited letter, see Rossiskaia Gosudarstvennaia Biblioteka Nauchno-issledovatel'skii otdel Rukopisei (Russian State Library, Manuscripts Collection, Moscow), f. 120 (M. N. Katkov), n. 22, ll. 42–44ob.

22. *G*, no. 121, May 3, 1866.

23. *Pokushenie Karakozova*, 2:266.

24. GARF f. 109, SA, op. 1, d. 270, l. 1.

25. *MV*, no. 76, April 12, 1866.

26. Ibid., no. 72, April 7, 1866.

27. Ibid.

28. Ibid., no. 73, April 8, 1866.

29. *G*, no. 102, April 14, 1866.

30. *SP*, no. 109, May 25, 1866.

31. *IG*, no. 15, April 21, 1866.

32. Cited in Kornei Chukovskii, *Poet i Palach (Nekrasov i Murav'ev)* (Petersburg: Epokha, 1922), 22; *The Poet and the Hangman (Nekrasov and Muravyov)*, trans. R. W. Rotsel (Ann Arbor: Ardis, 1977), 40.

33. See for example *G*, no. 121, May 3, 1866.

34. *MV,* no 85, April 22, 1866. My emphasis.

35. Ibid., no. 73, April 8, 1866.

36. Ibid., no. 132, June 25, 1866.

37. Ibid.

38. Ibid., no. 85, April 22, 1866.

39. Ibid., no. 75, April 10, 1866, and *G,* no. 223, August 14, 1866.

40. The article was reprinted in all major Russian newspapers, e.g. *PL,* no. 113, August 4, 1866, and *MV,* no. 163, August 4, 1866.

41. See for example, "Novosti iz Rossii," "Vsiakaia vsiachina iz nashei reaktsii," and "Zagovora ne bylo," in Herzen, *Sobranie sochinenii,* 19:69–70, 111–112, and 144.

42. *G,* 212, August 3, 1866. Or see *MV* 168, August 11, 1866.

43. *G,* no. 212, August 3, 1866.

44. *PL,* no. 120, August 20, 1866.

45. *MV,* no. 180, August 26, 1866. See also ibid., no. 163, August 4, 1866, and *G,* no. 212, August 3, 1866.

46. *MV,* no. 163, August 4, 1866. It is unclear whether this phrase of Katkov's invoked the image of a Polish political phenomenon well-known at that time, or whether he was simply referring to the relative foreignness of the word. Both the verb *organizovat'* and the noun *organizatsiia* had been entered into Russian dictionaries during the early years of the nineteenth century, and the noun *organizator* followed in the 1860s, but it is true that the terms were of Western origin, albeit more likely French than Polish. See P. Ia. Chernykh, *Istoriko-etimologicheskii slovar' sovremennogo russkogo iazyka,* vol. 1 (Moscow: Russkii iazyk, 1999), 603.

47. *G,* no. 223, August 14, 1866.

48. *MV,* no. 134, June 28, 1866.

49. Ibid.

50. The text to which Katkov refers is *Iosafat Ogryzko i Peterburgskii revoliutsionnyi rzhond v dele poslednego miatezha.* Sostavil chlen Vilenskoi osoboi po politicheskim delam komissii, 3-i artilleriiskoi brigady shtabs-kapitan N. V. Gogel' (Vilno, 1866). Penned by a police officer, this publication aimed to slander Ogryzko and the Polish cause.

51. *MV,* no. 181, August 28, 1866.

52. Reportedly, Nechaev's favorite book at the time he first became politically active was Theodor Griesinger's *Jesuits: The Complete History of Their Open and Secret Proceedings from the Foundation of the Order to the Present Time,* which was first published in Russia in 1868. Nechaev first took the book from Petr G. Uspenskii's library. V. V. Esipov, "Byl li Nechaev revoliutsionerom?" *Voprosy istorii,* no. 11 (1990): 182–185. For examples of Nechaev's fondness for embracing the Society of Jesus, see Philip Pomper, *Sergei Nechaev* (New Brunswick: Rutgers University Press, 1979), 51; Lur'e, *Nechaev,* 232.

53. Mikhail Katkov, "O nashem nigilizme po povodu romana Turgeneva," *Russkii vestnik* 40, no. 7 (1862), 402–426. Cited in Martin Katz, *Mikhail N. Katkov: A Political Biography, 1818–1887* (The Hague: Mouton, 1966), 75–76.

54. *MV,* no. 83, April 20, 1866.

55. *G,* no. 248, September 8, 1866. The essay in *Den'* provoked a defensive response from a Russian Jesuit, Martinov, to which *Den'* in turn responded. *Jesuits and their Relations to Russia* was the collected version of this exchange.

56. *MV,* no. 127, June 11, 1863.

57. *PL,* no. 120, August 20, 1866.

58. *Pokushenie Karakozova,* 2:345–346. My emphasis.

59. *MV,* no. 163, August 4, 1866. "Roman Chernyshevskogo byl dlia etikh porchennykh evangeliem." Katkov uses the terms *porchennyi* (spoiled) and *bol'noi ot porchi* (sick with a wasting disease bewitched, under the evil eye).

60. *MV,* no. 84, April 21, 1866 and, for the ad, see *IG,* no. 1, January 6, 1866.

61. *G,* no. 93, April 5, 1866.

62. Gustave Flaubert, *Dictionary of Received Ideas,* trans. Jacques Barzun (New York: New Directions, 1968), 52.

63. See Joseph Frank, *Dostoevsky: The Stir of Liberation 1860–1865* (Princeton: Princeton University Press, 1986), 310–347.

64. Cited in Paperno, *Chernyshevsky*, 27.

65. See the introduction and notes by Katz and Wagner to *What Is to be Done?* The notes are very thorough in their documentation of the novel's Christian symbolism. See also Paperno, *Chernyshevsky*, esp. 195–218; Clark, *The Soviet Novel*, esp. 50–51; and Frank, "N. G. Chernyshevsky," 78–79.

66. Herzen, *Sobranie sochinenii*, 20:337; *My Past and Thoughts*, trans. Constance Garnett (Berkeley: University of California Press, 1991), 631 n. 5.

67. For Russia's religious approach to reading during this period, see Jeffrey Brooks, *When Russia Learned to Read: Literacy and Popular Literature, 1861–1917* (Princeton: Princeton University Press, 1985), 22–34.

68. Paperno, *Chernyshevsky*, 9.

69. Ibid.

70. Ibid., 27.

71. Ibid., 27–28.

72. See Frank, "N. G. Chernyshevsky," 83; Paperno, *Chernyshevsky*, 29; Shcherbakova, "Roman N. G. Chernyshevskogo *Chto delat'?*," 62; Yarmolinsky, *Road to Revolution*, 135; and Drozd, *Chernyshevskii's What Is to Be Done?*, 10.

73. Cited in Shcherbakova, "Roman N. G. Chernyshevskogo *Chto delat'?*," 68. Or see Adam Ulam, *In the Name of the People. Prophets and Conspirators in Prerevolutionary Russia* (New York: Viking, 1977), 144.

74. Trial testimony of Ermolov, *Pokushenie Karakozova*, 1:73.

75. Trial testimony of Stranden, ibid., 79–81.

76. Ibid., 168.

77. Nikolaev's final statement before the Supreme Criminal Court, ibid., 2:334. See also trial testimony of Nikolaev, ibid., 1:220 and 2:334.

78. Trial testimony of Ermolov, ibid., 1:218.

79. Trial testimony of Nikolaev, Ibid., 219.

80. Nikolaev's final statement to the Supreme Criminal Court, ibid., 2:334. Though he testified that he could not recall who among them had used the term first, it was probably Nikolaev himself, not just because Ermolov testified that it had been Nikolaev who had explained the word to him, but also because Nikolaev, at that time a twenty-two-year-old Moscow University student of political economy, was well versed in political theory. His last words before the court included a speech about the differences between the theory of regicide and tsaricide as a revolutionary means and a government necessity. If we are to believe his testimonies, Nikolaev did not adhere to the "theory of regicide," but considered tsaricide legitimate "in some cases, as a government necessity."

81. Testimonies of Malinin on Ermolov's violence, *Pokushenie Karakozova*, ibid., 172, and Ishutin, ibid., 166.

82. Trial testimony of Malinin, ibid., 114.

83. Written testimony of Dmitry Ivanov, GARF f. 272, op. 1, d. 5, l. 410ob.

84. Trial testimony of Kichin, *Pokushenie Karakozova*, 1:177.

85. Ibid.

86. Ibid., 178.

87. Ibid., 2:77.

88. Shaganov testified that he had taken ideas for a program he had written for "The Organization" from an essay about either the Italian Carbonari, an Italian revolutionary group established in 1811, or about the French Charbonnerie, founded a decade later to oppose the Bourbon Restoration. Ibid., 190–192. For Nikolaev on the Jacobins, see ibid., 1:220 and 2:334.

89. See written testimony of D. Ivanov, GARF f. 272, op. 1, d. 13, l. 2, and trial testimony of Zagibalov, *Pokushenie Karakozova*, 1:89.

90. Written testimony D. Ivanov, GARF f. 272, op. 1, d. 13, l. 2.

91. Written testimony of Ermolov, April 29, 1866, reprinted in "Pokushenie 4 Aprelia 1866 g.," 112.

92. Trial testimony of Zagibalov, *Pokushenie Karakozova*, 1:89.

93. Written testimony of Ermolov, April 29, 1866 reprinted in "Pokushenie 4 Aprelia 1866 g.," 111.

94. Ibid.

95. Trial testimony Malinin, *Pokushenie Karakozova*, 2:29.

96. Karakozov's proclamation, "Druz'iam rabochim," GARF f. 95, op. 1, d. 163 T. I, l. 8.

97. Chernyshevsky, *What Is to Be Done?*, 33.

98. Chernyshevsky, *What Is to Be Done?*, 212; *Chto delat'?*, 149.

99. Chernyshevsky, *What Is to Be Done?*, 437; *Chto delat'?*, 339.

100. Chernyshevsky, *What Is to Be Done?*, 291; *Chto delat'?*, 213.

101. Chernyshevsky, *What Is to Be Done?*, 292; *Chto delat'?*, 214.

102. Chernyshevsky, *What Is to Be Done?*, 291; *Chto delat'?,*, 213.

103. Dostoevsky, *Notes from Underground*, trans. Richard Pevear and Larissa Volokhonsky (New York: Vintage, 1993), 35; *PSS* 5:120. The utopian structures appear in Vera Pavlovna's fourth dream: "What style of architecture? There's nothing at all like it now. No, there is one building that hints at it—the palace at Sydenham"—the Crystal Palace constructed for the 1851 Great Exhibition. Chernyshevsky, *What Is to Be Done?*, 370; *Chto delat'?*, 284. In *Notes from Underground*, therefore, the structures simply become "the crystal palace."

104. The novel's only suicide, in fact, is Lopukhov's, and it is faked; a few years later, he triumphantly returns incognito as an American businessman.

105. Chernyshevsky, *What Is to Be Done?*, 203; *Chto delat'?*, 143.

106. Chernyshevsky, *What Is to Be Done?*, 239; *Chto delat'?*, 173.

107. Chernyshevsky, *What Is to Be Done?*, 278; *Chto delat'?*, 204.

108. The attribute "rigorist" has attached itself like a barnacle solely to Rakhmetov's ascetic modus vivendi. See Frank, "N. G. Chernyshevsky," 83; Clark, *The Soviet Novel*, 218; N. G. O. Pereira, *The Thought and Teachings of N. G. Chernyshevsky* (The Hague: Mouton, 1975), 86, 80; and Geoffrey Hosking, *Russia: People and Empire 1552–1917* (Cambridge, Mass.: Harvard University Press, 1997), 346.

109. Chernyshevsky, *What Is to Be Done?*, 274; *Chto delat'?*, 202.

110. Chernyshevsky, *What Is to Be Done?*, 274; *Chto delat'?*, 202. For Vera Pavlovna's second dream and notes on Liebig, see *What Is to Be Done?*, 180–188; *Chto delat'?*, 123–130.

111. Chernyshevsky, *What Is to Be Done?*, 283; *Chto delat'?*, 208.

112. See Pereira, *Thoughts and Teachings*, 80; Ulam, *In The Name of the People*, 137.

113. Chernyshevsky, *What Is to Be Done?*, 273–274; *Chto delat'?*, 201.

114. Chernyshevsky, *What Is To Be Done?*, 274 and 293; *Chto delat'?*, 202 and 215.

115. Chernyshevsky, *What Is To Be Done?*, 290; *Chto delat'?*, 213.

Chapter 3. "A Life for the Tsar"

Epigraph: Joke reported by the German satirical newspaper *Kladderadatsch* in the summer of 1866. Cited in Veinberg, "4-e aprelia," 301.

1. *SP*, no. 71, April 6, 1866. The weather report for April 4 relates the lowest temperature as -0.2 degrees, the highest as + 0.4 degrees, and the skies as "cloudy." The entire week before, the temperature had hovered around freezing and the skies been just as gloomy. For death and illness statistics for April 4, see *SP*, no. 72, April 7, 1866: 3,768 ill; 244 newly ill; 164 recovered; and 68 dead. The figures for April 3 are 3,770; 252; 186; and, again, 68 dead.

2. *PL*, no. 53, April 12, 1866.

3. Ibid., no. 60, April 24, 1866.

4. Venturi, *Roots of Revolution*, 348; Ulam, *In the Name of the People*, 3–5; Abbot Gleason, *Young Russia: The Genesis of Russian Radicalism in the 1860s* (New York: Viking, 1980), 333.

5. Chukovskii, *Poet i palach*, 17–29; *The Poet and the Hangman*, 32–53.

6. Ilya E. Repin, *Dalekoe blizkoe*, ed. K. Chukovskii (Leningrad and Moscow: Iskusstvo, 1937), 195.

7. Cherevin, *Zapiski P. A. Cherevina*, 3–5.

8. Esipovich, "Zapiski Senatora Esipovicha," 268.

9. "Excerpt from a letter without signature from St. Petersburg, dated April 10, 1866, to Mikhail Nikiforovich Katkov in Moscow." GARF f. 109, SA, op. 1, d. 389, l. 5.

10. *G,* no. 105, April 17, 1866.

11. *PL,* no. 54, April 14, 1866. The tsar's decision had been made on April 4 itself and had been reported in *Severnaia Pochta* the next day, but was not registered by law until April 9. See *SP,* no. 70, April 5, 1866.

12. Law No. 43164 specifically included a sentence on Komisarov's and Susanin's shared place of origin. See *PSZ* 41 (part 2), 334.

13. *MV,* no. 78, April 14, 1866.

14. Ibid., no. 71, April 6, 1866 (includes lengthy description of *A Life for the Tsar* performance in the Bolshoi). Letter from Tchaikovsky to his brothers, A. and M. Tchaikovsky, dated April 7, 1866. P. I. Tchaikovsky, *Polnoe sobranie sochinenii: Literaturnye proizvedeniia i perepiska,* vol. 5 (Moscow: Gosudarstvennoe Muzykal'noe Izdatel'stvo, 1959), 105.

15. In June, the capital's main telegraph office boasted that the speed of its Hughes apparatus left "nothing to be desired" and managed to send more than a thousand messages per day. *SP,* no. 135.

16. Ibid., no. 121, June 7, 1866.

17. *PL,* no. 83, June 9, 1866.

18. Ibid., no. 64, May 1, 1866. See also *MV,* no. 88, April 22, 1866.

19. See *G,* no. 142, May 25, 1866; *MV,* no. 83, April 20, 1866; *G,* no. 143, May 26, 1866; and, for an assessment of Komisarov ("an awfully vulgar person . . . dull-witted in the extreme") by his tutor and guardian, A. S. Voronov, see A. V. Nikitenko, *Zapiski i dnevnik,* vol. 2 (Saint Petersburg: Knigoizdatel'stvo M. V. Pirozhkova, Istoricheskii otdel', 1905), 331–332.

20. *PL,* no. 53, April 12, 1866; *MV,* no. 78, April 14, 1866; and *SP,* no. 121, June 7, 1866.

21. *PL,* no. 71, May 15, 1866.

22. For Nekrasov's poem, see *Modnyi Magazin,* no. 11 (1866): 163; for Maikov's hymn, see *MV,* no. 90, April 28, 1866; and for popular verses, see GARF f 95, op. 1, d. 181.

23. *PL,* no. 55, April 16, 1866.

24. Ibid., no. 69, May 12, 1866.

25. *MV,* no. 79, April 15, 1866, no. 86, April 23, 1866, and no. 85, April 22, 1866; *PL,* no. 62, April 28, 1866.

26. *PL,* nos. 57, 58, and 60, April 19, 21, and 24, 1866; *MV,* no. 76, April 12, 1866, and no. 79, April 15, 1866.

27. *G,* no. 105, April 17, 1866.

28. *PL,* no. 67, May 7, 1866.

29. *G,* no. 97, April 9, 1866. *Severnaia Pochta* reported that Komisarov had his photograph taken on April 6 at Levitsky's. *SP,* no. 72, April 7, 1866.

30. *PL,* no. 53, April 12, 1866.

31. *G,* no. 101, April 13, 1866, and *PL,* no. 54, April 14, 1866.

32. *G,* no. 100, April 12, 1866.

33. *PL,* no. 54, April 14, 1866.

34. Ibid., no. 55, April 16, 1866.

35. *G,* no. 120, May 2, 1866.

36. "Excerpt from a letter with the initials 'I. S.' from Kazan, dated April 18, 1866, to Arkady Egorovich Bystrov, student at Petersburg's Agricultural Institute." GARF f. 109, SA, op. 1, d. 271, l. 3.

37. *G,* no. 98, April 10, 1866.

38. V. E. Genkel', A. & F. Ushakov, and S. A. Manukhin all charge fifty kopeks for *kar-*

tochki. PL, no. 83, June 7, 1866, and *MV,* no. 277, December 17, 1865 and no. 77, April 13, 1866.

39. The studios of S. A. Manukhin, M. V. Popov, and A. & F. Ushakov charge fifty kopeks. *MV,* no. 76, April 12, 1866; *G,* no. 100, April 12, 1866; and ibid., no. 77, April 13, 1866. Prices for photographs of Komisarov plus his wife vary from one ruble charged by Zaltsfish (ibid., no. 81, April 17, 1866) to Arbat Photography's fifty kopeks apiece (ibid., no. 83, April 20, 1866), to whole-sale deals offered by City Leipzig (100 for 16 rubles) and Nastiukov (100 for 15 rubles) (ibid., no. 84, April 21, 1866).

40. Tulinov offers 100 business cards complete with facsimiles and miniature portraits at a price of 10 rubles, i.e. 10 kopeks per card. *MV,* no. 276, December 16, 1865. He thus charges a rate slightly lower than "City Leipzig" and Nastiukov do for their *kartochki* of Komisarov and his wife, but 10 kopeks is probably still too high an estimate, for these 10 kopeks undoubtedly guarantee profit.

41. "Agenturnye zapiski," October 29, 1866. GARF f. 109, SA, op. 1, d. 269, l. 5.

42. "Agenturnye zapiski," April 15, 1866. GARF f. 109, SA, op. 1, d. 269, l. 3.

43. Note to Komisarov. No date, but from 1866. GARF f. 95, op. 1, d. 172, ll. 23–24.

44. Note addressed to Komisarov care of Kazan Cathedral. GARF f. 109, 1 eks., d. 100 ch. 116, l. 16.

45. Cited in Chukovskii, *Poet i Palach,* 21; *The Poet and the Hangman,* 39. Chukovsky cites "Belyi terror," *Russkie Vedomosti,* no. 8 (1909), but he probably meant "Moskovskii universitet v 60-kh godakh: Iz vospominanii starago studenta" in the same issue. "Belyi terror" was published in *Kolokol* (January 1867). In "Moskovskie universitet v 60-kh godakh," there are reports of public beatings and arrests of people who possessed photos of Chernyshevsky. Normally, Chukovsky's references check out; he probably confused the citations.

46. Case 11 ch. 61 for 1866. GARF f. 109, op. 222, d. 5, ll. 177–177ob.

47. Case 11 ch. 224 for 1867. GARF f. 109, op. 222, d. 7, ll. 689–91.

48. "Gorodskie slukhi," April 29, 1866. GARF f. 109, SA, op. 1, d, 270, l. 3.

49. Ibid., l. 5.

50. "Agenturnye zapiski," May 19, 1866. GARF f. 109, SA, op. 1, d. 269, l. 4.

51. Ibid.

52. Ibid., l. 7.

53. "Regarding the noble Komisarov." No date, but from 1866. GARF f. 109, 1 eks., op. 1, d. 100 ch. 18.

54. Veinberg, "4-e aprelia," 301; Chukovskii, *Poet i Palach,* 20; *The Poet and the Hangman,* 38. Chukovsky cites K. A. Skal'kovskii, *V teatral'nom mire* (Saint Petersburg: Tipografiia A. S. Suvorina, 1899), xii–xiii.

55. Chukovskii, *Poet i Palach,* 20; *The Poet and the Hangman,* 37.

56. Repin, *Dalekoe blizkoe,* 195.

57. For information on Komisarov's father, see B. Bukhshtab, "Posle vystrela Karakozova," *Katorga i ssylka,* no. 5 (1931): 54–61.

58. Memo to the head of the gendarmes dated May 27, 1866. GARF f. 109, 1 eks., op. 1, d. 100 ch. 18, ll. 10–11ob.

59. Bukhshtab, "Posle vystrela Karakozova," 56.

60. "Agenturnye zapiski," November 12, 1866. GARF SA f. 109, op. 1, d. 269, l. 6.

61. "Agenturnye zapiski," November 23, 1866. Ibid., l. 8.

62. "Agenturnye zapiski," April 4, 1867. Ibid., l. 11.

63. "Agenturnye zapiski," February 2, 1868. Ibid., l. 1.

64. "Agenturnye zapiski," April 6, 1868. Ibid., ll. 13–13ob.

65. Memo, 1877. GARF f. 109, 1 eks., op. 1, d. 100 ch. 18, l. 39.

66. Ibid.

67. Ibid.

68. "Excerpt from a letter without signature . . . to Katkov in Moscow." GARF f. 109, SA, op. 1, d. 389, l. 5.

69. See Repin, *Dalekoe blizkoe,* 194.

70. See S. Morozov, *Russkaia khudozhestvennaia fotografiia: Ocherki iz istorii fotografii 1839–1917* (Moscow: Gosudarstvennoe Izdatel'stvo Iskusstvo, 1955), 19–20; "Delo o fotograficheskom vosproizvedenii revoliutsionnykh relikvii," in M. K. Lemke, *Politicheskie protsessy v Rossii v 60-kh godakh* (Moscow: Gosudarstvennoe izdatel'stvo, 1923).

71. "Agenturnye zapiski," May 18, 1866. GARF f. 109, SA, op. 1, d. 270, l. 17.

Chapter 4. Raskolnikov, Karakozov, and the Etiology of a "New Word"

Epigraph 1: *CP,* 4; *PSS* 6: 6.
Epigraph 2: Trial testimony of Ishutin, *Pokushenie Karakozova,* 1:69.
1. *Crime and Punishment*'s publication history will be taken up below. As what was intended as a novella morphed into a major novel, its composition naturally required much more time than anticipated: the first installment was published in January 1866, the last not until February of the following calendar year.

2. *Prestuplenie i nakazanie: Rukopisnye redaktsii, PSS* 7:310–311; Dostoevsky, *Complete Letters,* no. 266, vol. 2: *1860–1867,* trans. David A. Lowe (Ann Arbor: Ardis, 1989), 174–175.

3. Veinberg, "4-e aprelia," 299–300. For a slightly truncated version, see Joseph Frank, *Dostoevsky: The Miraculous Years, 1865–1871* (Princeton: Princeton University Press, 1995), 48. See also Iakubovich, *Letopis',* 2:61–62.

4. Cited in Iakubovich, *Letopis',* 2:63.

5. See M. S. Gus, *Idei i obrazy F. M. Dostoevskogo* (Moscow: Khudozhestvennaia literatura, 1971), 290–294.

6. Iakubovich, *Letopis',* 2:63.

7. Dostoevsky, *Complete Letters,* no. 275, 2:192.

8. Although nowhere recorded, an epileptic fit in the wake of Karakozov's failed assassination seems both possible and likely, not only because of the above-cited documentary evidence pointing to Dostoevsky's "fever," "bad health," and "illness" after April 4, but also because when, one year later, in May 1867, Anton Berezovsky made a second failed attempt on Alexander II in Paris, this event also unleashed an epileptic episode. See Frank, *Dostoevsky: The Miraculous Years,* 198.

9. With obvious reference to John 1:1 ("In the beginning was the Word"), what Dostoevsky called a "new word" really means a whole new poetics, knowledge, or *nomos,* and is thus as devastating an event as in the beginning. Dostoevsky's "new word" also contains a touch of irony: it is a common Russian idiom, namely "skazat' novoe slovo v nauke, v iskusstve," etc. ("to say something new in science, art," etc.).

10. *CP,* 258; *PSS* 6:198–199.

11. *CP,* 259; *PSS* 6:199.

12. My translation of the original: "V stat'e vsego etogo net, tam tol'ko nameki." *PSS* 6:203. The Coulson translation reads: "You will not find all this in the article; it is only hinted at there." *CP* (Coulson), 223. The Pevear and Volokhonsky translation reads, "That's not all in the article; it's only hinted at." *CP,* 263.

13. *CP,* 260; *CP* (Coulson), 221; *PSS* 6:199–200.

14. *CP* (Coulson), 223; *PSS* 6:202–3.

15. *CP* (Coulson), 220 and 223; *PSS* 6:200 and 202.

16. *CP* (Coulson), 223; *PSS* 6:202.

17. For the specific form Dostoevsky was targeting, see Frank, *Dostoevsky: The Miraculous Years,* 70–79.

18. Frank suggests that "no other source provides so perfect a fit" for *Crime and Punishment* as Pisarev's reading of Turgenev's *Fathers and Sons,* "Bazarov," published in 1862 in *Russkoe Slovo.* Ibid., 70–79. As for the stock phrase of radical criticism: Paperno writes that what was known at that time as "real criticism" held that "an author can reveal things in reality (such as future types) that are independent or even contrary to his intentions . . . the

literary critic had to play the role of scientist in literature and 'complete' the artistic analysis of reality." Paperno, *Chernyshevsky,* 10.

19. Mikhail Bakhtin, *Problems of Dostoevsky's Poetics,* ed. and trans. Caryl Emerson (Minneapolis: University of Minnesota Press, 1984), 90.

20. Dostoevsky, *Complete Letters,* no. 275, in 2:194.

21. *CP,* 389; *PSS* 6:351.

22. "Molodaia Rossiia," reprinted in *Revoliutsionnyi radikalizm v Rossii: Vek deviatnadtsatyi,* ed. E. L. Rudnitskoi (Moscow: Arkheograficheskii Tsentr, 1997), 142–150.

23. Frank, *Dostoevsky: The Miraculous Years,* 72–73.

24. *Iskra,* no. 14 (1867). Cited in Iakubovich, *Letopis',* 2: 107.

25. Iakubovich, *Letopis',* 2:39–40.

26. "Once a source is found, according to positivist logic, the originality of the passage is destroyed. This is the fallacy of 'source study,' in which poetry is reduced to content and its form is neglected." Leo Spitzer, "Development of a Method," in *Representative Essays,* ed. Alban K. Forcione, Herbert Lindenberger, and Madeline Sutherland (Stanford: Stanford University Press, 1988), 431.

27. Undated; *PSS* 27:65.

28. Cited in Frank, *Dostoevsky: The Miraculous Years,* 308. *PSS* 28/2:329; December 11/23, 1868.

29. See *MV,* no. 16, January 21, 1866.

30. See *G,* no. 95, April 7, 1866. For references to the Danilov case, see Iakubovich, *Letopis',* 2:51, 55, 93, 95–96, 150.

31. For trial transcripts, see for example *MV,* nos. 37–40, February 15–18, 1867; *Russkii Invalid,* nos. 48–58, 18–27 February 1867; or *G,* nos. 49–52, 18–21 1867.

32. *Russkii Invalid,* no. 63, March 4, 1867. The article was by Aleksei Sergeevich Suvorin. Iakubovich, *Letopis',* 2:95.

33. See *G,* no. 67, March 8, 1867.

34. *MV,* no. 168, August 11, 1866.

35. A. Volodin, "Raskolnikov i Karakozov," 221. For Bor'ba za zhizn'," see D. I. Pisarev, *Sochineniia,* 4 vols. (Moscow: Gosudarstvennoe izdatel'stvo Khudozhestvennoi literatury, 1955–56), 4:316–367.

36. Frank, *Dostoevsky: The Miraculous Years,* 42.

37. Dostoevsky, *Complete Letters,* nos. 283 and 284, 2:205 and 207.

38. Publication history of *Crime and Punishment* (based on references found in Iakubovich, *Letopis',* vol. 2):

	Written	Published
Part One	Mid-Dec. 1865	Jan. 30, 1866
Part Two	Jan.–Feb.	March 11
Part Three	March–April–May	May 20 (delayed)
Part Four, chs. 1–4	By May	Delayed
Part Four, chs. 1–4, Revised	By July 18	July 20
Part Four, chs. 5–6; Part V, chs. 1–3	July 22	Aug. 21
Part Five, chs. 4–5	Aug.–Sept.	Sept. 24
Part Six, chs. 1–6	From Nov. 8	Dec. 29
Part Six, chs. 7–8; Epilogues	By Dec. 27	Feb. 14, 1867

This took place against the background of the following events. January 12–14, in the midst of writing Part Two, news of the Danilov case breaks. April 4, as Dostoevsky writes Part Three, Karakozov attempts to assassinate Alexander II. August 30 and September 3, Karakozov sentenced and executed. September 24, members of "The Organization" sentenced. October 4, Ishutin pardoned as Dostoevsky writes the latter part of Part Five, Part Six, and the Epilogues.

39. History of *Crime and Punishment*'s composition based on Iakubovich, *Letopis'*, 2:38, 13; Dostoevsky, *Complete Letters*, 2:188 or Iakubovich, *Letopis'*, 2:45; Dostoevsky, *Complete Letters*, 2:200; and Iakubovich, *Letopis'*, 2:73.

40. See D. V. Stasov, "Karakozovskii protsess (Nekotoryia svedeniia i vospominaniia)," *Byloe*, no. 4 (1906): 290.

41. Shchegolev, "D. V. Karakozov v raveline," in *Alekseevskii ravelin: Sekretnaia gosudarstvennaia tiur'ma Rossii v XIX veke*, ed. A. A. Matyshev, vol. 2 (Leningrad: Lenizdat, 1990), 2:19n. Originally published in the collection *Muzei revoliutsii*, no. 1 (1923).

42. *CP*, 444–446; *PSS* 6:340–341.

43. *IG*, no. 14, April 14, 1866.

44. *CP*, 261; *PSS* 6:200.

45. *CP*, 261; *PSS* 6:201.

46. *CP*, 262; *PSS* 6:202.

47. Ibid.

Chapter 5. Armiak; *or, "So Many Things in an Overcoat!"*

Chapter title: "'So many things in a minuet!' a celebrated dancer used to say. So many things in an overcoat!—when circumstances and men make it speak." H. de Pène, *Paris intime* (Paris, 1859), 236. Cited in Walter Benjamin, *Arcades Project*, trans. Howard Eiland and Kevin McLaughlin (Cambridge, Mass.: The Belknap Press of Harvard University Press, 1999), 223.

Epigraph: Esipovich, "Zapiski Senatora Esipovicha," 134.

1. N. V. Gogol, "The Overcoat," in *The Overcoat and Other Tales of Good and Evil*, trans. David Magarshack (Cambridge, Mass.: Robert Bentley, 1979), 265; "Shinel'," in *Polnoe sobranie sochinenii v desiati tomakh* (Berlin: Slovo, 1921), 3:167.

2. Gogol, "The Overcoat," 236; *"Shinel',"* 132.

3. Gogol, "The Overcoat," 239; *"Shinel',"* 136.

4. Gogol, "The Overcoat," 267; *"Shinel',"* 169.

5. Cf. Carl Schmitt, *Theorie des Partisanen: Zwischenbemerkung zum Begriff des Politischen* (Berlin: Duncker & Humblot, 1992), 72–73; *The Concept of the Political*, trans. George Schwab, expanded ed. (Chicago: University of Chicago Press, 2007), 67.

6. "Posledniia Mody," *IG*, no. 9, March 3, 1866.

7. This was an epoch that, quite literally, dug up the past while creating the future. This fashion column stands in the company of manifold articles on Pompeii's excavations, cretinism evidenced by unearthed skeletons, the exposure of corpses at the new Parisian morgue, etc. Across the page, they face lithos of telegraphs, monorails, etc. At a time that is about to tear itself loose from tradition, fashion remembers whatever threatens to be lost. "Fashions are a collective medicament for the ravages of oblivion," noted Benjamin. *Arcades Project*, 80.

8. Written testimony of Zabalotin, April 4, 1866. GARF, f. 272, op. 1, d. 10, l. 12. Some of Karakozov's police photographs, taken on the day of the attempted assassination, show him with a hat.

9. *PL*, no. 49, April 5, 1866; *SP*, no. 70, April 5, 1866; and *MV*, no. 72, April 7, 1866.

10. *MV*, no. 70, April 5, 1866; *SP*, no. 71, April 6, 1866; *G*, no. 98, April 10, 1866; and *MV*, no. 76, April 12, 1866.

11. *MV*, no. 72, April 7, 1866.

12. "Ishutin himself told me it was Karakozov who had shot when he read the description of Karakozov in *Moskovskie Vedomosti*," testified Korevo, "and he regretted that Karakozov had not taken off the *galanskaia* [*sic: gollandskaia*, Dutch] shirt." Written testimony of Korevo, April 22, 1866, cited in "Pokushenie Karakozova," 101.

13. Written testimony of Ermolov. GARF f. 272, op. 1, d. 12, ll. 123–132.

14. See V. Ryndin, *ed., Russkii Kostium 1850–1870* (Moscow: Vserossiiskoe Teatral'noe

Obshchestvo, 1963), 146–152; Iu. A. Fedosiuk, *Chto neponiatno u klassikov ili Entsiklopediia russkogo byta XIX veka* (Moscow: Nauka, 2003), 187; R. M. Kirsanova, *Rozovaia ksandreika i dradedamovyi platok: Kostium-veshch' i obraz v russkom literature XIX veka* (Moscow: Kniga, 1989), 25.

15. Ryndin, *Russkii Kostium,* 164; Fedosiuk, *Chto neponiatno,* 192 and 193; Kirsanova, *Rozovaia ksandreika,* 20–22 and 177.

16. *MV,* no. 72, April 7, 1866.

17. GARF f. 272, op. 1, ll. 66, 67, 69, 71–72, 73, 77–78ob, 106, 109.

18. See Ryndin, *Russkii Kostium,* 146–150.

19. Ekaterina Allenova, *Ilia Repin* (Moscow: Belyi gorod, 2001), 33.

20. *PSS* 6:7. The English of the first sentence is from *CP,* 5, except that I have preferred to translate "smeshnaia" as "funny" rather than as Pevear and Volokhonsky's "ludicrous." The rest of the English is from *CP* (Coulson), 3.

21. *CP,* 81; *PSS 6:*76.

22. GARF f. 272, op. 1, d. 10, l. 67.

23. *CP,* 81; *PSS 6:*76.

24. Paperno, *Chernyshevsky,* 18.

25. Herzen, *My Past and Thoughts,* 606; *Sobranie sochinenii,* 11:464.

26. Georg Simmel, "Philosophy of Fashion," in *Simmel on Culture* (London: SAGE Publications, 1997), 189.

27. I. S. Turgenev, *Fathers and Sons,* trans. Ralph E. Matlaw (New York: Norton, 1989), 4 and 11; *Polnoe sobranie sochinenii i pisem v tridtsati tomakh,* vol. 7 (Moscow: Nauka, 1981), 11 and 19.

28. Turgenev, *Fathers and Sons,* 13 and 19; *Polnoe sobranie sochinenii,* 7:11 and 18.

29. Paperno, *Chernyshevsky,* 18.

30. Lev Tikhomirov, "The Term Nihilism," in *Russia Political and Social,* trans. Edward Aveling, vol. 2 (London: Swan Sonnenschein, 1892), Appendix B, 271–272.

31. Ibid.

32. GARF f. 109, SA, op. 1, d. 299, ll. 16–16ob.

33. Herzen, *My Past and Thoughts,* 607; *Sobranie sochinenii,* 11:466.

34. Vorms, "Belyi terror," 1894.

35. *PL,* no. 168, November 20, 1866.

36. Herzen, *My Past and Thoughts,* 608–609; *Sobranie sochinenii,* 11:467.

37. See Ryndin, *Russkii Kostium,* 6.

38. Cited ibid., 6.

39. See "Delo o fotograficheskom vosproizvedenii revoliutsionnykh relikvii," in Lemke, *Politicheskie protsessy,* 633–634.

40. Ibid., 639 and 640–641.

41. Ibid., 639.

42. Repin, *Dalekoe blizkoe,* 194.

43. Ibid., 195.

44. Photograph of Zagibalov. GARF f. 272, op. 1, d. 12, l. 255zh.

45. Photograph of Ermolov. GARF f. 272, op. 1, d. 11, l. 136a.

46. Simmel put it nicely: "The widely projecting limbs of the Baroque statue are, as it were, always in perpetual danger of being broken off . . ." Simmel, "Philosophy of Fashion," 205.

47. Section title: Luke 12:35. *The New Testament and Other Early Christian Writings: A Reader,* ed. Bart D. Ehrman (New York: Oxford University Press, 1998), 77. Joseph A. Fitzmeyer offers the following remarks on Luke 12:35: "Lit. 'let your loins be girded' (pf. ptc., expressing condition), i.e. let the long, ankle-length robe be adjusted by a waist-belt to ensure readiness for action or departure." See *The Gospel According to Luke (X–XXIV),* trans. Joseph A. Fitzmyer, S.J., Anchor Bible, vol. 28A (New York: Doubleday, 1985), 987.

48. Written testimony of Karakozov, April 4, 1866. GARF f. 272, op. 1, d. 10, l. 21ob.

49. Written testimony of Karakozov, April 28, 1866. GARF f. 272, op. 1, d. 12, ll. 17–17ob.

50. Ibid., 17ob. Notably, Karakozov and friends often address each other with the formal, un-nihilist *vy.*

51. Trial testimony of Stranden, *Pokushenie Karakozova,* 1:78. Written testimony of Ermolov. GARF f. 272, op. 1, d. 12, ll. 123–132.

52. Written testimony of Karakozov, April 28, 1866. GARF, f. 272, 1, 12, l. 20.

53. Ibid., ll. 19ob–20.

54. Written testimony of Kobylin, April 6, 1866. GARF f. 272, op. 1, d. 10, ll. 63–65.

55. Trial testimony of Kobylin, *Pokushenie Karakozova,* 1:235.

56. See trial testimony of Komarova, ibid., 249–250.

57. Trial Testimony of Kobylin, ibid., 234.

58. Ibid.

59. *MV,* no. 76, April 12, 1866.

60. Trial testimony of Nikolsky, *Pokushenie Karakozova,* 2:246. Lebedev had stated that Nikolsky had discussed with him "that general rumor . . . that [Karakozov] was dressed in a gray *armiak,* that he had on him a double-barreled pistol." Trial testimony of Lebedev, ibid., 245.

61. Trial testimony of Kobylin, *Pokushenie Karakozova,* 1:233. Written testimony of Karakozov, June 15, 1866. GARF f. 272, op. 1, d. 16, l. 244.

62. Investigative Commission journal entry for April 7, 1866. GARF f. 272, op. 1, d. 10, l. 99.

63. Report of A. Trofimov-Trokhimovich on Khudiakov in Siberia. GARF f. 95, op. 1, delo 340, l. 13ob.

64. V. I. Lenin, "Sovremennoe polozhenie Rossii i taktika rabochei partii," *Polnoe Sobranie sochinenii,* 5th ed., 55 vols. (Moscow: Gosudarstvennoe izdatel′stvo politicheskoi literatury, 1958–65) 12:180. Originally published in *Partiinye Izvestiia,* no. 1, February 7, 1906. "Terror byl sovershenno ne sviazan ni s kakim nastroeniem mass. Terror ne podgotovlial nikakikh boevykh rukovoditelei mass. Terror byl rezul′tatom—a takzhe simptomom i sputnikom—neveriia v vosstanie, otsutstviia uslovii dlia vosstaniia."

65. Lur′e, *Nechaev,* 171–172.

66. Ibid., 140, citing Alexandra Uspenskaia, "Vospominaniia shestidesiatnitsy," *Byloe,* no. 18 (1922): 19–45.

67. Cited in Lur′e, *Nechaev,* 171. Nechaev sometimes wore an officer's uniform to convince members of *Narodnaia Rasprava* that he had just come from a secret meeting with military officers. Ibid., 160.

68. Everyone mentions his nail-bitten fingers. See, for example, ibid., 98 and 256.

69. N. A. Morozov, cited ibid., 319.

70. Ibid.

71. L. G. Praisman, *Terroristy i revoliutsionery, okhranniki i provokatory* (Moscow: Rosspen, 2001), 289–290.

72. Ibid., 60–61.

73. Ibid., 359.

74. Charles Baudelaire, "The Painter of Modern Life," in *The Painter of Modern Life and Other Essays,* trans, Jonathan Mayne (London: Phaedon, 1995), 9. Flaubert, *Dictionary of Received Ideas,* 52.

Chapter 6. "Factual Propaganda," an Autopsy

Epigraph: *CP* (Coulson), 287. *CP,* 339–340; *PSS* 6:261.

1. *CP* (Coulson), 452. *CP,* 536; *PSS* 6:411.

2. *CP* (Coulson), 294. *CP,* 348; *PSS* 6:268.

3. Karakozov's last letter (second draft). September 1, 1866. GARF, f. 272, op. 1, d. 5, l. 597.

4. Investigative Commission journal, April 7, 1866. GARF f. 272, op. 1, d. 10, l. 98.

5. "Druz'iam rabochim." GARF f. 272, op.1, d. 10, ll. 6–7ob. Or, for a copy made by a clerk, see GARF f. 95, op. 1, d. 163 T. I, ll. 7–7ob.

6. Karakozov's Letter to Ishutin. GARF f. 272, op. 1, d. 10, ll. 4–5.

7. Trapp, report to Investigative Commission, April 6, 1866. GARF f. 272, op. 1, d. 10, l. 44.

8. Ibid., l. 44ob. Trapp probably meant *The New Pitaval,* not the original collection of "causes célèbres et intéressantes" written up by Francis Gayot de Pitaval during the mid-eighteenth century. *Der Neue Pitaval: Eine Sammlung der interessantesten Criminalgeschichten aller Länder aus älterer und neuerer Zeit,* ed. Julius Eduard Hitzig and Wilhelm Häring, 60 vols. (Leipzig: Brockhaus, 1842–90).

9. GARF f. 272, op. 1, d. 10, ll. 44–45.

10. Karakozov identified Kobylin thus on April 4 and 5, 1866. Ibid., ll. 23–24 and 37.

11. *IG,* no. 14, April 14, 1866; *PL,* no. 54, April 14, 1866.

12. Ibid., no. 13, April 7, 1866.

13. *PL,* no. 120, August 4, 1866.

14. Trial protocols, August 10, 1866. GARF f. 272, op. 1, d. 5, ll. 293–294.

15. *Polnyi svod zakonov ugolovnykh,* 32.

16. Trial proceedings, *Pokushenie Karakozova,* 1:6.

17. Ibid., 10. The reference is to Dr. L. U. Pogozhev's *historia morbi,* which was read aloud to the court on August 18, 1866. See also trial protocols, August 18, 1866. GARF f.272, op. 1, d. 5, ll. 279–280.

18. *Pokushenie Karakozova,* 1:260.

19. Ibid., 263–264.

20. Ibid., 263.

21. Ibid., 264.

22. Ibid., 281. Or see, for example, *PL,* no. 126, September 3, 1866.

23. *Pokushenie Karakozova,* 1:281.

24. Ibid., 282.

25. Trial protocols, August 11, 1866. GARF f. 272, op. 1, d. 5, l. 379. *Pokushenie Karakozova,* 1:10.

26. Vorms, "Belyi terror," 1890.

27. Khudiakov, *Zapiski Karakozovtsa,* 114. Although this story is told above by people partial to the revolutionary movement, Karakozov's attempt to starve himself to death receives confirmation from much less sympathetic sources. See for example Ioann Nikitich Polisadov, *Slovo pred soversheniem torzhestvennago blagodareniia Gospodu Bogu za spasenie zhizni Gosudaria Imperatora skazannoe sviashchennikom Ioannom Polisadovym 9ogo Aprelia 1866 goda* (Saint Petersburg, 1866).

28. Cherevin, *Zapiski P. A. Cherevina,* 24.

29. Written testimonies of Karakozov, April 5–6, 1866. GARF f. 272, op. 1, d. 10, ll. 39ob and 33ob; written statement addressed to Alexander II April 10, 1866. GARF f. 95, op. 1, d. 163 T I, l. 79.

30. Report by physicians Ovel' and Vil'ms, May 27, 1866. GARF f. 272, op. 1, d. 15, l. 163.

31. Report by Sorokin, June 1, 1866. Ibid., l. 162.

32. Reports by physicians Ovel' and Vil'ms for May 27–June 7, 1866. Ibid., ll. 163, 229, 317, 325, 426, 427. Or see GARF f. 109 op. 1, d. 100 ch. 1, ll. 73–90.

33. Report of June 7, 1866. GARF f. 95, op. 1, d. 439, ll. 54–55. Or see GARF f. 272, op. 1, d. 15, l. 427.

34. Cherevin, *Zapiski P. A. Cherevina,* 10–11.

35. Written testimony of Stranden. GARF f. 272, op.1, d. 11, l. 197. See also written testimony of Dmitry Ivanov. GARF f. 272, op. 1, d. 13, l. 2ob; written testimony of Iurasov. GARF f. 272, op.1, d. 11, l. 193.

36. See for example written testimony of Dmitry Ivanov. GARF f. 272, op. 1, d. 13, l. 2ob. Also written testimony of Ermolov. GARF f. 272, op. 1, d. 11, l. 149ob.

37. Written testimony of Zagibalov. Ibid., ll. 208ob.

38. Moscow University Clinic, *historia morbi* of Karakozov. Ibid., ll. 303–310. Karakozov's *historia morbi* consist of two (slightly different) sets of medical records written by a fourth-year student resident named Auerbach and by Dr. L. U. Pogozhev. Pogozhev's diagnosis reads as follows: "zheludochno-kishechnyi katar, khronicheskii pereloi, obshchee istoshchenie v umerennoi stepene." Auerbach's does not mention the general exhaustion, but includes the relapsing fever: "*urethritis et catarrhus ventriculi et intestinorum;* pozdnee *febris recurrens.*"

39. Ibid., ll. 305 and 307.

40. Ibid., l. 307.

41. Ibid., l. 305.

42. Ibid., ll. 307–308.

43. Ibid., ll. 308–308ob. Auerbach's *historia morbi* includes not only admission documents (symptoms, diagnoses, and anamnesis), but also these daily observations.

44. Ibid., l. 306. This was not the first time Karakozov had problems with his ears: from age fourteen to nineteen, he had suffered a painful infection that eventually left him deaf in his right ear. Ibid., l. 304.

45. Moscow University Clinic pulse, breath, and temperature chart for Karakozov. Ibid., l. 310.

46. Written testimony of Ermolov. Ibid., l. 149ob.

47. Written testimony of Dmitry Ivanov. GARF f. 272, op. 1, d. 13, ll. 2–5. Written testimony of Iurasov. GARF f. 272, op.1, d. 11, l. 193ob.

48. Written testimony of Ermolov. Ibid., l. 149ob. See also written testimony of Zagibalov. Ibid., l. 209.

49. Written testimony of Iurasov. Ibid., l. 194. Written testimony of Ermolov. Ibid., l. 149ob.

50. Written testimony of Ermolov. Ibid., ll. 149–150. Written testimony of Iurasov. Ibid., l. 193ob.

51. Written testimony of Iurasov. Ibid., l. 194. It should be borne in mind that this was hearsay, via Stranden, and Iurasov actually placed this episode after Karakozov's second suicide note was found (see below).

52. Written testimony of Ermolov. Ibid., l. 149ob. Written testimony of Dmitry Ivanov. GARF f. 272, op. 1, d. 13, ll. 2ob–3.

53. Written testimony of Iurasov. GARF f. 272, op.1, d. 11, l. 193.

54. Written testimony of Dmitry Ivanov. GARF f. 272, op. 1, d. 13, ll. 3–3ob.

55. Written testimony of Ermolov. GARF f. 272, op. 1, d. 11, l. 150.

56. *Pokushenie Karakozova,* 1:30.

57. Written testimony of Dmitry Ivanov. GARF f. 272, op. 1, d. 13, ll. 3ob–4.

58. Written testimony of Ermolov, April 12. GARF f. 272, op. 1, d. 11, l. 150. Cf. trial testimony of Iurasov, *Pokushenie Karakozova,* 1:133–134.

59. Trial testimony of Zagibalov, *Pokushenie Karakozova,* 1:89.

60. Written testimony of Ermolov. GARF f. 272, op. 1, d. 11, l. 150ob.

61. Written testimony of Standen. Ibid., l. 197.

62. Written testimony of Iurasov. April 14, 1866. Ibid., l. 193.

63. Written testimony of Dmitry Ivanov. GARF f. 272, op. 1, d. 13, l. 3ob.

64. Written testimony of Zagibalov. GARF f. 272, op. 1, d. 11, l. 209ob.

65. Written testimonies of Khudiakov, April 11, 13, and 25, 1866. GARF f. 272, op. 1, d. 11. ll. 73ob (not exact), 155, 198 (not exact), 215, 462ob, and 465–467ob.

66. Trial testimony of Motkov, *Pokushenie Karakozova,* 1:163–164.

67. Trial testimony of Karakozov, ibid., 1:16. Written testimony of Karakozov, April 28–29, 1866. GARF f. 272, op. 1, d. 12, ll. 21 and 21–21ob.

68. See for example written testimonies of Karakozov, April 15–16 and 28–29, 1866. GARF f. 272, op. 1, d. 11, ll. 219–238ob and 7–46.

69. Written testimony of Karakozov, June 24, 1866. GARF f. 272, op. 1, d. 17, l. 56.

70. Written testimony of Kobylin, April 6, 1866. GARF f. 272, op. 1, d. 10, ll. 63–63ob; trial testimony of Kobylin, *Pokushenie Karakozova,* 1:229.

71. Trial testimony of Kobylin, *Pokushenie Karakozova,* 1:229.

72. Cf. written testimony of Karakozov, April 5, 1866. GARF f. 272, op. d. 10, l. 37; trial testimony of Kobylin, *Pokushenie Karakozova,* 1:230.

73. Written testimony of Kobylin, April 6, 1866. GARF f. 272, op. 1, d. 10, l. 163ob.

74. Written testimony of Karakozov, April 5–6, 1866. GARF f. 272, op. 1, d. 10, ll. 230b–224. For attestations by the pharmacist Schmitt and his assistant Kreis, see ibid., ll. 71–73.

75. Report of Trapp to Investigative Commission, April 6, 1866. GARF f. 272, op. 1, d. 10, l. 45.

76. Written testimony of Kobylin, April 6, 1866. Ibid., l. 64.

77. Trial testimony of Kobylin, *Pokushenie Karakozova,* 1:230.

78. Written testimony of Karakozov, April 6, 1866. GARF f. 272, op. 1, d. 10, l. 38.

79. Written testimony of Kobylin, April 6, 1866. Ibid., ll. 63–65.

80. Trial testimony of Kobylin, *Pokushenie Karakozova,* 1:232.

81. Ibid., 234.

82. Ibid.

83. All the above from written testimonies of Karakozov, April 28–29, 1866. GARF f. 272, op. 1, d. 12, ll. 39–39ob.

84. Trial testimony of Karakozov, *Pokushenie Karakozova,* 1:19–20.

85. Written testimony of Karakozov, April 5, 1866. GARF f. 272, op. 1, d. 10, l. 39ob.

86. "Druz'iam rabochim." GARF f. 272, op. 1, d. 10, ll. 7–7ob.

87. Written statement of Karakozov to Alexander II, April 10, 1866. GARF f. 95, op. 1, d. 163 T. I, l. 78ob.

88. Written testimony of Karakozov, April 10, 1866. GARF f. 95, op. 1, d. 163 T. I, l. 72. See also written testimony of Karakozov, April 15–16, 1866. GARF f. 272, op. 1, d. 11, l. 232.

89. Khudiakov, *Zapiski Karakozovtsa,* 114.

90. Note from Ishutin to Karakozov, late April 1866. GARF, f. 95, op. 1, d. 163 T. I, l. 279. See ll. 280–280ob for the second note dated April 28, 1866.

91. Written testimony of Karakozov, April 4, 1866. GARF, f. 272, op. 1, d. 10, ll. 23ob–24.

92. Written testimony of Karakozov, April 5–6, 1866. Ibid., l. 35.

93. Written testimony of Karakozov, April 10, 1866. GARF f. 95, op. 1, d. 163 T. I., l. 75.

94. Written testimony of Karakozov, April 10, 1866. Ibid. Karakozov repeated this testimony on April 15–16, 1866. GARF f. 272, op. 1, d. 11, l. 233.

95. Written testimonies of Karakozov, June 12, 1866. GARF f. 272 op. 1, d. 16, ll. 149–151.

96. Written testimonies of Karakozov, June 14–15, 1866. GARF, f. 272, op. 1, d. 16, ll. 224–225 and 244–244ob.

97. Trial testimony of Karakozov, *Pokushenie Karakozova,* 1:241 and 240. See also written testimony of Karakozov, June 12, 1866. GARF f. 272, op. 1, d. 16, l. 149.

98. Trial testimony of Karakozov, *Pokushenie Karakozova,* 1:244.

99. Written testimony of Karakozov, April 28–29, 1866. GARF f. 272, op. 1, d.12, ll. 25–26 and 40–42. Written testimony of Karakozov, April 10, 1866. GARF f. 95, op. 1, d. 163 T. I, l. 74ob.

100. Trial testimony of Karakozov, *Pokushenie Karakozova,* 1:237.

101. Someone, though, told Karakozov something serious: in Moscow, Ishutin told the

court, Karakozov said some doctor had told him that he had trichinosis—and had only days left to live. Trial testimony of Ishutin, *Pokushenie Karakozova,* 1:155. Trichinosis, or trichinellosis, is a roundworm infection. Caused by ingestion of raw or undercooked meat infected with the larvae of the Trichinella worm, symptoms include nausea, diarrhea, fatigue, fever, abdominal pain, aching joints and muscles, itchiness, and constipation. At present, the disease is rarely fatal, but early editions of Brokgaus and Efron, the leading encyclopedia in pre-revolutionary Russia, still cited a 50 percent mortality rate.

102. Karakozov's written testimony of April 28–29, 1866. GARF f. 272, op. 1, d. 12, l. 23ob. See also written testimony of Karakozov, June 24, 1866. GARF f. 272, op. 1, d. 17, ll. 56–57.

103. Written testimony of Karakozov, April 15–16, 1866. GARF f. 272, op. 1, d. 11, l. 230.

104. Written testimony of Karakozov, April 29, 1866. GARF f. 272, op. 1, d. 12, l. 22.

105. Written testimony of Karakozov (and Khudiakov), June 12, 1866. GARF f. 272, op. 1, d. 16, l. 202. Earlier that day, Karakozov had already characterized "factual propaganda" as follows: "that is, propaganda by means of a crime, and precisely I am someone who—because he hasn't got long to live—can commit that crime." Written testimony of Karakozov, June 12, 1866. Ibid., l. 147.

106. "Propaganda by the deed" usually refers to the anarcho-terrorism of the global fin de siècle. Scholarship says that this doctrine of direct action was first promoted by Italian revolutionaries Carlo Pisacane and, later, Enrico Malatesta and Carlo Cafiero, though coinage of the phrase itself has been attributed to French anarchist Paul Brousse and dated to 1877. Originally, it meant collective action: the "facts" of the Kazan and Berne demonstrations (1876), or of the Benevento rebellion (1877)—these were *propaganda par le fait;* by contrast, assassination attempts like those of Fieschi (1835), Orsini (1858), Hödel* and Nobiling* (1878) were not. But because *Narodnaia Volia*'s "emperor hunt" and the anarchist "outrages" of the 1890s were so sensational, the meaning of "propaganda by the deed" was forever altered: after the *ère des attentats,* it meant political assassination. See Rudolf Rocker, *Johann Most: Das Leben eines Rebellen* (Berlin: Der Syndikalist, 1924), 102; and David Stafford, *From Anarchism to Reformism: A Study of the Political Activities of Paul Brousse within the First International and the French Socialist Movement 1870–90* (London: Weidenfeld & Nicolson, 1971), 84–86 and 123–124. This history should be modified, for it was in fact Karakozov who coined the phrase in 1866: *fakticheskaia propaganda.* And he meant by it precisely singular, serial assassinations.

107. Written testimony of Karakozov, June 12, 1866. GARF f. 272, op. 1, d. 16, l. 148.

108. Ibid., l. 149.

109. Written testimony of Khudiakov, April 23, 1866. GARF f. 272, op. 1, d. 11, l. 431.

110. Report of A. Trofimov-Trokhimovich on Khudiakov in Siberia. GARF f. 95, op. 1, d. 340, ll. 3 and 13.

Chapter 7. The Head of the Tsaricide

Epigraph: I. N. Polisadov, *Slovo pred soversheniem torzhestvennago blagodareniia gospodu bogu za spasenie zhizni Gosudaria Imperatora skazannoe Sviashchennikom Ioannom Polisadovym 9ogo Aprelia 1866 g.* (Saint Petersburg, 1866). These words were spoken by Ioann Polisadov, *not* Vasily Polisadov, the priest featured in this chapter. Evidently, the Polisadovs were an ecclesiastic family.

1. GARF f. 109, SA, op. 1, d. 295. Golodai ("Hunger") was renamed Ostrov Dekabristov (Island of the Decembrists) after the Revolution.

2. See GARF f. 109, SA, op. 1, d. 270, ll. 11ob and 12.

3. Ibid., l. 10.

4. Ibid., l. 13.

5. See Repin, *Dalekoe blizkoe,* 198–201.

6. Cited in Allenova, *Ilia Repin,* 32.

7. Repin, *Dalekoe blizkoe,* 198.

8. Ibid., 20.

9. Ibid., 197. Literally, "Etot poklon srazu perevernul vse eto mnogoglovoe pole" translates as "This bow immediately turned the many-headed floor upside-down." Given that this "turning" follows Karakozov's bowing, I chose the expression "to turn on its head" in order to have the crowd's movement echo that of the criminal.

10. Ibid.

11. "Agenturnye zapiski," September 3, 1866. GARF f. 109, SA, op. 1, d. 270, l. 9; *Birzhevie Vedomosti* (*Stockmarket News*) article reprinted in *IG*, no. 35, 8 September 1866; and *G* article reprinted in *MV*, no. 186, 6 September 1866.

12. Esipovich, "Zapiski Senatora Esipovicha," 277.

13. *Russkii Invalid* article reprinted in *MV*, no. 186, 6 September 1866.

14. *G*, no. 244, 4 September 1866.

15. *PL*, no. 127, 4 September 1866.

16. *Birzhevye Vedomosti* article reprinted in *IG*, no. 35, 8 September 1866.

17. Ibid.

18. *G*, no. 4, 4 September 1866.

19. Written testimony of Peterson. GARF f. 95, op. 1, d. 384, l. 7.

20. *Pokushenie Karakozova*, 1:17.

21. Written testimony of Dmitry Ivanov. GARF f. 272, op. 1, d. 13, ll. 2–5.

22. *Pokushenie Karakozova*, 1:16.

23. Ibid.

24. Written testimony of Karakozov, April 15, 1866. GARF f. 272, op. 1, d. 11, l. 236.

25. Ibid.

26. Investigative Commission journal, June 16, 1866. GARF f. 95, op. 1, d. 439, l. 56.

27. *Pokushenie Karakozova*, 1:17.

28. Stasov, "Karakozovskii protsess," 290.

29. Karakozov's last letter, September 1, 1866. GARF f. 272, op. 1, d. 5, l. 571; Esipovich, "Zapiski Senatora Esipovicha," 275–276.

30. GARF f. 109, SA, op. 1, d. 268.

31. Investigative Commission journal for April 6, 1866. GARF f. 95, op. 1, d. 163 T. 1, p. 16. Investigative Commission, note to Alexander II from April 5, 1866. GARF f. 272, op. 1, d. 10, l. 32.

32. The only other discussion of Polisadov's role in the Karakozov case is Pavel E. Shchegolev's "D. V. Karakozov v raveline." Part of *Alekseevskii ravelin*, a two-volume set devoted to the history of the Peter-Paul Fortress, Shchegolev's article aims to illuminate prison life through a focus on "the use of religion as a means of coercion." Fair on the whole, Shchegolev sometimes overstrains the documentary record in order to achieve the impression that Polisadov *only* functioned as an instrument of coercion.

33. For Polisadov's estimation of 1848–49, see "Otvet na stat'iu N. A. Serno-Solov'evicha, 'Neskol'ko razmyshlenii, vyzvannykh poucheniem, slyshannym 8 sentiabria," 13 sent. 1863 g." RNB OR) f. 727, ed. khr. 43, l. 6ob. For his German connections, see RGIA f. 796, op. 139, d. 486, g. 1863, l. 5–8ob; Polisadov, "Sobesedovaniia s protestantom v Berline po sluchaiu publichnykh ego chtenii o russkoi tserkvi," *Strannik* 3, no. 8 (August 1860): 85; and Polisadov, "Pis'mo iz Parizhe ot 27 Avgusta (8 Sentiabria), 1861 g. k Sviashchenniku Smolensko-kladbishchenskoi Tserkvi Ioannu Efimovichu Flerovu," *Pis'ma Protoiereia V. P. Polisadova o puteshestvii nashei dukhovnoi missii v Parizhe i ob osviashchenii parizhkoi tserkvi* (Saint Petersburg: Lermantov & Co., 1861), 3 and 9.

34. RGIA f. 796, op. 139, d. 486, g. 1859, ll. 1–10b.

35. See GARF f. 109, 1 eks., op. 41, d. 141, ll. 2–3.

36. On May 2, 1866, Polisadov remarked in a footnote to a letter addressed to General Sorokin that his sermons to Karakozov were improvised. GARF f. 109, 1 eks., op. 1, d. 100 ch. 1, l. 41.

37. Polisadov, "Smert' prestupnika Gudzevicha," *Dukhovnaia beseda* 21, no. 31 (1864): 449 and 453.

38. Polisadov's December 4, 1859 letter to the University. RGIA f. 796, op. 139, d. 486, l. 2.

39. Ibid., l. 2ob.

40. Ibid., ll. 5–8ob.

41. Ibid., l. 6.

42. Ibid.

43. Mezentsev to Sorokin, April 18 or 19, 1866. GARF f. 109, 1 eks., op. 1, d. 100 ch. 1, ll. 16–16ob.

44. Shuvalov to Alexander II and to Sorokin, April 20, 1866. Ibid., ll. 18–19.

45. See Sorokin to Alexander II, April 20, 1866. Ibid., l. 20.

46. Sorokin to Mezentsev, April 20, 1866. Ibid., l. 17ob.

47. Sorokin to Shuvalov, April 24, 1866. Ibid., l. 24ob.

48. Mezentsev to Sorokin, April 18 or 19, 1866. Ibid., l. 16ob.

49. Polisadov's April 23, 1866, report to Sorokin. Ibid., ll. 25–26.

50. For a precedent for Polisadov's attempt to distance himself from Russian official-dom via a suspension of formalities, see Polisadov, "Smert' prestupnika Gudzevicha," 451 and 452.

51. When two people *rassushdaiut,* the term has the meaning of debate or argue. When one person employs the verb for him/herself, it implies that he/she will expound on or discuss a subject in detail. The latter is implied the second time Polisadov uses the term ("permit myself to *rassushdat'*"), but in the context of "I want in my personal *sobesedovaniiakh* with him to enter into *rassushdeniia,*" it is clear that an exchange of ideas will take place. This meaning of *besedovat', besedy, sobesedovanie,* etc., is confirmed by Polisadov's above-cited 1863 letter to a university official and his article, "Sobesedovaniia s protestantom," 83–108.

52. Shchegolev, "D. V. Karakozov v raveline," 16.

53. Polisadov's May 2, 1866 report to Sorokin. GARF f. 109, 1 eks., op. 1, d. 100 ch. 1, ll. 41–42. Sorokin's May 4, 1866 report to Shuvalov. Ibid., l. 40.

54. Polisadov's May 2, 1866, report to Sorokin. Ibid., l. 42.

55. For Karakozov, see reports by the physicians Ovel' and Vil'ms, May 27–June 7, 1866. GARF f. 272, op. 1, d. 15, ll. 163, 229, 317, 325, 426, and 427. For Polisadov, see Dr. Do-broliubov's, Polisadov's, and Sorokin's letters from May 5, June 11, and June 12, 1866. GARF f. 109, 1 eks., op. 1, d. 141, ll. 1–4.

56. Polisadov's September 4, 1866, letter to Shuvalov. GARF f. 109, 1 eks., op. 1, d. 100 ch. 1, ll. 112–113ob. The role assigned to "Your predecessor, Prince Andreevich," i.e. Prince V. A. Dolgorukov, is probably incorrect, for Dolgorukov had already been transferred to Moscow by the time of Polisadov's earliest correspondences about Karakozov.

57. *The New Oxford Annotated Bible with the Apocrypha, Revised Standard Version* (New York: Oxford University Press, 1977), 1381–1382.

58. "Pis'ma Polisadova 1862–1865." RNB OR f. 727, ed. khr. 88, ll. 6 and 4.

59. Polisadov, September 4, 1866, letter to Shuvalov, GARF f. 109, 1 eks., op. 1, d. 100 ch. 1, l. 113. *Suetnyi* means, first, *pustoi* or *neznachitel'nyi* (empty, vain) and second, *khlopotlivyi* and *besporiadochnyi* (fussy, rushed). The first meaning comes from the biblical usage: "vanity of vanities," for example, is translated as *sueta suet.*

60. Polisadov, "Smert' prestupnika Gudzevicha," 459.

61. Ibid., 463.

62. Polisadov, 1863 letter to the University. RGIA f. 796, op. 139, d. 486, l. 8ob.

63. Polisadov, "Proekt predsmertnogo ob'iasneniia gosudarstvennogo prestupnika D. V. Karakozova." RNB OR f. 727, ed. khr. 36., l. 1.

64. Ibid., ll. 1ob–2ob.

65. Ibid., 1ob.

66. Karakozov's last letter, September 1, 1866. GARF f. 272, op. 1, d. 5, l. 571. Esipovich, "Zapiski Senatora Esipovicha," 275–276, or see *Pokushenie Karakozova,* 1:287, which cites a penciled note by Alexander II on the Supreme Criminal Court's verdict: "Personally, I have in my soul long forgiven him, but as the representative of supreme power, I do not consider myself entitled to forgive such a criminal."

67. Resolution of the Supreme Criminal Court, September 1, 1866, *Pokushenie Karakozova,* 1:287.

68. Letter dated November 10, 1866. GARF f. 112, op. 2, d. 2376, ll. 2–2ob.

69. *G,* no. 244, 4 September 1866.

70. Ibid.

Conclusion

1. Cicero, for example, declared: "[Who] would say that he commits a crime who assassinates a tyrant, however close a friend? The people of Rome, I tell you, think it no crime, but the noblest of all noble deeds." Cicero, *De officiis,* cited in *Voices of Terror,* ed. Walter Laqueur (New York: Reed Press, 2004), 18.

2. Attacks on nonstate actors—civilians—belong to a more democratically developed age, an age in which the demos, at least nominally, possesses political power.

3. David C. Rapoport, *Assassination and Terrorism* (Toronto: Canadian Broadcasting Corporation, 1971), 37.

4. Walter Benjamin, "On the Concept of History (Theses on the Philosophy of History)," in *Illuminations,* trans. Harry Zorn (London: Pimlico, 1999), 252–253.

5. See Maximilien Robespierre, *Virtue and Terror,* ed. Slavoj Žižek (London: Verso, 2007), 115. In defining terror as such, Robespierre was taking off from Montesquieu's *The Spirit of the Laws,* which had defined the nature and principles of governments: democracy, monarchy, and despotism, and, respectively, virtue, honor, and fear (*peur*). See Montesquieu, *The Spirit of the Laws* (Cambridge: Cambridge University Press, 1989), 21–30.

6. Shilov (1919), Venturi (1952), Vilenskaia (1969), and Gleason (1980), for example, all tell such a story. See A. A. Shilov, *D. V. Karakozov i pokushenie 4 aprelia 1866 goda* (Petrograd: Gosudarstvennoe izdatel'svo, 1919), 11; Venturi, *Roots of Revolution,* 347; E. S. Vilenskaia, *Khudiakov* (Moscow: Molodaia Gvardiia, 1969), 102; and Gleason, *Young Russia,* 329.

7. Shilov, *D. V. Karakozov,* 11. Cf. Venturi, *Roots of Revolution,* 347; Vilenskaia, *Khudiakov,* 102; Gleason, *Young Russia,* 329.

8. Khudiakov, *Zapiski Karakozovtsa,* 114.

9. *MV,* no. 72, 7 April 1866.

10. Testimony of Nikifor Fedotov. April 4, 1866. GARF f. 272, op. 1, d. 10, l. 15.

11. *Pokushenie Karakozova,* 1:263.

12. According to Zabolotin, the tsar had responded to the exchange about the assassin's identity ("Who are you?" "A Russian.") by putting his hand on Karakozov's head and saying, "What have you done, you unfortunate one?" Written testimony of Zabolotin. April 4, 1866. GARF f. 272 op. 1, d. 10, l. 12ob. Slesarchuk had heard the following: "What do you want?" the tsar asked the assassin (or rather: "What do you need?" "Chto tebe nuzhno?"). "I don't want anything," he answered (or: "I don't need anything." "'Nichego,' govorit, 'ne nuzhno'"). *Pokushenie Karakozova,* 1:13–14. During the trial, Zabolitin confirmed Slesarchuk's version. When Karakozov was asked to respond to their testimonies, he only said he did not remember them, and therefore did not contest their accounts in any way. Ibid., 14–15.

13. Ulam, *In the Name of the People,* 168.

14. Cherevin, *Zapiski P. A. Cherevina,* 11.

15. Letter of Karakozov to Alexander II, undated, but probably April 10, 1866. GARF f. 95, op. 1, d. 163 T. I, l. 78.

16. This has been "official" since at least 1907, when Brokgaus and Efron's encyclopedia, in its entry on terror, wrote that "Separate terrorist acts also occurred earlier, but as a system, terror got its push from the shooting of General Trepov by Vera Zasulich on January 24, 1878." *Entsiklopedicheskii slovar'*, ed. F. A. Brokgauz and I. A. Efron, vol. 2 (Saint Petersburg, 1907), 753.

17. Zasulich cited in Jay Bergman, "Vera Zasulich, The Shooting of Trepov, and the Growth of Political Terrorism in Russia, 1878–1881," *Terrorism: An International Journal* 4 (1980): 31 and 37.

18. Ibid., 28.

19. "Druz'iam rabochim." GARF, f. 95, op. 1, d. 163 T. I, l. 8.

Appendix C. The Karakozov Case, 1866–Present

1. See for example A. Thun, *Geschichte der revolutionären Bewegungen in Russland* (Leipzig: Duncker & Humblot, 1883); L. Kul'chitskii (Mazovetskii), *Istoriia russkogo revoliutsionnogo dvizheniia (1801–1870)*, vol. 1 (Saint Petersburg: Elektropechatnia Ia. Levenshtein, 1908); L. Barrive, *Obshchestvennoe dvizhenie v tsarstvovanie Aleksandra Vtorogo* (Moscow: Izdatel'stvo Tovarishchestva "Obrazovanie," 1911); and B. B. Glinskii, *Revoliutsionnyi period russkoi istorii: 1861–1881 gg.* (Saint Petersburg: Tipografiia Tovarishchestva A. S. Suvorina "Novoe Vremiia," 1913).

2. *Za Sto Let (1800–1896): Sbornik po istorii politicheskikh i obshchestvennykh dvizhenii v Rossii*, ed. V. Burtsev and S. M. Kravchinskii (Stepniak) (London: Russian Free Press Fund, 1897), 85–87; *Gosudarstvennyia prestupleniia v Rossii v XIX veke: Sbornik iz offitsial'nykh izdanii pravitel'stvennykh soobshchenii*, ed. B. Bazilevskii, vol. 1: *1825–1876 goda* (Stuttgart: J. H. W. Dietz, 1903), 242–275.

3. P. F. Nikolaev, *Lichnye vospominaniia o prebyvanii Chernyshevskogo v katorge v Aleksandrovskom zavode* (Moscow: Knigoizdatel'stvo E. D. Miagkova "Kolokol," 1906); V. Shaganov, *Nikolai Gavrilovich Chernyshevskii na katorge i v ssylke* (Saint Petersburg: Izdatel'stvo E. G. Pekarskago, 1907); Esipovich, "Zapiski senatora Esipovicha"; D. V. Stasov, "Karakozovskii protsess"; Veinberg, "4-e aprelia"; and Murav'ev, "Zapiska M. N. Murav'eva," *Byloe*, no. 1 (1907).

4. Kul'chitskii, *Istoriia russkogo revoliutsionnogo dvizheniia;* Glinskii, *Revoliutsionnyi period russkoi istorii;* A. A. Kornilov, *Obshchestvennoe dvizhenie pri Aleksandre II (1855–1881)* (Moscow: Tovarishchestvo tipografiia A. I. Mamontova, 1909); V. E. Cheshikhina-Vetrinskii, "N. G. Chernyshevskii i karakozovtsy," *Russkaia mysl'*, no. 2 (1913); Evgen'ev-Maksimov, "Delo Karakozova."

5. A. A. Shilov, "Iz istorii revoliutsionnago dvizheniia 1860-kh gg.: Proklamatsiia "Druzh'iam-rabochim" D. V. Karakozova, *Golos Minuvshego*, no. 5 (1918); Shilov, *D. V. Karakozov.*

6. M. M. Klevenskii, *M. M. Ishutinskii kruzhok i pokushenie Karakozova* (Moscow: Izdatel'stvo Vsesoiuznogo obshchestva politkatorzhan i ssylnykh-poselentsev, 1927; 2d ed., 1928); *I. A. Khudiakov, revoliutsioner i uchenyi* (Moscow: Izdatel'stvo Vsesoiuznogo obshchestva politkatorzhan i ssylnykh-poselentsev, 1929). See also Klevensky's article, "*Evropeiskii revoliutsionnyi komitet* v dele Karakozova," and introductory notes to "Iz vospominanii Z. K. Ralli," *Revoliutsionnoe dvizhenie 1860 godov: Sbornik*, ed. B. I. Gorev and B. P. Koz'min (Moscow: Politkatorzhan, 1932), 147–167 and 135–146.

7. *Pokushenie Karakozov;* Klevenskii, "Malen'kaia zametka ob Iv. Al. Khudiakove" and "Materialy ob I. A. Khudiakove," *Katorga i ssylka* 8–9 (1928); "Ishutintsy v tiur'me i ssylke," *Krasnyi Arkhiv* 2 (1929). See also N. Tiutchev, "Poslednii iz karakozovtsev—Maksimilian Nikolaevich Zagibalov," and E. Pekarskii, "Iz vospominanii o karakozovtse V. N. Shaganove," both in *Katorga i ssylka* 3, no. 10 (1924): 207–211 and 213–217; V. Nikiforov, "Karakozovtsy v ssylke i ikh vliianie na iakutov," and B. Kybalov, "Karakozovets I. A. Khudiakov v ssylke,"

both in *Katorga i ssylka* nos. 7–8 (1926): 153–157 and 166–192; and Bukhshtab, "Posle Vystrela Karakozova." The notes of P. A. Cherevin were also published around this time: Cherevin, *Zapiski P. A. Cherevina.*

8. This statement should be qualified by underlining that, first, no Soviet was ever very impressed with Karakozov's mind, either, and most of them characterized him as "ahead of his time," "impatient," etc. Second, if recurrent reference to Karakozov's psycho-logic has enjoyed popularity in the West, then mostly as a stock answer to the question, "Why April 4?"; not so much to dismiss the possibility that the members of the Moscow circle were real Jacobins, Blanquists, or Bolsheviks in the making.

9. Lur'e, *Nechaev*, 95–96; Budnitskii, *Terrorizm*, 339.

10. Venturi's is the classic account. It characterizes "the movement which can be personified by the three names of Ishutin, Khudyakov, and Karakozov" as "both Socialist and terrorist and—because of the way in which it combined these two elements—it constituted the first typically and purely Populist nucleus." Venturi, *Roots of Revolution*, 331. For Pomper, Karakozov and friends are evangelical and Chernyshevsky-ist nihilists who created a "little community of saints." Pomper, *The Russian Revolutionary Intelligentsia*, 85. Pomper's is probably the first of the major non-Russian accounts to really underline the "aberrant" nature of the mid-1860s conspiracies and draw an explicit parallel between the nihilists and Bolsheviks. Ulam's chapter combines his own reading of the trial records, Vilenskaia's conspiratorial interpretation of the case (see below), and a very heavy emphasis on the group's psycho-logic, perversion, and criminality. "Karakozov himself would today doubtless be declared not responsible for his actions by reason of insanity," is how Ulam introduces the story of April 4, "and he was a tool in the hands of two people who had exhibited signs of serious mental instability and who were to end their lives mad: Nicholas Ishutin and Ivan Khudyakov." Ulam, *In the Name of the People*, 148. Gleason's chapters in *Young Russia* also draw much from Vilenskaia's monograph, but his source-base is broader than Ulam's and his narrative much more balanced. Gleason's, in fact, is the only text that attempts to suspend its judgment as far as the existence of "The Organization" and "Hell" is concerned. His account also includes some good information on the backgrounds and early activities of Karakozov and friends, especially Ivan Khudiakov.

11. Riasanovsky, *A History of Russia*, 380.

12. For Shilov, for example, Karakozov's shooting was "too early" (*prezhdevremennyi*) but nevertheless, "the first step from the word to the act: the next big case—the Nechaev case— was closely connected with the Muscovite *Organization;* Karakozov's idea, in altered form, was brought into life by our "active populists" of the 70s; and finally, invisible threads connect Karakozov with the activities of *The People's Will*, which continued on his path." Shilov, *D. V. Karakozov*, 52 and 55. Klevensky, in a more subtle argument, noted that the idea of tsaricide was not peculiar to Karakozov, but that tsaricide was hardly the raison d'être of "The Organization" and, in fact, did not enjoy the support of other members. According to Klevensky, the historical relevance of the Moscow circle is that it holds all later ideas in embryo. See his introduction to *Pokushenie Karakozova*, v.

13. See for example R. V. Filippov's introduction to *Revoliutsionnaia narodnicheskaia organizatsiia N. A. Ishutina–I. A. Khudiakova (1863–1866)* (Petrozavodsk: Karel'skoe Knizhnoe Izdatel'stvo, 1964), esp. 5–15.

14. B. G. Bazanov, "I. A. Khudiakov i pokushenie Karakozova," *Russkaia literatura*, no. 2 (1959); S. S. Shusterman, "Podvig revoliutsionera," *Voprosy istorii*, no. 11 (1961). Filippov, *Revoliutsionnaia narodnicheskaia organizatsiia;* E. S. Vilenskaia, *Revoliutsionnoe podpol'e v Rossii (60-e gody XIX v.)* (Moscow: Nauka, 1965). Four years later, Vilenskaia published *Khudiakov.*

15. Shcherbakova, "Roman N. G. Chernyshevskogo *Chto delat'?*," 34.

16. Khudiakov, *Zapiski Karakozovtsa*, 104.

Bibliography

This bibliography includes all works cited except archival references.

Published Documents and Periodicals

Golos. 1866–1867.

Gosudarstvennye prestupleniia v Rossii v XIX veke. Sbornik iz offitsial'nykh izdanii pravitel'stvennykh soobshchenii. Ed. B. Bazilevskii. Vol. 1: *1825–1876 goda.* Stuttgart: J. H. W. Dietz, 1903.

Illiustrirovannaia Gazeta. 1866.

Iskra. 1867.

Kolokol. 1866–1867.

Literatura Partii Narodnoi Voli, ed. B. Bazilevskii. Paris: Société nouvelle de librairie et d'édition, 1905.

Modnyi Magazin. 1866.

Moskovskie Vedomosti. 1863, 1866–1867.

Peterburgskii Listok. 1866.

Pokushenie Karakozova: Stenograficheskii otchet po delu D. Karakozova, I. Khudiakova, N. Ishutina i dr. Ed. M. M. Klevenskii and K. G. Kotel'nikov. Seriia Politicheskie protsessy 60–80 gg., ed. V. V. Maksakov and V. I. Nevskii. 2 vols. Moscow and Leningrad: Izdatel'stvo Tsentrarkhiva RSFSR, 1928–30.

"Pokushenie Karakozova 4 aprelia 1866." Introd. A. A. Shilov. *Krasnyi Arkhiv* 4, no. 17 (1926): 91–137.

Politicheskie protsessy 60-kh g.g. Ed. V. P. Alekseev and B. P. Koz'min. Vol. 1. Moscow and Petrograd: Gosudarstvennoe izdatel'stvo, 1923.

Polnoe sobranie zakonov Rossiskoi Imperii. 2d ser.: 1825–1881. Saint Petersburg, 1830–84.

Polnyi Svod Zakonov Ugolovnykh. Ulozhenie o nakazaniiakh ugolovnykh i ispravi-
tel'nykh, s vkliucheniem teksta vsekh statei Svoda zakonov, na kotoryia ukazany
ssylki v ulozhenii o nakazaniiakh starago 1857 i novago 1866 g. izdaniia.
Moscow, 1867.
Revoliutsionnoe dvizhenie 1860 godov: Sbornik. Ed. B. I. Gorev and B. P. Koz'min.
Moscow: Politkatorzhan, 1932.
Revoliutsionnyi radikalizm v Rossii: Vek deviatnadtsatyi. Ed. E. L. Rudnitskii. Moscow:
Arkheograficheskii Tsentr, 1997.
Russkii Invalid. 1867.
Severnaia Pochta. 1866–1867.
*Za Sto Let (1800–1896): Sbornik po istorii politicheskikh i obshchestvennykh dvizhenii v
Rossii.* Ed. V. Burtsev and S. M. Kravchinkskii (Stepniak). London: Russian Free
Press Fund, 1897.

Secondary Sources

Alexander Mikhailovich, Grand Duke. *Velikii kniaz' Aleksandr Mikhailovich, 1866–
1933: Kniga vospominanii.* Moscow: Zakharov-AST, 1991.
Allenova, Ekaterina. *Ilia Repin.* Moscow: Belyi gorod, 2001.
Bakhtin, Mikhail. *Problems of Dostoevsky's Poetics.* Ed. and trans. Caryl Emerson. Min-
neapolis: University of Minnesota Press, 1984.
Barrive, L. *Obshchestvennoe dvizhenie v tsarstvovanie Aleksandra Vtorogo.* Moscow: Iz-
datel'stvo Tovarishchestva "Obrazovanie," 1911.
Baudelaire, Charles. *The Painter of Modern Life and Other Essays.* Trans. Jonathan
Mayne. London: Phaedon, 1995.
Bazanov, B. G. "I. A. Khudiakov i pokushenie Karakozova." *Russkaia literatura,* no.
4 (1959): 146–163.
Benjamin, Walter. *The Arcades Project.* Trans. Howard Eiland and Kevin McLaugh-
lin. Cambridge, Mass.: The Belknap Press of Harvard University Press, 1999.
———. *Illuminations.* Trans. Harry Zorn. London: Pimlico, 1999.
Bergman, Jay. "Vera Zasulich, The Shooting of Trepov and the Growth of Politi-
cal Terrorism in Russia, 1878–1881." *Terrorism: An International Journal* 4 (1980):
25–51.
Bhat, G. N. "Trial by Jury in the Reign of Alexander II: A Study in the Legal Cul-
ture of Late Imperial Russia, 1864–1881." Ph.D. diss., University of California
Berkeley, 1995.
Brooks, Jeffrey. *When Russia Learned to Read: Literacy and Popular Literature, 1861–
1917.* Princeton: Princeton University Press, 1985.
Budnitskii, O. V. *Terrorizm v rossiiskom osvoboditel'nom dvizhenii: Ideologiia, etika,
psikhologiia (vtoraia polovina XIX–nachalo XX v.).* Moscow: Rosspen, 2000.
Bukhshtab, B. "Posle vystrela Karakozova." *Katorga i ssylka,* no. 5 (1931): 50–
88.
Cherevin, P. A. *Zapiski P. A. Cherevina (Novye materialy po delu Karakozova).* Kos-
troma: Izdanie "Kostromskogo Nauchnogo Obshchestva po izucheniiu mest-
nogo kraia," 1918.
Chernykh, P. Ia. *Istoriko-etimologicheskii slovar' sovremennogo russkogo iazyka.* 2 vols.
Moscow: Russkii iazyk, 1999.
Chernyshevskii, N. G. *Chto delat'?* Ed. T. I. Ornatskaia and S. A. Reiser. Leningrad:
Nauka, 1975.

——. *What Is to Be Done?* Trans. Michael R. Katz and William G. Wagner. Ithaca: Cornell University Press, 1989.

Chukovskii, Kornei. *Poet i palach (Nekrasov i Murav'ev).* Petersburg: Epokha, 1922.

——. *The Poet and the Hangman (Nekrasov and Muravyov).* Trans. R. W. Rotsel. Ann Arbor: Ardis, 1977.

Clark, Katerina. *The Soviet Novel: History as Ritual.* Chicago: University of Chicago Press, 1981.

Daly, Jonathan. *Autocracy Under Siege: Security Police and Opposition in Russia, 1866– 1905.* DeKalb: Northern Illinois University Press, 1998.

Dostoevskii, F. M. *Polnoe sobranie sochinenii v tridtsati tomakh.* 30 vols. Leningrad: Nauka, 1972–90.

——. *Complete Letters,* vol. 2: *1860–1867.* Trans. David A. Lowe. Ann Arbor: Ardis, 1989.

——. *Crime and Punishment: The Coulson Translation. Backgrounds and Sources. Essays in Criticism.* Trans. Jessie Coulson. New York: Norton, 1989.

——. *The Brothers Karamazov.* Trans. Richard Pevear and Larissa Volokhonsky. New York: Farrar, Straus and Giroux, 1990.

——. *Crime and Punishment.* Trans. Richard Pevear and Larissa Volokhonsky. New York: Vintage Classics, 1992.

——. *Notes from Underground.* Trans. Richard Pevear and Larissa Volokhonsky. New York: Vintage Books, 1993.

Drozd, Andrew M. *Chernyshevskii's What Is To Be Done? A Reevaluation.* Evanston: Northwestern University Press, 2001.

Entsiklopedicheskii slovar'. Saint Petersburg: Izdatel'stvo F. A. Brokgauz i I. A. Efron, 1890–1907.

Esipov, V. V. "Byl li Nechaev revoliutsionerom?" *Voprosy istorii,* no. 11 (1990): 182– 185.

Esipovich, Ia. G. "Zapiski Senatora Esipovicha." *Russkaia Starina 137,* nos. 1–3 (1909): 123–144, 259–278, and 555–564.

Evgen'ev-Maksimov, V. "Delo Karakozova i redaktsiia *Sovremennika.*" *Zavety,* no. 6 (1914): 77–98.

Fedosiuk, Iu. A. *Chto neponiatno u klassikov ili Entsiklopediia russkogo byta XIX veka.* Moscow: Nauka, 2003.

Filippov, R. V. *Revoliutsionnaia narodnicheskaia organizatsiia N. A. Ishutina–I. A. Khudiakova (1863–1866).* Petrozavodsk: Karel'skoe Knizhnoe Izdatel'stvo, 1964.

Flaubert, Gustave. *Dictionary of Received Ideas.* Trans. Jacques Barzun. New York: New Directions, 1968.

Frank, Joseph. "N. G. Chernyshevsky: A Russian Utopia." *Southern Review* 3, no. 1 (1967): 68–84.

——. *Dostoevsky: The Stir of Liberation 1860–1865.* Princeton: Princeton University Press, 1986.

——. *Dostoevsky: The Miraculous Years, 1865–1871.* Princeton: Princeton University Press, 1995.

——. *Dostoevsky: The Mantle of the Prophet, 1871–1881.* Princeton: Princeton University Press, 2002.

Gleason, Abbot. *Young Russia: The Genesis of Russian Radicalism in the 1860s.* New York: Viking, 1980.

Glinskii, B. B. *Revoliutsionnyi period russkoi istorii (1861–1881 gg.).* Saint Petersburg: Tipografiia Tovarishchestva A. S. Suvorina "Novoe Vremiia," 1913.

Gogol', N. V. *Polnoe sobranie sochinenii v desiati tomakh*. Berlin: Slovo, 1921.

——. *The Overcoat and Other Tales of Good and Evil*. Trans. David Magarshack. Cambridge, Mass.: Robert Bentley, 1979.

The Gospel According to Luke (X–XXIV). Trans. Joseph A. Fitzmyer, S.J. New York: Doubleday, 1985.

Griesinger, Theodor. *The Jesuits: The Complete History of their Open and Secret Proceedings From the Foundation of the Order to the Present Time*. Trans. A. J. Scott, M. D. 3d ed. London: W. H. Allen & Co., 1903.

Gus, M. *Idei i obrazy F. M. Dostoevskogo*. Moscow: Khudozhestvennaia literatura, 1971.

Herzen, Alexander. *Sobranie sochinenii v tridtsati tomakh*. Moscow: Izdatel'stvo Akademii Nauk SSSR, 1954–65.

——. *My Past and Thoughts*. Trans. Constance Garnett. Berkeley: University of California Press, 1991.

Hosking, Geoffrey. *Russia: People and Empire 1552–1917*. Cambridge, Mass.: Harvard University Press, 1997.

Iakubovich, I. D. *Letopis' zhizni i tvorchestva F. M. Dostoevskogo*. 3 vols. Saint Petersburg: Akademicheskii proekt, 1993–95.

Iosafat Ogryzko i Peterburgskii revoliutsionnyi rzhond v dele poslednego miatezha. Sostavil chlen Vilenskoi osoboi po politicheskim delam komissii, 3-i artilleriiskoi brigady shtabs-kapitan N. V. Gogel'. Vilno, 1866.

Katz, Martin. *Mikhail N. Katkov: A Political Biography, 1818–1887*. The Hague: Mouton, 1966.

Khudiakov, Ivan. Zapiski Karakozovtsa. Moscow: Molodaia gvardiia, 1930. Written in 1867 and originally published as *Opyt avtobiografii*. Geneva: Vol'naia russkaia tipografiia, 1882.

Kirsanova, R. M. *Rozovaia ksandreika i dradedamovyi platok: Kostium-vesh' i obraz v russkoi literature XIX veka*. Moscow: Kniga, 1989.

Klevenskii, M. M. *Ishutinskii kruzhok i pokushenie Karakozova*. Moscow, 1927; 2nd ed., Moscow: Izdatel'stvo Vsesoiuznogo obshchestva politkatorzhan i ssylnykh-poselentsev, 1928.

——. "Malen'kaia zametka ob Iv. Al. Khudiakove." *Katorga i ssylka*, nos. 8–9 (1928): 221–231.

——. "Materialy ob I. A. Khudiakove." *Katorga i ssylka*, nos. 8–9 (1928): 218–220.

——. "*Evropeiskii revoliutsionnyi komitet* v dele Karakozova." *Revoliutsionnoe dvizhenie 1860 godov: Sbornik*, ed. B. I. Gorev and B. P. Koz'min (Moscow: Politkatorzhan, 1932), 147–167.

——. *I. A. Khudiakov, revoliutsioner i uchenyi*. Moscow: Izdatel'stvo Vsesoiuznogo obshchestva politkatorzhan i ssylnykh-poselentsev, 1929.

——. Introductory notes to "Iz vospominanii Z. K. Ralli," *Revoliutsionnoe dvizhenie 1860 godov: Sbornik*, ed. B. I. Gorev and B. P. Koz'min (Moscow: Politkatorzhan, 1932), 135–146.

——. "Ishutintsy v tiur'me i ssylke." in Krasnyi Arkhiv 2 (1929): 213–221.

Kornilov, A. A. *Obshchestvennoe dvizhenie pri Aleksandre II (1855–1881)*. Moscow: Tovarishchestvo tipografii A. I. Mamontova, 1909.

Kucherov, Samuel. *Courts, Lawyers and Trials under the Last Three Tsars*. New York: Praeger, 1953.

Kul'chitskii, Ludwik. *Istoriia russkogo revoliutsionnogo dvizheniia (1801–1870)*. Vol. 1. Saint Petersburg: Elektropechatnia Ia. Levenshtein, 1908.

Kybalov, B. "Karakozovets I. A. Khudiakov v ssylke." *Katorga i ssylka,* nos. 7–8 (1926): 166–192.

Laqueur, Walter. *The Age of Terrorism.* Boston: Little, Brown, 1987.

——, ed. *Voices of Terror.* New York: Reed Press, 2004.

LeDonne, John P. "Criminal Investigations before the Great Reforms." *Russian History,* no. 1 (1974): 101–118.

Lemke, M. K. *Politicheskie protsessy v Rossii v 60-kh godakh.* Moscow: Gosudarstvennoe izdatel'stvo, 1923.

Lenin, V. I. *Polnoe sobranie sochinenii.* 5th ed. 55 vols. Moscow: Gosudarstvennoe izdatel'stvo politicheskoi literatury, 1958–65.

Lur'e, F. M. *Nechaev: Sozidatel' razrusheniia.* Moscow: Molodaia Gvardiia, 2001.

Malevich, K. S. *The World as Non-Objectivity. Unpublished Writings 1922–25.* Vol. 3, ed. Troels Andersen. Copenhagen: Borgen, 1976.

Margolis, A. D. *Tiur'ma i ssylka v imperatorskoi rossii.* Moscow: Lanterna Vita, 1995.

Montesquieu, Charles de Secondat. *The Spirit of the Laws.* Cambridge, U.K.: Cambridge University Press, 1989.

Morozov, S. *Russkaia khudozhestvennaia fotografiia. Ocherki iz istorii fotografii 1839–1917.* Moscow: Gosudarstvennoe Izdatel'stvo Iskusstvo, 1955.

Moss, Walter G. *Russia in the Age of Alexander II, Tolstoy, and Dostoevsky.* London: Anthem Press, 2002.

Murav'ev, M. N. "Zapiska M. N. Murav'eva." *Byloe,* no. 1 (1907), 153–157.

Nabokov, Vladimir. *The Gift.* Trans. Michael Scammell. New York: Vintage, 1991.

Der Neue Pitaval: Eine Sammlung der interessantesten Criminalgeschichten aller Länder aus älterer und neuerer Zeit. Ed. Julius Eduard Hitzig and Wilhelm Häring. 60 vols. Leipzig: Brockhaus, 1842–90.

The New Oxford Annotated Bible with the Apocrypha, Revised Standard Version. New York: Oxford University Press, 1977.

The New Testament and Other Early Christian Writings: A Reader. Ed. Bart D. Ehrman. New York: Oxford University Press, 1998.

Nikiforov, V. "Karakozovtsy v ssylke i ikh vliianie na iakutov." *Katorga i ssylka,* nos. 7–8 (1926): 153–157.

Nikitenko, A. V. *Zapiski i dnevnik.* Vol. 2. Saint Petersburg: Knigoizdatel'stvo M. V. Pirozhkova, Istoricheskii otdel', 1905.

Nikolaev, P. F. *Lichnye vospominaniia o prebyvanii Chernyshevskogo v katorge v Aleksandrovskom zavode.* Moscow: Knigoizdatel'stvo E. D. Miagkova "Kolokol," 1906.

——. "N. G. Chernyshevskii i Karakozovtsy." *Russkaia Mysl'* 34, no. 2 (1913): 102–106.

Paperno, Irina. *Chernyshevsky and the Age of Realism: A Study in the Semiotics of Behavior.* Stanford: Stanford University Press, 1988.

——. *Suicide as a Cultural Institution in Dostoevsky's Russia.* Ithaca: Cornell University Press, 1997.

Pekarskii, E. "Iz vospominanii o karakozovtse V. N. Shaganove." *Katorga i ssylka* 3, no. 10 (1924): 212–217.

Pereira, N. G. O. *The Thought and Teachings of N. G. Chernyshevsky.* The Hague: Mouton, 1975.

Pisarev, D. I. *Sochineniia.* 4 vols. Moscow: Gosudarstvennoe izdatel'stvo khudozhestvennoi literatury, 1955–56.

Polisadov, I. N. *Slovo pred soversheniem torzhestvennago blagodareniia gospodu bogu za*

*spasenie zhizni Gosudaria Imperatora skazannoe Sviashchennikom Ioannom Polisa-
dovym 9ogo Aprelia 1866 g.* Saint Petersburg, 1866.

Polisadov, V. P. *Pis'ma Protoiereia V. P. Polisadova o puteshestvii nashei dukhovnoi missii v Parizhe i ob osviashchenii parizhkoi tserkvi.* Saint Petersburg, 1861.

———. "Smert' prestupnika Gudzevicha." *Dukhovnaia beseda* 21, no. 31 (1864): 445–
464.

———. "Sobesedovaniia s protestantom v Berline." *Strannik* 3, no. 8 (August 1860):
83–108.

Pomper, Phillip. *Sergei Nechaev.* New Brunswick, N.J.: Rutgers University Press,
1979.

———. *The Russian Revolutionary Intelligentsia.* Wheeling, Ill.: Harlan Davidson,
1993.

Praisman, L. G. *Terroristy i revoliutsionery, okhranniki i provokatory.* Moscow: Rosspen,
2001.

Rapoport, David C. *Assassination and Terrorism.* Toronto: Canadian Broadcasting
Corporation, 1971.

Repin, Ilya E. *Dalekoe blizkoe.* Ed. and introd. K. Chukovskii. Leningrad and
Moscow: Iskusstvo, 1937.

Riasanovsky, Nicholas V. *A History of Russia.* Oxford: Oxford University Pres, 1993.

Robespierre, Maximilien. *Virtue and Terror.* Ed. Slavoj Žižek. London: Verso, 2007.

Rocker, Rudolf. *Johann Most: Das Leben Eines Rebellen.* Berlin: Der Syndikalist, 1924.

Ryndin, V., ed. Russkii Kostium 1850–1870. Moscow: Vserossiiskoe Teatral'noe Obshchestvo, 1963.

Schmitt, Carl. *Theorie des Partisanen: Zwischenbemerkung zum Begriff des Politischen.*
Berlin: Duncker & Humblot, 1992.

———. *The Concept of the Political.* Trans. George Schwab. Expanded ed. Chicago:
University of Chicago Press, 2007.

Seneca. *Epistles.* Cambridge, Mass.: Loeb Classical Library. 1996.

Shaganov, V. *Nikolai Gavrilovich Chernyshevskii na katorge i v ssylke.* Saint Petersburg:
Izdatel'stvo E. G. Pekarskago, 1907.

Shchegolev, P. E. *Alekseevskii ravelin: Sekretnaia gosudarstvennaia tiur'ma Rossii v XIX
veke,* ed. A. A. Matyshev. Vol. 2. Leningrad: Lenizdat, 1990. Originally published
in *Muzei revoliutsii,* no. 1 (1923).

Shcherbakova E. I. "Roman N. G. Chernyshevskogo *Chto delat'?* v vospriiatii
radikal'noi molodezhi serediny 60-kh godov XIX v." *Vestnik Moskovskogo Universiteta* 8 (Istoriia) no. 1 (1998): 59–68.

Shilov, A. A. "Iz istorii revoliutsionnago dvizheniia 1860-kh gg.: Proklamatsiia
"Druzh'iam-rabochim" D. V. Karakozova." *Golos Minuvshego,* no. 5 (1918): 159–
168.

———. *D. V. Karakozov i pokushenie 4 aprelia 1866 goda.* Petrograd: Gosudarstvennoe
izdatel'svo, 1919.

Shusterman, S. S. "Podvig revoliutsionera." *Voprosy istorii,* no. 11 (1961): 210–213.

Simmel, Georg. *Simmel on Culture.* London: SAGE Publications, 1997.

Skal'kovskii, Kostantin A. *V teatral' nom mire.* Saint Petersburg: Tipografiia A. S. Suvorina, 1899.

Spitzer, Leo. *Representative Essays.* Ed. Alban K. Forcione, Herbert Lindenberger,
and Madeline Sutherland. Stanford: Stanford University Press, 1988.

Stafford, David. *From Anarchism to Reformism: A Study of the Political Activities of Paul*

Brousse within the First International and the French Socialist Movement 1870–90. London: Weidenfeld & Nicolson, 1971.

Stasov, D. V. "Karakozovskii protsess (Nekotoryia svedeniia i vospominaniia)." *Byloe*, no. 4 (1906): 276–290.

Suvorin, A. S. *Dnevnik A. S. Suvorina*, ed. M. G. Krichevskii. Moscow and Petrograd: Izadetel'stvo L. D. Frenkel', 1923.

Tchaikovsky, P. I. *Polnoe sobranie sochinenii: Literaturnye proizvedeniia i perepiska.* Vol. 5. Moscow: Gosudarstevennoe muzykal'noe izdatel'stvo, 1959.

Thun, A. *Geschichte der revolutionären Bewegungen in Russland.* Leipzig: Duncker & Humblot, 1883.

Tikhomirov, L. A. Russia Political and Social. Vol. 2. Trans. from the French by Edward Aveling. London: Swan Sonnenschein, 1892.

Tiutchev N. "Poslednii iz karakozovtsev—Maksimilian Nikolaevich Zagibalov." *Katorga i ssylka* 3, no. 10 (1924): 207–211.

Troitskii, N. A. "Vosem' popytok osvobozhdeniia N. G. Chernyshevskogo." *Voprosy istorii*, no. 7 (1978): 122–141.

Turgenev, I. S. *Fathers and Sons.* Trans. Ralph E. Matlaw New York: Norton, 1989.

——. *Polnoe sobranie sochinenii i pisem v tridtsati tomakh.* Vol. 7. Moscow: Nauka, 1981.

Ulam, Adam. *In the Name of the People: Prophets and Conspirators in Prerevolutionary Russia.* New York: Viking, 1977.

Valuev, P. A. *Dnevnik P. A. Valueva Ministra Vnutrennikh Del.* 2 Vols. Moscow: Izdatel'stvo Akademii Nauk SSSR, 1961.

Veinberg, Petr. "4-e aprelia 1866 g. (Iz moikh vospominanii)." *Byloe*, no. 4 (1906): 299–303.

Venturi, Franco. *Roots of Revolution: A History of the Populist and Socialist Movements in Nineteenth-Century Russia.* Trans. Francis Haskell. London: Phoenix Press, 2001.

Vilenskaia, E. S. *Revoliutsionnoe podpol'e v Rossii (60-e gody XIX v.).* Moscow: Nauka, 1965.

——. *Khudiakov.* Moscow: Molodaia Gvardiia, 1969.

Volodin A. "Raskol'nikov i Karakozov: K tvorchestkoi istorii D. Pisareva *Bor'ba za zhizn'*." *Novyi Mir*, no. 11 (1969): 212–231.

Vorms, N. A. "Belyi Terror." *Kolokol*, nos. 231–232 (1 January 1867): 1889–1895; nos. 233–234 (1 February 1867): 1905–1913; nos. 235–236 (1 March 1867): 1923–1931.

W. "Karakozov, tsar, i publika." *Kolokol*, no. 224 (15 July 1866): 1829–1334.

Yarmolinsky, Avrahm. *Road to Revolution: A Century of Russian Radicalism.* New York: Collier Books, 1962.

INDEX

Page numbers in italics refer to illustrations.